HUMANIZING
SOCIAL PSYCHOLOGY

M. Brewster Smith

HUMANIZING
SOCIAL
PSYCHOLOGY

Jossey-Bass Publishers
San Francisco • Washington • London • 1974

HUMANIZING SOCIAL PSYCHOLOGY
by M. Brewster Smith

Copyright © 1974 by: Jossey-Bass, Inc., Publishers
615 Montgomery Street
San Francisco, California 94111
&
Jossey-Bass Limited
3 Henrietta Street
London WC2E 8LU

Library of Congress Catalogue Card Number LC 73-21076

International Standard Book Number ISBN 0-87589-229-9

Manufactured in the United States of America

JACKET DESIGN BY WILLI BAUM

FIRST EDITION

Code 7422

232967

The Jossey-Bass
Behavioral Science Series

FOR
HENRY A. MURRAY

CELEBRANT, EXPLORER,
AND CHEMIST OF PERSONALITY;
PSYCHOLOGIST AND PERSON PREEMINENT

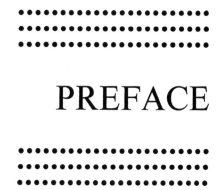

PREFACE

*T*o call for "humanizing social psychology" is to voice a perspective that is emerging as increasingly important in the social sciences generally. The attempt to carry over to the social sciences the spirit and some of the trappings of inquiry in the natural sciences has attained only modest success. The positivist-empiricist epistemology that guided it no longer seems sacrosanct—though it can still marshal vigorous support. The emerging awareness of worldwide critical problems in the human condition that call for radical solutions, the insistent new voices of minorities and women (former objects of social science who demand to be subjects), our increasing articulateness about the dehumanizing features of our technological-bureaucratic society—all call into question the viability of business as usual in the social sciences, social psychology among them.

The sense of crisis encourages polarization. For some, hope appears to lie in more and better of the same: with B. F. Skinner, more and better tough-minded behavioral science and technology "beyond freedom and dignity" toward the solution of human problems. For others, science itself is rejected, along with its technology. A countercultural mysticism is afoot—sometimes flying the banner of humanism—which looks more like a symptomatic escapist reaction to problems felt to be beyond rational solution rather than a proposal of new directions in which solutions may be sought.

Humanizing Social Psychology is written from a point of view that rejects this Hobson's choice. In the broad area of social psychology (construed to include the study of personality and self-hood), it argues that a humane social science is urgently desirable and possible, and indeed already incipiently exists. The chapters here illustrate this perspective as well as argue for it. Chapter One develops the rationale for the book. Brief introductions to the several parts provide context and framework for the individual chapters.

The book makes generally accessible in revised form essays and chapters that have appeared since 1968 in widely scattered books and journals. In addition to Chapter One, Chapters Ten and Twelve have not been published previously. In spite of their occasional origins, all the chapters were written in the service of a personal agenda, to carry forward and apply a point of view in personality-and-social psychology and, indeed, in psychology in general that seems to me badly in need of spokesmen. I hope that this book may have more influence than scattered papers could in this task of humanizing social psychology.

Santa Cruz, California   M. BREWSTER SMITH
August 1974

CONTENTS

HUMANIZING
SOCIAL PSYCHOLOGY

Chapter One

•••••••••••••••••••••••
•••••••••••••••••••••••••
•••••••••••••••••••••••••••

HUMANISM AND SOCIAL PSYCHOLOGY

•••••••••••••••••••••••••
•••••••••••••••••••••••••
•••••••••••••••••••••••••

*S*ocial psychology as a subdiscipline of psychology is in crisis—on that there is wide agreement. Symposia on "Whither Social Psychology?" have become regular features of meetings of the American Psychological Association. The self-confidence of the previous era has been replaced by self-doubt.

In the two postwar decades, social psychology emerged in the United States as a field of vigorous laboratory experimentation that applied self-consciously scientific methodology to the clarification and elaboration of small theories about such topics as social influence, social comparison processes, strains toward consistency in beliefs and feelings, and the perception of other persons or the attribution to them of psychological states and dispositions. Lindzey and Aronson (1968–1969) codify the results of this productive period in five volumes.

Near the end of the 1960s, doubt and self-criticism became increasingly evident among American social psychologists—about the lack of gains compared with the large collective effort expended, about the failure to arrive at consensual paradigms to define the growing edge of scientific advance, about the artificiality and

1

irrelevance of some of the problems that had been pursued with great theoretical and technical sophistication, about the instability of laboratory findings insofar as they often turned out to depend upon unexamined interpretations of the experimental situation by the human subjects, and about the questionable ethics involved in the deceptive manipulations typically required to attain some control over these interpretations. The field is still in crisis, with no predominant new directions clearly apparent, though there is greater emphasis on observation and experiment in real-life settings and on applied concerns.

The chapters in this volume partly reflect this crisis in the field of psychological social psychology narrowly construed. Certainly, I write with an assurance that would have been hard to muster in the heyday of the experimental pursuit of subtle implications of dissonance theory. But the conception of social psychology that I am addressing is an older and broader one than that which became prevalent in the period of laboratory experimentalism. In the tradition of William McDougall, G. H. Mead, and Gordon Allport, this concept embraces man's experience and behavior as a social, culture-bearing, symbolizing animal. I therefore find the distinction between social and personality psychology artificial and constrictive. Personality-and-social psychology, as these terms enter the title of Division 8 of the American Psychological Association and of one of the central scientific journals of the association, is what I am talking about. And the discontent that partly motivates a number of these chapters is symbolized by the fact that I have been finding myself frankly uninterested in many of the research papers delivered in meetings of that division or published in the tightly refereed pages of that journal. They don't seem to me to contribute sufficiently to understanding man's experience and behavior as a social, culture-bearing, symbolizing animal. Instead, person and group get lost to sight in the pursuit of variables via meticulously elaborated experimental designs—designs that incidentally impose a snap-shot linear causal model on social behavior that does violence to what, on other occasions, we think we know about its interactive, recursive nature. We should expect and demand more of our science and try to contribute more to an understanding that becomes increasingly urgent for human survival.

I now address some general issues in order to clarify what I mean by humanizing social psychology, and why I think it is desirable. I comment briefly on the humanistic tradition and its implications for psychology, and conclude with an introductory discussion of extrascientific, metapsychological models of man as they shape and in turn may be modified by the scientific enterprise —a matter with which several of the chapters deal.

Organized humanistic psychology has given humanism in psychology a connotation far removed from its Renaissance origins. As it has flowered in my adopted state of California and spread widely in affluent urban America, the humanistic psychology that is linked with the sensitivity training, encounter, and personal growth movement (Back, 1972) is in the main antiscientific, even anti-rational, and in an excess of anti-Puritan flight from human responsibility into the here-and-now. It opens itself chaotically to a shallow eclectic mysticism or occultism without the spiritual discipline by which the great mystics of the religious past left intelligible peaks of human experience in their wake rather than ephemeral and escapist peak experiences that dissolve in alienation. I agree with Sigmund Koch (1973), a first-rate scientific psychologist and philosopher of science become humanist in the traditional sense, that much of the touchy-feely activity sponsored in the name of humanistic psychology is a shoddy, mindless substitute for the actualization of our human potential, for the realization of our possibilities for truly human relationships. (People are complex, obscure creatures who must work to understand and cherish one another. Instant communion comes cheap and may temporarily relieve a desperate sense of lack; it cannot substitute for love.)

The excesses of humanistic psychology are understandable, if not entirely excusable, as a reaction against the extremely dehumanizing impact of our technological-bureaucratic commercial society. (I do not say capitalist, because the society of our Soviet counterparts is no better.) Historically, those who have raised the banner of humanism have been embattled with an opposition that they regard as antihuman. For the humanists of the Renaissance, who gave enduring honor to the name, it was the medieval Church. Revelling in the newly recovered pagan classics, they celebrated the miracle of the whole man as Microcosm in an anthropocentric

Cosmos in which the beginnings of scientific inquiry jostled happily with hermetic mysticism. Later on with Vico, humanism achieved a historical perspective, the vision of a grand drama in which Man creates his own nature on the stage of history.

Recent academic humanism has been a pallid reflection of academic political organization, in which the humanities face (and typically oppose) the social and natural sciences in a rear-guard action to defend the remnants of the older humanistic tradition (minus the classics) as the basis for liberal education. Partly they have forfeited their claim by mimicking the sciences in pedantic scholarship. Insofar as they have been true to their heritage, they conserve it as a reservoir of objectified human experience to sensitize incoming generations to the wide range of potential that has in fact been realized in history and culture (far wider and deeper than can be discerned unaided in the here-and-now). They also foster the creative arts and letters, with respect for the discipline that is required if the creative impulse is to be brought to realization and for the traditions that must be mastered if innovation is to be significant.

The academic politics of resource allocation aside, the humanities of the present day complement the natural and social sciences as joint successors to the integral humanism of the Renaissance; there is no intrinsic basis for opposition. In principle, there should be room for a humanistic psychology within the humanities so conceived, one that would draw upon literature and the arts as well as on living experience to sensitize our awareness to human potential. Such a venture would not need to be committed to the self-corrective social program of observation, abstract conceptualization, test, and reformulation that by successive approximation and occasional revolutions yields a progressively firmer and more comprehensive grasp on reality—the scientific enterprise. A few psychologists have devoted themselves to such a humanistic undertaking, which is far from characteristic of humanistic psychology. Perhaps the trouble is that writers like Shakespeare, Dostoevski, Henry James, Nietzsche, and Proust, and the critics who have commented upon their work, have done this kind of humanistic psychology so well that little remains for the psychologist who follows in their tracks. He is likely to sound like a second-rate literary critic, not a creative psychologist-humanist.

When I call for humanizing social psychology, then, I am not asking my colleagues and students to stop doing science. I certainly am not inviting them to make the pilgrimage to Esalen, though it might help some of them. I want rather to nudge our faltering social science toward close attention to human experience and human problems. Since, after all, our subject matter is Man, our science may even be the better for it.

In my undergraduate days of just-post-Watsonian behaviorism, anthropomorphism was a serious charge to bring against a theorizing psychologist. As late as the 1940s, psychological reputations were built by validating psychoanalytic hypotheses via the bizarre procedure of seeing whether analogues could be found in the behavior of the laboratory rat. In its eagerness to be scientific, psychology has rather ridiculously modeled its theories on what it understood of the sophisticated physical sciences and has respected findings about rats and pigeons more than ones about people. If the situation in psychology is better in this respect today than when I was a sophomore, as it surely is, I doubt that it is because we let our reverence for the harder sciences intrude any less irrelevantly. Rather, our cousins the apes now compete successfully with rats for our scientific attention, and the model of the electronic computer has supplanted that of the telephone switchboard. Far more sophisticated models, both the beast and the machine—ones that fortunately tend to liberate and legitimize our attention to intrinsically human processes.

An anthropomorphic social psychology need not rely on a ghost in the machine, an imaginary homunculus on whom we load our puzzles of psychological explanation. It is rather a psychology in which terms like *wish, intention, belief, commitment,* and *feeling* and corresponding inferred dispositions appropriate to people can have their place. By the same token, it is a psychology that can play a role in self-understanding, in the critical guidance of social action.

A humanized social psychology would be anthropomorphic in this sense. (The special attention given in several of the chapters that follow to the causal relevance of feelings of efficacy and, more generally, to attitudes of hope and self-respect is an illustration.) It would also seek to contribute in the context of the unprecedented predicaments and dilemmas that are faced by mankind. In part this contribution will be technical, toward the solution of urgent social problems in which there is a psychological ingredient. But in part, and by no means unimportantly, it can also be interpretative, helping people to achieve creative redefinition of their problems and helping them to understand themselves in their historic situation so that wise social action is possible. Although this interpretative role of social psychology and social science has fallen into disrepute since the early days of speculative theory, especially among scientific psychologists, I suggest in Chapter Eleven that some of the most impressive recent contributions of psychology with respect to social problems have in fact been of this sort. The interpretative role (based on the best attainable scientific understanding) is in turn congruent with humanistic ethics; the psychologist should serve to the extent that he can as collaborator rather than as technocratic expert in relation to the people whom he helps (Chapter Twelve), so as to enhance human freedom and dignity.

If social psychology is to address itself cogently to social problems and matters of human significance, it will need to become rather less muscle-bound methodologically than it has been in the recent past. Too often the triviality of research problems has been ignored because of fascination with the elegance of experimental or statistical techniques, sometimes even with the audacity and complexity of stage management and experimental manipulations. But more, not less, scientific and technical competence will be required of us if we are to have useful things to say about the complex problems of social behavior in the real world. McGuire (1973) makes valuable suggestions about directions in which social psychology ought to develop for the health of the science; these suggestions seem to me equally applicable to increasing its human relevance.

The social psychology that I favor and seek to promote is thus both scientific and humanistic. The attractive simplicities of ideological polarization have the result that effective spokesmen for this junction are in short supply, at least in the public arena. (Many good psychologists work quietly on a scientific agenda that contributes to humane ends.) Since irrationalism and denial of science seem to have a strong appeal to the disaffected young (some of whose attitudes are explored in Chapter Four), we must speak out

if we believe that our best grounds for hope lie in human rationality
—especially as developed in the scientific enterprise.

The humanist philosopher Frankel (1973) most articulately
examines the appeals and fallacies of irrationalism, including the
psychological variety. As he puts it, the countercultural spokesmen
of irrationalism "offer a vision of how men should live [that] is
essentially passive and wistful. It is that of the Lotus-Eater. The
dream is of a scheme of things in which human beings face no
difficult dilemmas and all good things are equally possible. What,
after all, is the imperative for rationality in action? It is simply that,
in human life, appearances are deceptive, impulses and desires at
cross-purposes, and time, energy, and resources limited. Irrationalism asks us to believe that these constraints do not exist in the
world, not when it is rightly understood; irrationalism asks us
further to believe that rational methods, which emerge to mitigate
these constraints, are their cause" (pp. 930–931).

Contemporary philosophers of science increasingly agree that
any knowledge-seeking inquiry begins with stipulations or assumptions that determine what will be regarded as data and evidence,
that set the questions for investigation, and that establish the nature of acceptable explanations. The scientist's commitment to rationality rests on such a basis. The various sorts of positivism that
assert the inherent primacy or exclusive legitimacy of certain kinds
of data have no claim to special privilege from this perspective; we
can note the assertion without any compulsion to accept it. For the
scientist, the merit of one or another set of epistemological assumptions is assessed pragmatically in terms of their elaborated consequences as worked out in the collective process of inquiry and
criticism.

The models of man entertained by the personality-and-social
psychologist have this character of preempirical stipulation, which
sets the terms of inquiry and shapes its strategy and tactics. In a
playfully brilliant paper, Little (1972) makes a serious distinction
between reflexive and nonreflexive models of man. In the nonreflexive type, the implicit model entertained by the psychologist of
himself as investigator has nothing in common with his explicit
model of the subjects of his investigation. A good case is B. F.

Skinner's metapsychology, in which Skinner the scientist, polemicist, and novelist and his alter ego, the Utopian Frazier, exemplify an implicit model of man radically different from the explicit model that his theory promulgated for the rest of us (see Chapter Eleven). In the reflexive type however, essentially the same model is proposed by the psychologist for himself and for his subjects. Little considers a variety of reflexive models, starting with George Kelly's man as scientist. He obviously enjoys juggling a multiplicity of models each entertained with "as-if" half seriousness; the paper exemplifies how such a theoretical attitude can free the conceptual imagination and open new vistas for inquiry.

In the thought that underlies this book, however, I find such an as-if attitude foreign. I feel quite square and unplayful about the selection of models. It seems to me that any nonreflexive model of social man is just plain wrong: inconsistent in its treatment of psychological data and inadequate to the task of a human psychology. And I want to struggle as best I can toward a relatively comprehensive reflexive model that points up with some adequacy what we think we know and can discover about people, including ourselves. This is for me a central goal of a humanistic social psychology.

My prior stipulations commit me to this less playful endeavor as having more than academic importance. Following in this respect Mead (1934), I see man's linked species-specific capacities of symbolization and self-awareness as implying reflexivity in another sense: man's commentary on his own behavior—and on his nature—enters into the guidance of what he does and what he becomes. Not only do our theoretical models of man govern our research behavior as psychologists, but the models of man that we believe in and promulgate enter the culture (albeit simplified and caricatured: behold the fate of Freud!) and can have historical human consequences. Whether we see man as a passive pawn of environmental contingencies or as capable of meaningful active choice can entail momentous self-confirming consequences in the risky world that we face. This theme is elaborated in all three parts of this book.

PART I

•••••••••••••••••••••
•••••••••••••••••••••
•••••••••••••••••••••••

EMPHASIS: SOCIAL

•••••••••••••••••••••
•••••••••••••••••••••••
•••••••••••••••••••••••

The five chapters in this part have in common a concern with topics that would conventionally be regarded as sociopsychological, although they were mostly not the topics conventionally studied by leading social psychologists during the period in which they were written.

The part begins with an attempt to give perspective to psychological contributions to the theory of public opinion. I include it because it introduces themes that recur throughout the book in a sociohistorical context that now appears as a great divide in the shifting social orientations of the American public, particularly the young: the short period in 1970 after President Nixon's announcement of the invasion of Cambodia and the killings of students at Kent State University and Jackson State College—a period when the wave of reflex destructiveness that swept the campuses was transmuted into a short-lived episode of fervent political activity.

Chapter Three, on political attitudes, surveys the contributions of attitude research and theory to political psychology in depth. The critical perspective is that of the present, after the close of the epoch of self-confident laboratory experimentation on attitude change. In the chapter I also update my favored version of functional theory and relate it to my present metapsychological concerns

9

with man as an actor, political and otherwise—concerns that have supplanted my earlier involvement with the psychology of attitudes.

Chapter Four, written in collaboration with two former colleagues at the Institute of Human Development, University of California, Berkeley, reexamines research and theory concerning activism and alienation among college youth from the perspective of the early 1970's, when the tide of protest had receded but the basis for hopeful participation in society was by no means reestablished.

Chapters Five and Six, which deal with population issues, seek to involve psychologists in this challenging problem area. The need to control the expansion of the human species on a finite planet poses difficult ethical and political questions (that I attempt to clarify) which have psychological components (that I try to shape so as to be accessible to research).

The treatment of sociopsychological issues in this part follows from the high priority I give to human freedom—a respect for people's individual values, whatever they may be. It also draws on a theoretical commitment to a view of man's nature as a social animal, in which his capacity for reflexive self-awareness is central and his beliefs about his identity and potential are therefore seen as tending to be self-confirming. The model of man implied is examined explicitly in the two last parts of the volume.

Chapter Two

●●●●●●●●●●●●●●●●●●●●●●
●●●●●●●●●●●●●●●●●●●●●●●
●●●●●●●●●●●●●●●●●●●●●●●

PUBLIC-OPINION
THEORY

●●●●●●●●●●●●●●●●●●●●●●●
●●●●●●●●●●●●●●●●●●●●●●●
●●●●●●●●●●●●●●●●●●●●●●●

A time that has generated Panthers and Weathermen, eruptive dissent, and a newly vocal "silent majority," is not a good one for the old weatherman's prediction that today's political alignments will persist tomorrow. Such a time compels attention to the causal dynamics of opinion processes because existing empirical regularities may cease to hold.

Public-opinion research as an approach to these causal dynamics has mainly meant survey research. For psychologists, it has meant attitude research. Over the past generation, survey research has amply proved its utility, but neither survey research nor experimental attitude research has greatly advanced our formulations of public opinion as a social force. Here I first briefly take stock of psychological contributions to the understanding of public opinion and then emphasize the need for psychologists to join forces with sociologists and political scientists in the attempt to understand how the opinions of individuals articulate to become a politically effective force—a problem that psychologists may have a trained incapacity to face. I conclude with some suggestions from the psychologist's own territory that bear on politically effective opinion in our present day.

An honest stocktaking of psychological research on opinion processes should be the occasion for considerable modesty. We can now look back on a double wave of theoretically interesting research on persuasive communication and opinion change, associated with Carl Hovland and Leon Festinger. As we scan what this double wave has left behind on the beach as it recedes, we cannot be self-satisfied. True, many factors that affect the formation and change of individual opinion have been identified and mapped, and accounts of these processes have been brought into contact with theories about general psychological processes of learning, judgment, cognitive organization, and personality dynamics. These advances are all to the good and not to be minimized. They have shaped the discipline of experimental social psychology as we have known it in the past two decades. But Maccoby's (1963) metaphor of the "new scientific rhetoric" overstates what psychologists are in a position to export to students of public opinion.

A quarter century of experimental research actually leaves us quite vulnerable. The initial experimental work appropriately focused on trivial, superficial beliefs and opinions, where measurable change could be produced efficiently by brief and easily conducted "manipulations." This procedure made good sense in a preliminary mapping of the terrain. But there has been little follow-through on consequential attitudes and with parametric studies of several variables in interaction, although there have been some notable exceptions in the work of Sherif (for example Sherif, 1967; Sherif, Sherif, and Nebergal, 1965) and of Janis (for example, Janis, 1967; Janis and Mann, 1968). The result is that a quite comprehensive map is filled in with entries that are suggestive rather than definitive. And meanwhile, Orne, Rosenthal, and Rosenberg (see Rosenthal and Rosnow, 1969) have come on the scene with their skeptical "social psychology of the psychological experiment," implying that subjects in many of our experiments may unwittingly have been conning the experimenter rather than vice versa.

Apart from these uncertainties, three general features of this line of psychological research limit its relevance for the understanding of consequential public opinion. First, the prevailing emphasis on experimental manipulation has deflected attention from the long-term processes by which a person's deep commitments and orientations become established and may subsequently be dislodged. Second—this point is stressed by Festinger (1964)—the relevance of opinion change to behavior change is still shockingly in doubt. While we have learned to talk about the relation of attitudes to behavior in more sophisticated terms than we did at the time of La-Piere's (1934) study (see D. T. Campbell, 1963; Fishbein, 1967; Wicker, 1969; Dillehay, 1973), the realm of psychological research on opinions and attitudes largely remains an encapsulated verbal world. And, third, psychologists have not concerned themselves with how individual opinions aggregate or articulate to produce social and political consequences. They have not dealt with public opinion as a social force. This fault can hardly be charged to laboratory research; psychologists are likely to be biased by training and preoccupation against taking the problem of articulation seriously.

According to the old individualistic view that used to be the psychologist's predictable bias—the view that Floyd Allport (1933) once proclaimed—the very concept of public opinion is a reification. All we can deal with scientifically are distributions of individual opinions, and that is that. While our methodological premises have become less dogmatic, our habits of research still take for granted the doctrine of one man–one vote, which is fine for voting but not for the processes of influence and decision-making that constitute the stuff of politics outside the voting booth.

A skeptical, reductionist view of public opinion in this individualist tradition has its constructive side. We do well to doubt the substantiality of public opinion as a supraindividual entity. That is, the opinions of individuals do not necessarily articulate in the same way in different political contexts. In maintaining or questioning the legitimacy of the political and legal order; in influencing Congress, the President, the military, or local government; in the different content spheres of domestic and foreign policy issues, effective public opinion is surely composed from individual opinions along different lines. The relevant attentive publics are different, as is the role of the inattentive citizenry; the paths from opinion to influence likely differ. This set of relationships has to be worked out empirically, and I take it that the job falls in the customary sphere of political science and political sociology.

One component of the problem of articulation is sociopsychological. According to Kurt Lewin's methodological premise, anything that has effects is "real," and this premise surely applies to reifications of public opinion as they enter the belief systems of legislators and policy-makers, as they are purveyed by the mass media, and as they are entertained by different segments of the general citizenry. What people in these various roles believe public opinion to be obviously affects what they do.

Events of the past few years provide some interesting illustrations of how beliefs about public opinion can influence realities. One involves President Nixon's invention of the silent majority, which has my grudging admiration as an inspired political tactic. By giving an explicit label to a segment of the population whose general agreement with many of his less liberal policies would otherwise be neutralized by its normal tendency to be politically inert, Nixon would seem to have reaped an immediate dividend in self-fulfilling political perception. Verbal magic is obviously only part of the story, but I think it improves the prospects of his intended new coalition. I admire the strategy but fear for the consequences. I hope that public-opinion research in progress may capture enough of what is happening to advance our understanding of how the manipulation of political perception can alter the political facts.

The events on our campuses in the spring of 1970 as I interpreted them at the time provide another example of feedback processes whereby perceptions of public opinion change political realities. After the assassinations of Martin Luther King, Jr., and the Kennedys, the playing out of the McCarthy crusade, the police riot at the 1968 Democratic National Convention, and the fragmentation of the Students for a Democratic Society (SDS), the campuses that had previously been swept by activist protest seemed to be settling into a kind of sullen peace. Although American Council on Education data (see Bayer, Astin, and Baruch, 1970) showed some trends toward increasing polarization among students, those sympathetic to the left were tending toward hopelessness—copping out in quietism and drugs or exploding in nihilistic expressive violence.

Nixon's speech on Cambodia and the Kent State and Jackson State killings of students that followed in close sequence, at the height of spring, evoked an immediate response of outrage. The common and compelling stimulus triggered a simultaneous response that organized and made manifest what had previously been latent and disorganized—and also brought into the picture the less elite campuses that had thus far been quite inactive. In good part, the initial response had the destructiveness of a reflex reaction by the hopeless; it was more expressive than instrumental. But campus perception of this massive response, by students, faculties, and administrators, paradoxically created grounds for new hope and expectations of political effectiveness that substantially changed the setting and nature of student protest and involved faculties and administrators as well to an unprecedented extent. The initial expressive reaction laid the basis for a burst of instrumental activity. The floundering student-protest movement found new life, and student energies on many campuses were for a while directed once more toward normal political channels. Unfortunately, this burst of energy proved short-lived.

According to this interpretation, the visibility of widespread immediate reaction to a common stimulus created a sense of efficacy that started a new chain of political events. The perception of public opinion is a fact, describable at the individual level, that mediates and complicates how individual opinions aggregate or articulate to produce political effects.

My final point bears on perceived and real efficacy as involved in the spring 1970 example. Research and theory have brought psychology at long last to a position in which it can contribute to formulating the conditions and consequences of individual self-determination, an issue at the heart of normative political theory and also basic to protest politics on and off the campus. Claims for self-determination are involved not only in the rebellious protests of students, blacks, and former colonials but also in the reactive backlash of people whose own freedom and privilege seem threatened by the new claims pressed by the insurgent groups. Can self-determination be given an intelligible psychological meaning? Can the gap between the normative theory of democracy and the deterministic theories of the behavioral sciences be bridged?

This problem has long been before the American Association for Public Opinion Research (AAPOR). Berelson (1952) devoted his presidential address to democratic theory and public opinion. After tallying point by point the imperfect match between facts gleaned in public-opinion research and the ideal requirements for a democratic polity, he noted as a problem for negotiation that "the theorists tend to use descriptive categories (for example, rationality) and the researchers prefer predictive categories (for example, group memberships) in 'explaining' political preferences" (p. 330). Is there a place for rational choice in a causal theory of opinion and political behavior?

More recently, that master of political research, Key (1966), argued from presidential voting data that "in the large, the electorate behaves about as rationally and responsibly as we should expect, given the clarity of the alternatives presented to it and the character of the information available to it. In American presidential campaigns of recent decades the portrait that emerges is not one of an electorate strait-jacketed by social determinants or moved by subconscious urges. . . . It is rather one of an electorate moved by concern about central and relevant questions of public policy, of governmental performance, and of executive personality" (pp. 7–8). Key proclaimed the importance of rational choice, but saw it as antithetical to the role of social and psychological determinants.

As I note in Chapter Three, Key's characteristically vivid rhetoric creates a needless theoretical dilemma. Social determinants, to the extent that they do indeed have effects, do not exert their influence by any mysterious process of strait-jacketing the electorate. Social determination occurs primarily through a process in which people who share important aspects of social position and social experience tend to develop similar perceptions of interest. Over time norms emerge that reflect these perceptions. Social determination is thus by no means incompatible with political rationality. Nor is psychological determination.

Glock (1964), in his AAPOR presidential address, raised the problem that I want to highlight still more pointedly—"How much free will is man thought to have?" For Glock as for Key, freedom or rationality and causal determination are at opposite, mutually exclusive poles. This way of thinking is so much a part of our intellectual heritage that we can hardly escape from it.

My suggestion is that the time has come for us to break free of what I think is a false polarity; we now have the conceptual resources to do so. As social scientists, true enough, we must be committed to determinism as a methodological premise. But freedom, in the sense of self-determination, is not a matter of chance and randomness; it is itself subject to causal analysis. Psychological research is beginning to treat free will not as a paradox or as an illusion, but as an empirical variable that has causes and consequences. Some people have more free will than others. Some people who have had little of it for obvious reasons are now developing more of it; they are getting pushy.

I draw upon the ideas and research of R. W. White (1959, 1963) and De Charms (1968) and evidence from Rotter (1966) to propose that, to a considerable extent, how much self-determination a person exercises is bound up in a self-fulfilling prophecy. His feelings of efficacy, rooted in attitudes and concepts about the self, have much to do with what he will try and what he will accomplish (see Smith, 1968c). And these feelings of efficacy have their own social and personal determinants. The other side of the coin, psychological reactance as a motivational state produced when a person's perceived options or degrees of freedom are reduced, is explored by Brehm (1966).

What has this way of viewing matters to do with the theory of public opinion? The close relationship between general feelings of personal effectiveness and the sense of political efficacy has been established by Douvan and Walker (1956). Almond and Verba (1963) make it clear that the sense of political efficacy is a key ingredient that differentiates political cultures. Seeman (1966), another contributor to this line of development, draws on Rotter's work to relate psychological propositions about a person's sense of control over the outcomes of his endeavors to sociological propositions about alienation in mass society. I am therefore not adding new ideas or facts: I am rather trying to put what we are beginning to know in a new focus. I am suggesting that a psychological ingredient unknown to the deterministic psychologies of the past, be they behavioristic or psychoanalytic, and not explicitly encompassed in my early work (Smith, Bruner, and White, 1956) is turning out to be important in psychological research and relevant to political analysis. The sense of personal control or efficacy as a self-fulfilling source of initiative and political action is a psychological variable about which I predict we will be hearing much more.

It would be good for the ethical and political posture of the theory of public opinion if I am right. Accounts of psychological and social determinants seem to have a strait-jacketing effect on individual political freedom even though, as I maintain, this is a metatheoretical mistake. Behavioral science has projected a mechanistic view of man, which again in a self-fulfilling prophecy has lent weight of dehumanizing trends in modern life and to disrespectful, manipulative trends in the marketplace and political arena. My colleagues in experimental social psychology have focused on the techniques of manipulating opinions and behavior, and in the very style of their research they have unintentionally advanced the dehumanizing trend (see Kelman, 1968). Now that the young and the movement types are calling stridently for self-determination, it behooves our behavioral science to push ahead with the attempt to understand the phenomena of self-determination systematically and causally. Additions to our knowledge of the conditions and consequences of personal control and autonomy in politics should help to prepare us for some difficult times to come.

Chapter Three

•••••••••••••••••••••••
•••••••••••••••••••••••
•••••••••••••••••••••••

POLITICAL
ATTITUDES

•••••••••••••••••••••••
•••••••••••••••••••••••
•••••••••••••••••••••••

*I*n the initial, classical review of
the topic of attitudes, written at a time that from present perspectives seems almost antediluvian, G. W. Allport (1935) began
by saying, "The concept of attitude is probably the most distinctive
and indispensable concept in contemporary American social psychology." Through many vicissitudes during the intervening years,
attitudes have remained a central topic in the psychologist's social
psychology; they have also figured prominently in the sociologist's
variant of this interdisciplinary field. Although the social psychologists of whatever persuasion who have used the term seem to have
known what they were talking about, the vast literature concerning
attitudes includes a substantial controversial literature about their
definition. In this case, as in so many others, definitional controversy is a tedious, but not wholly sterile, enterprise. As we shall see,
fundamental issues of conceptual strategy are involved.

Conception of Attitudes

For present purposes, a working definition that is as un-
pretentious as I can make it seems desirable: "The concept of

attitude, although variously defined, is most commonly employed
to designate inferred *dispositions,* attributed to an individual, according to which his thoughts, feelings, and perhaps action tendencies are organized with respect to a psychological object" (Smith,
1968a, p. 458). Even such an informal definition embraces a
controversial theoretical commitment to a strategy that accounts for
observed social behavior by extracting analytically two classes of
inferred, reconstructed determinants: features of the *situation* of
action, and inferred *dispositions* or properties of the behaving *person*
(see Lewin, 1951). This strategy, which is one that I feel at home
with and prefer, is by no means necessary for social psychology and
behavioral science. It has never been attractive to behaviorists and
other positivists, who like to stay as close as possible to observables.
In fact, the truly radical behaviorist (Skinner, 1957; Bem, 1967)
has no use at all for the concept of attitude, which he dissolves into
particular behaviors, verbal and otherwise, viewed as under the
control of particular discriminative stimuli and contingencies of
reinforcement. Various compromise positions—for instance, merging
attitudes with habits (Doob, 1947) or treating attitudes not as
dispositions but as a special class of behaviors—have been taken by
theorists influenced by positivism. (See D. T. Campbell, 1963, for
a view that holds cognitive and behavioral concepts of attitudinal
dispositions to be essentially equivalent.)

The choice between a dispositional or a positivistic-behav-
ioral commitment can hardly be based on established fact. It is not
a matter of right or wrong. Certainly, the Skinnerians have shown
that they are able to push their approach surprisingly far into the
precincts of human action—though I think only by letting a good
deal of commonsense "dispositional" psychology in through the
back door (see Chapter Eleven). My own commitment to a dispositional orientation rests on two grounds.

One has to do with a broad view of the image of man
(Chein, 1972) that is compatible with human freedom and dignity,
and therefore with politics, and also with empirical, self-corrective,
and thus on the whole cumulative science. The reductive, positivistic
view of Skinner (1971) has no meaningful place for politics, which
concerns the allocation of power among human actors in a polity.
The values of liberty and justice, traditional to normative political

theory, require a concept of human agency. And a view of man as an actor, politically and otherwise, needs concepts to formulate man's more enduring dispositions. Such an analysis of variable social behavior into more or less stable personal attributes and variable properties of the situation of action corresponds with Heider's (1958) analysis of "common-sense psychology," and I take that as an advantage if our aim is to give a systematic account of human action in the world of living human concerns.

The second is pragmatic. Because human beings as we know them grow up in language communities in which, however imperfectly and mysteriously, communication takes place, we do have approximate access to one another's thoughts and feelings, from which we can make approximate inferences about each other's more enduring orientations. Neither as naïve human actors nor as social scientists are we restricted to the Skinnerian world of fragmented behaviors. We can listen to one another; we can even conduct systematic interviews and administer verbal scales. Although inferences from the data of communication can mislead as well as inform, we have good warrant to depend on them in social science as in everyday life. A conceptual framework that excludes inferred psychological dispositions from any legitimate place is so severely restrictive that in practice even the committed behaviorist does not stay consistently within it. Henceforth, therefore, I will take for granted a dispositional view of attitudes.

To return to my working definition, a few additional comments are in order. Definitions of attitudes often specify that attitudes are relatively enduring learned dispositions. But it seems unnecessary to build duration or, for that matter, learned acquisition into the definition. The crux of the definition, and also the point on which virtually all proposed definitions agree, is that attitudes are organized with respect to a psychological object. Attitudes are toward something: a thing, a concept, a policy, a person, a political party—or even the self. They also involve organization—a structured set of beliefs held in readiness; a readiness to feel and to act toward the object in different but coherently specifiable ways depending upon features of the immediate situation in which the object is encountered. One of the founders of social psychology, William McDougall (1921), a great and presently underrated theorist, adapted this concept from Shand (1914) as the basis upon which mental life is organized, though he and Shand used the term *sentiment* instead of attitude.

The dispositions with which we are concerned govern both thoughts (beliefs) and feelings (affect), which are hardly separable. As Osgood, Suci, and Tannenbaum (1957) have shown with the semantic differential, the primary, preemptive dimension of connotative meaning for any concept tends to be evaluative, pro or con. The main tradition of psychological research in attitude measurement has overwhelmingly stressed this pro-con dimension (see Scott, 1968). If one were to attend only to this tradition, a working definition of attitude might restrict it to dispositions of favorableness or unfavorableness toward objects. But survey research and qualitative studies, including studies of particular relevance to politics, are equally concerned with the cognitive content of beliefs.

My working definition fudges in its reference to action tendencies, because I do not want to take the route of definition to decide empirical-theoretical issues that are very much alive. In political psychology, we are of course ultimately interested in behavior—what the person does (which includes what he says on a given occasion). The complexities involved in the relation between attitudes and behavior will be touched upon below. It is still not clear, however, whether behavioral consequences are more profitably viewed as following from a given set of beliefs and feelings, given the person's appraisal of his immediate situation, or whether a "behavioral component" needs to be built into the conception of attitude itself (Katz and Stotland, 1959).

In this chapter I do not take seriously the specification of *political* attitudes. This term could obviously be given either a narrow reading (attitudes toward political objects such as issues, parties, candidates, or leaders) or a broad one (attitudes of political actors thought to be relevant to their political actions). I generally have the broader meaning in mind, with no concern about boundaries. I am concerned rather with interpreting the sociopsychological literature on attitudes for its relevance to political psychology—focusing mainly on the nature of attitudes and the processes involved in their development and change.

My review is perforce selective and personal. There are

forty-three pages of references in McGuire's (1968) definitive chapter on attitudes and attitude change. Two excellent books (Insko, 1967; Kiesler, Collins, and Miller, 1969) have been devoted to a critical examination of theories of attitude change, the main focus of recent psychological attention; and a very fat one (Abelson and others, 1968) treats the single topic of consistency theories. Sears' (1969) chapter on political behavior is in fact mainly a substantive treatment of political attitudes as they bear on voting in national American politics; it has sixteen pages of references. Clearly, then, I must aim more at perspective than at summary.

Some History

The scholarly history of the concept of attitudes is shorter than G. W. Allport's (1935) review suggests. In his day, Allport felt the need for legitimizing the concept by tracing ambiguous linkages to the history of experimental psychology. Given the solid sociopsychological use of the concept since his chapter was written, we can forgo such legitimizing pseudohistory. I have already mentioned a more germane theoretical antecedent in McDougall's (1921) concept of sentiment. The term *attitude* was launched in social psychology (sociological version), however, by Thomas and Znaniecki (1918) in the methodological preface to their classic monographic study *The Polish Peasant*. For Thomas and Znaniecki, attitude and *value* are complementary terms. Attitude refers to any disposition of a person toward an object, while any object becomes a value by virtue of being target of a person's attitude. Thus launched conceptually, attitudes became fully established in social psychology when Thurstone (1928) directed his sophistication in psychophysics to the problem of their measurement. What could be more legitimizing? In fact, a sophisticated theory of attitude measurement has developed from the beginnings launched by Thurstone (see Scott, 1968), a line of development that has thus far mainly served the legitimizing function. For better or worse, the theoretically interesting experimental studies of attitude of the last two decades have mostly used very simple, even naïve indices of attitude: single items presented for agreement or disagreement, or ad hoc and a priori "scales" assembled without regard for psychometric nicety. The methodological inventiveness of the experimenters has been invested almost wholly in the manipulations of experimentation, not in the mapping and measurement of attitudinal variables. As for descriptive analyses of public attitudes, particularly relevant to political psychology, these have mainly drawn upon the techniques of survey design and analysis, not of attitude scaling (see Hyman, 1955, 1973).

The research of the early period—reviewed by Allport (1935) and by Murphy, Murphy, and Newcomb (1937), who each declared attitudes to be a central topic of social psychology—was in fact not very interesting or substantial. The characteristic approach was descriptive and correlational (mainly on college sophomores, at that), with little sustained attention to the conditions under which attitudes are formed and modified and little effort to connect the psychology of attitudes with general explanatory principles.

One of the substantial studies of this period (Murphy and Likert, 1938) came up with little that was more solid or reliable than the finding that among college students radicalism was somehow associated with dissatisfaction. (Strictly speaking, radicalism-conservatism is a personality trait rather than an attitude, since it lacks a psychological object. As a trait, however, it is defined by consistencies among attitudes toward a variety of social objects.) It was popular to correlate radicalism-conservatism with personality traits like introversion-extraversion—also being newly and crudely measured. There was little by way of theory to guide the venture, and little by way of theory resulted from it. Eysenck (1954) pursued a similar strategy with explicit theory and more sophisticated methods, but his study is badly faulted and its conclusions cannot be accepted (see Christie, 1956).

About the time of World War II, then, the psychology of attitudes was at low ebb. Maybe it was still the central topic of social psychology, but it did not attract the bright young investigators, some of whom were finding exciting new directions in the experimental group dynamics of Kurt Lewin. Several developments in the late 1930s and the 1940s radically changed the complexion of the field. As a result, during the 1950s and 1960s attitudes at last really earned a central place in the heart of a burgeoning, primarily experimental social psychology.

One development, which began in the late 1930s with the invention of public-opinion polls (later rechristened for scientific purposes as sample surveys), carried the study of attitudes off the campus into the territory of real political life. The major thrust was under sociological auspices. Paul Lazarsfeld in particular introduced analytic methods for treating successive interviews with "panels" of respondents, and employed this approach in studying the determinants of voting decisions in presidential campaigns (see, for example, Lazarsfeld, Berelson, and Gaudet, 1944). The emphasis was on demographic predictors of the voting decision, such as rural-urban residence, socioeconomic status, and religious affiliation. Survey methodology in the study of attitudes (though not directly political ones) was substantially advanced in the wartime studies, directed by the sociologist Stouffer, that resulted in the volumes of *The American Soldier* (Stouffer and others, 1949).

But psychologists too were employing the new survey technology—initially, under the leadership of Rensis Likert and Angus Campbell, in the Bureau of Program Surveys of the United States Department of Agriculture and later at the Survey Research Center of the University of Michigan. When these psychologists turned their attention to the study of voting decisions, they placed focal emphasis on attitudes—such as toward candidate, toward party, and toward campaign issues. (For a classic later example in this tradition, see A. Campbell and others, 1960; see also the review by Sears, 1969.) They typically paid much more attention than sociologists to beliefs—cognitive structures—embedded in these attitudes. Whether under psychological or sociological auspices, survey research has provided the major descriptive substantive content of the psychology of political attitudes. More than any other research tradition, it has brought their study into contact with the realities of political life.

A second development followed from the surge of academic interest in psychoanalytic theory that, in the immediate postwar years, accompanied the launching of a self-conscious clinical psychology. The studies brought together in *The Authoritarian Per-*

sonality (Adorno and others, 1950) drew upon a liberalized psycho-analytic theory (in keeping with the emerging dominance of "ego psychology" in psychoanalytic circles) to give a motivational inter-pretation of anti-Semitic and more generalized ethnocentric atti-tudes in terms of defensive personality processes. En route, the au-thors extended their interpretation to antidemocratic or "fascist" orientations generally. The F scale, devised to measure these orienta-tions, staked a claim for itself in an ambiguous common ground overlapping attitudes, ideology, and personality. Over the ensuing decade, its availability led to a large amount of research, much of which was unfortunately consumed in exploring the scale's technical defects. The tide of research interest in the topic unfortunately waned at about the point when more adequate measures were be-coming available (Kirscht and Dillehay, 1967). In the present con-text, *The Authoritarian Personality* is important because it reintro-duced interest in the psychodynamic basis of political attitudes, emphasizing more systematic methods and more explicitly delimited and elaborated theory than was characteristic of Lasswell's (1930) initial ground-breaking foray. (See Sanford, 1973.)

The third major development began with wartime experi-mental studies of the impact of army films for internal propaganda, and emerged full-blown shortly after the war as a new laboratory-based experimental social psychology, in which attitude change was the focal topic of experiment and theory. Carl Hovland, a brilliant experimental psychologist who was drawn in as a consultant to direct a program of research on army orientation films (Hovland, Lumsdaine, and Sheffield, 1949), carried forward the research at Yale after the war in a vigorous collaborative program on persuasive communication. Unlike the earlier studies of propaganda and atti-tude change (Murphy, Murphy, and Newcomb, 1937), the Yale studies were guided by theories drawn from general psychology. The predilection of Hovland and his closest collaborators was for the kind of learning theory identified with Yale and the names of Clark Hull and Kenneth Spence, but the program was actually guided by a theoretically neutral empirical scheme that mapped the effects of persuasive communication into those attributable to the source of the communication, to the content of the communication, to the predispositions of the audience, and to responses induced to the communication. (This scheme can be traced to Lasswell.) Different theoretical models could be drawn upon, and were, for hypotheses. A programmatic statement that presented an impressive initial series of experiments (Hovland, Janis, and Kelley, 1953) was followed by a series of monographs that filled in much of the picture sketched in the initial volume. (See Hovland and Janis, 1959; Rosenberg and Abelson, 1960; M. Sherif and Hovland, 1961.)

Added to this manifestly fruitful research program, which seemed to be yielding a new experimental rhetoric, was a simple, new, imperialistic theory pushed with proselytizing enthusiasm by an incomparably ingenious experimentalist. The proselytizing experimentalist was Leon Festinger, the theory concerned "cognitive dissonance" (Festinger, 1957), and the heyday of experimental social psychology (the late 1950s and the 1960s) followed. In other respects the timing was right: through the National Institute of Mental Health and the National Science Foundation, the federal government released unprecedented resources to train researchers in the behavioral sciences and to support their basic research. That the new laboratory studies of attitude change came to concern themselves with abstruse theoretical and methodological issues was for the time being an advantage, not a handicap. Under the system of research grants by peer review, the new field expanded under its own directives, with few external brakes applied.

The study of attitude change, then, suddenly became integrally linked with the competitive extension and elaboration (not just the application) of general theories in psychology. But these process-oriented developments proceeded in virtual isolation from the content-oriented tradition of field research using survey methods.

Toward the end of the decade, disillusionment began to set in (Ring, 1967). There were a variety of grounds for discontent. It became apparent to those who did not already know it that experimentation is no royal road to truth: ambiguities abound in the experimental realization of theoretical concepts. Although the heavy social investment in experimental social psychology produced gains in the sophistication of experimental design and in alertness to alternative possibilities of interpretation, experimentation (which came to involve increasingly intricate stage management) did not seem to be paying off as much as hoped in replicable results. And the issues to which the experiments were being addressed were getting increasingly detached from the real world of social—and political—behavior.

The preciousness of much work in experimental social psychology also ran afoul of the tide of social concern and discontent that was sweeping the campuses with its call for "relevance." Newly aroused ethical sensitivities were disturbed by the manipulative cast of sociopsychological experimentation, especially by its heavy reliance upon deception to bring social reality into the laboratory. And questions were raised, too, as to whether the experimenters themselves were being deceived (Rosenthal and Rosnow, 1969). Meanwhile, cold winds from Washington added their force to these intrinsic trends. "Basic" research no longer could enjoy a growth economy, and the carrot of funds began to point in the direction of problem-focused studies.

Concommitantly with these developments, social psychologists who had sequestered themselves in the laboratory were becoming interested in field studies. Ingenuity was being directed to stage-managing field experiments that tested sociopsychological hypotheses in real-life settings with unwitting participants. (Ethical problems here, too!) An influential early example, which displayed the value and the great appeal of such an approach, was the exploration of the unresponsive bystander problem—why he so often remains uninvolved when help is urgently needed (Latané and Darley, 1970). D. T. Campbell (1969) was providing a rationale for social psychologists to regard "reforms as experiments" and contributing to the development of techniques for doing so. Field experimentation was thus added to survey research as an alternative—or a complement—to the laboratory.

As I write this chapter, it is too early to predict the extent to which the pendulum will swing. I hope that a better balance in research strategies will result, not just a change of fashion (Smith, 1972). It is already clear, however, that the substantial recent reviews of theoretically oriented experimental studies of attitudes (Abelson and others, 1968; Insko, 1967; Kiesler, Collins, and

Miller, 1969; McGuire, 1968) adopted a more sanguine view of past and future achievements than comes easily to us today.

The Yield of Attitude Research

My own appraisal, as the reader surely understands, is cast in the emerging, more skeptical mode. There have been gains from two decades of eager experimentation, but their contribution to political psychology is surely far less than that of the steady, relatively untheoretical progress toward describing and in part understanding the attitudinal determinants of political behavior, especially voting, by means of sampling surveys (see the review by Sears, 1969). I discuss the yield of experimental attitude research for political psychology under two headings: empirical generalizations and the relevance of theory.

Empirical Generalizations. Experimental studies of persuasive communication have yielded a number of generalizations that can be fitted into an untheoretical map, like the one with which Hovland, Janis, and Kelley (1953) began. For a readable summary of this "scientific rhetoric" I quote at length from Zimbardo and Ebbesen's (1969, pp. 20–23) introduction to the psychology of attitude change. (Zimbardo and Ebbesen draw, in turn, from Karlins and Abelson, 1970.) The backup for these dogmatically phrased statements is most fully available in McGuire's (1968) compendious chapter.

A. The Persuader
1. There will be more opinion change in the desired direction if the communicator has high credibility.
Credibility is:
    a. Expertise (ability to know correct stand on issue).
    b. Trustworthiness (motivation to communicate knowledge without bias).
2. The credibility of the persuader is less of a factor in opinion change later on than it is immediately after exposure.
3. A communicator's effectiveness is increased if he initially expressed some views that are also held by his audience.
4. What [the members of] an audience [think] of a persuader may be directly influenced by what they think of his message.

5. The more extreme the opinion change that the communicator asks for, the more actual change he is likely to get.
   a. The greater the discrepancy (between communication and recipient's initial position), the greater the attitude change, up to extremely discrepant points.
   b. With extreme discrepancy, and with low-credibility sources, there is a falling off in attitude change.
6. Communicator characteristics irrelevant to the topic of his message can influence acceptance of its conclusion.

B. How to Present the Issues

1. Present one side of the argument when the audience is generally friendly, or when your position is the only one that will be presented, or when you want immediate, though temporary, opinion change.
2. Present both sides of the argument when the audience starts out disagreeing with you, or when it is probable that the audience will hear the other side from someone else.
3. When opposite views are presented one after another, the one presented last will probably be more effective. . . .
4. There will probably be more opinion change in the direction you want if you explicitly state your conclusions than if you let the audience draw their own, except when they are rather intelligent. Then implicit conclusion drawing is better.
5. Sometimes emotional appeals are more influential, sometimes factual ones. It all depends on the kind of audience.
6. Fear appeals: The findings generally show a positive relationship between intensity of fear arousal and amount of attitude change, if recommendations for action are explicit and possible, but a negative reaction otherwise.
7. The fewer the extrinsic justifications provided in the communication for engaging in counternorm behavior, the greater the attitude change after actual compliance [if it occurs].
8. No final conclusion can be drawn about whether the opening or closing parts of the communication should contain the more important material.
9. Cues which forewarn the audience of the manipulative intent of the communication increase resistance to it, while the presence of distractors simultaneously presented with the message decreases resistance.

C. The Audience as Individuals

1. The people you want most in your audience are often least likely to be there. There is evidence for selective seeking and

exposure to information consonant with one's position, but not for selective avoidance of information dissonant with one's position.

2. The level of intelligence of an audience determines the effectiveness of some kinds of appeals.

3. Successful persuasion takes into account the reasons underlying attitudes as well as the attitudes themselves. That is, the techniques used must be tailored to the basis for developing the attitude.

4. The individual's personality traits affect his susceptibility to persuasion; he is more easily influenced when his self-esteem is low.

5. There are individuals who are highly persuasible and who will be easily changed by any influence attempt, but who are equally influenceable when faced with countercommunications.

6. Ego involvement with the content of communication (its relation to ideological values of the audience) decreases the acceptance of its conclusions. Involvement with the consequences of one's response increases the probability of change and does so more when source-audience discrepancy is greater.

7. Actively role-playing a previously unacceptable position increases its acceptability.

D. The Influence of Groups

1. A person's opinions and attitudes are strongly influenced by groups to which he belongs and wants to belong.

2. A person is rewarded for conforming to the standards of the group and punished for deviating from them.

3. People who are most attached to the group are probably least influenced by communications which conflict with group norms.

4. Opinions which people make known to others are harder to change than opinions which people hold privately.

5. Audience participation (group discussion and decision-making) helps to overcome resistance.

6. Resistance to a counternorm communication increases with the salience of one's group identification.

7. The support of even one other person weakens the powerful effect of a majority opinion on an individual.

8. A minority of two people can influence the majority if they are consistent in their deviant responses. [The last two propositions pertain to small face-to-face groups.]

E. The Persistence of Opinion Change
1. In time, the effects of a persuasive communication tend to wear off.
   a. A communication from a positive source leads to more rapid decay of attitude change over time than one from a negative source.
   b. A complex or subtle message produces slower decay of attitude change.
   c. Attitude change is more persistent over time if the receiver actively participates in, rather than passively receives, the communication.
2. Repeating a communication tends to prolong its influence.
3. More of the desired opinion change may be found some time after exposure to the communication than right after exposure (sleeper effect) [which is greater for communications from less trustworthy or negatively evaluated communicators].

How the reader reacts to such a list must be a virtual Rorschach test of his orientation to social research. Most of the points seem obvious, yet the contraries of many of them could reasonably be maintained. The passage quoted is a fair rendition of the empirical outcome of an enormous amount of research—some of it directed primarily to more esoteric theoretical issues. As a rhetoric of political communication, it surely contributes to political psychology. Yet qualifications must be introduced about the evidential status of these assertions and about the adequacy of this account of persuasive communication for political psychology.

Some of the propositions quoted (for instance, A-2, B-1, E-1, E-2, E-3) concern the longer-run consequences of exposure to a communication. But most of the research on which this summary is based tests the immediate effects of very brief and therefore, in the long run, inconsequential communications. A confident scientific rhetoric would have to be based upon research that followed the effects of more extensive exposure to persuasive communication through longer time.

As proposition C-1 recognizes implicitly, research on attitude change pertains mostly to what can be done to captive audiences. Except under totalitarian circumstances, political communication in the real world faces conditions quite other than those studied in the laboratory. (See Hovland, 1959, for a discussion that attempts to reconcile the contrasting results of experimental studies of attitude change in response to attempts at persuasive influence, which typically find change to spare and sample surveys in the field, which typically do not.) Only McGuire (1964) makes a concerted attempt to study the conditions under which communication can induce resistance to counterpersuasion, and he limits his research to the special case of cultural truisms (like the precepts of good hygiene) that are not normally exposed to attack in the ordinary arena of communication.

A more important empirical reservation is that the propositions listed do not give sufficient prominence to the underlying fact of psychological inertia—resistance to change—which, after all, is the sensible response to any isolated new fact that challenges a person's existing attitudes (Janis and Smith, 1965). Particularly when the issue is important and therefore engages with well-established systems of belief and attitude, or with the norms of groups with which the person is identified, resistance make sense from the perspective of adaptation, unless or until compelling evidence or social pressure is introduced. The fact of resistance, in persuasive communication as well as in psychotherapy, makes the claims of would-be persuaders less menacing than they would otherwise be if taken at face value.

More seriously, this experimental rhetoric is incomplete. It utterly ignores the impact of rational argument, such as cogent versus irrelevant considerations, weighty versus trivial arguments, logical versus illogical reasoning. If the set of propositions gives the global impression of manipulativeness and disrespect for the political actor, the impression is fair. Although, to be sure, most political actors do operate at a discouragingly low level of rationality (Sears, 1969), the fact is that researchers have not brought the intrinsic features of rational argument under experimental scrutiny. The manipulative flavor of the conclusions drawn has to be understood in this context.

Relevance of Theory. Since attitudes are learned in the first place, and enduring change in attitudes is a matter of further learning, *theories of learning* are one major approach to the conceptualization of attitude change. Attitudes can also be seen as embodying the results of information processing and in turn affect the way that a person conceives and judges aspects of his world. *Theories of the cognitive processes* are therefore a second source of hypotheses about attitude change. And as organized dispositions toward psychological objects, attitudes are important components of personality. A third group of theoretical orientations to attitude change thus have their roots in *personality theory*. These differing theoretical orientations highlight different research questions that involve different variables, so they are perhaps best regarded as complementary rather than competitive.

Let us first look briefly at learning theories. We have already noted that Skinner's radically behavioristic treatment of learning bypasses attitudes, along with all other dispositional concepts, and focuses on the stimulus control of discrete responses as it is established and maintained by specified contingencies of "reinforcement" (Skinner, 1957). This is a program that can be argued in principle, and illustrated, but hardly carried out in adequate detail to meet the needs of students of political behavior. The analyst of political behavior can nevertheless learn from the Skinnerians to attend closely to the payoff contingencies of reward and punishment (reinforcement) under which particular politically relevant behaviors are "acquired" and to the current contingencies under which they are maintained. Such attention to significant detail can be a healthy corrective to the sloppy habits that a global functionalism may seem to countenance. (The functionalist perspective is presented at some length below.) As a critical perspective, moreover, Skinnerian behaviorism usefully questions the assumption that attitudes are intrinsically structured. (The degree to which public beliefs and attitudes *are* structured in the sense of patterns of correlations across persons is readily exaggerated; see Converse, 1964.) To the extent that the coherence of beliefs, attitudes, and behavior can be accounted for by external contingencies, the concept of intrinsic structure can be misleading. What people *say* and what they *do* are surely governed in part by different contingencies, different positive and negative sanctions. The Skinnerians usefully remind us of this, though I do not believe that their theoretical strategy can be extended to deal adequately with the domain of political psychology.

Psychologists have drawn on the broader framework of

stimulus-response (S-R) learning theory for a conceptual language to apply in the study of attitude change, which they analyze in terms of the familiar categories of stimulus and response, incentives, reinforcement, generalization, discrimination, and conflict. As illustrated in the work of the Yale group (Hovland, Janis, and Kelley, 1953), the categories of learning theory serve heuristically to set the terms of empirical problems and to suggest lines of interpretation that give direction to subsequent investigation—rather than to generate specific hypotheses. Campbell (1963) suggests that in this kind of use, the S-R and cognitive languages may well be intertranslatable and equivalent for most purposes. The student of political psychology need feel under no obligation to learn the S-R language, I think, unless he wishes to pursue some of the technical psychological literature. The recent stream of interest in the experimental psychology of verbal learning has yet to influence attitude research and theory, to which it might be thought to be especially relevant.

As mentioned, cognitive theories are another source of hypotheses about attitude change. There has always been a strong cognitive emphasis in the psychology of attitudes. As the philosophical basis for dogmatic positivism lost its legitimacy and psychologists ceased to be cowed by its dictates (see Koch, 1959), cognitively oriented theories of attitudes came into greater prominence.

In the traditional alignment of controversy in systematic psychology, learning theories were linked with behaviorism and cognitive theories with Gestalt psychology. During the period of behavioristic predominance, the Gestalt psychologist Asch attacked the stimulus-response account of "prestige suggestion" (a traditional topic in the earlier literature on attitude change) in a series of studies that are described in his excellent textbook (Asch, 1952). The controversy centered on how to interpret the empirical fact that people tend to evaluate a slogan or literary passage more highly when it is attributed to a prestigious source than when it is attributed to a source toward whom they feel less favorable. The S-R account asserted an essentially mechanical process of associative learning, in which the positive or negative affect aroused by the source adheres to the message (on the model of classical conditioning). Asch's Gestalt-oriented view held, to the contrary, that attribution serves rather to provide a new context of meaning; this new context induces changes in the cognitive object, so that changed evaluative judgments and accompanying affect are then appropriate. At least two issues apparently are involved. One has to do with the priority of cognitive as compared with affective factors in attitude change. Do people change their feelings about an object because they have come to see it differently, or do they change their beliefs about it to fit prior alterations in their feelings? The evidence now seems clear that both processes occur; what may be primary is a tendency to bring beliefs and feelings into congruence (Rosenberg, 1960). From present perspectives, the second issue also seems less clearly drawn than it did in 1950: Are the processes of influence to be interpreted in associative or in meaningful terms? Recent elaborations of associative theory, which emphasize central media-tional processes intervening between stimulus and response, tend to converge with the older cognitive theories. Heat has dissipated from controversy as theorists socialized to feel at home with stimulus-response or with cognitive terminologies came to see their differences as more a matter of linguistic preference and conceptual strategy and less a question of truth versus falsity.[1]

During the heyday of experimental research on attitude change, the main focus of attention concerned theories of cognitive consistency (Abelson and others, 1968). The topic became elabo-rated to such an extreme that it defies responsible summary in my allotted space. I therefore restrict myself to identifying a few of the main contenders in the barest terms, preparatory to venturing some judgments about the contribution of consistency theories to political psychology.

One kind of consistency that seems firmly established but be-cause of its obviousness (once established) has not attracted a great deal of research is that between beliefs and feelings (Rosenberg, 1960); that is, there is a strong tendency for people to bring their beliefs and feelings into line. The tendency of voters to support the issue stands of their preferred party has been interpreted by Sears (1969) as reflecting such a rationalizing trend toward consistency. Along somewhat similar lines, Rosenberg and Abelson (1960) de-

---

[1] The discussion of Asch is adapted from Smith, 1968a, p. 461.

veloped a formal model for assessing the degree of "balance" in attitudinal structures, conceived as networks in which affectively evaluated cognitive elements are linked by positive, negative, or null relations. Thus, to draw on one of their examples, a state of imbalance is illustrated by a student who favors coeds at Yale, wants good grades, yet believes that having coeds at Yale would interfere with getting good grades. The imbalance motivates a search for a balance-producing resolution, which might be attained by changing the affective sign (+ or −) of "coeds at Yale" or of "good grades" or of the imputed relation between the terms, or by introducing further cognitive differentiation in one or the other term. Attitude change is accounted for by pressures to restore balance when new information has upset it. The formal model, which develops widely influential ideas suggested by Heider (1958), has not been extensively tested.

The ability of cognitive-affective consistency theory, taken rather loosely, to suggest political strategies is illustrated by Rosenberg (1967) in regard to peace-oriented politics of the cold war era (Rosenberg also draws on the broader gamut of empirical generalizations and theories about attitude change) and by Rosenberg, Verba, and Converse (1970) in regard to peace advocacy during the Vietnam war. In a handbook for doves, the latter authors urge that "the great persuasion task is to show Americans that some of the doubts they already feel are indeed very legitimate ones, and that the [hawkish] Southeast Asian policy which they still endorse and mildly favor does, in fact, violate their positive values and advance negative ones" (p. 97). The relative lack of firmly crystallized, consistent structure in dovish or hawkish attitudes (Converse and Schumann, 1970) suggested to the authors that the appropriate cultivation of inconsistencies could change public attitudes in the direction they favored.

By far the greatest experimental attention has been devoted to Festinger's (1957) theory of cognitive dissonance. The theory itself is simple (too simple, its critics maintain). Any two cognitive elements—beliefs or bits of knowledge—may be either *consonant, dissonant,* or *irrelevant* to one another. Dissonance occurs when one element follows psychologically from the contrary of the other. Thus, my knowledge that I have irretrievably purchased a new house is dissonant with my awareness of each of the disadvantages entailed in my purchase. The total amount of dissonance that a person experiences is a function of the importance of the elements in a dissonant relationship and of the proportion of relevant relations that are dissonant. People tend to attempt to reduce dissonance when it arises: states of dissonance have motivational properties. Dissonance may be reduced in three major ways: by changing one or more of the elements involved in dissonant relations, by adding new cognitive elements that are consonant with already existing cognitions, and by decreasing the importance of the dissonant elements. A general tendency for cognitions to be brought into correspondence with impinging reality is assumed.[2]

In many respects this capsule summary is misleading, though accurate. One could never guess from it the main preoccupations of dissonance research or the nature of its contribution. In the first place, dissonance theory has been applied by Festinger and others to a much narrower range of phenomena than was implied by Festinger's initial general statement: mainly to the case in which a person's knowledge of what he has just done is dissonant with his awareness of grounds for not having done it—a special case indeed. Thus, the smaller the bribe or threat used to induce a person to take a public stand contrary to his private attitude, the more likely he is subsequently to change his private attitude in the direction of public action. Knowledge that one has sold out for a small price is more dissonant with knowledge of one's discrepant private attitude than is knowledge that the price is right, and it therefore results in greater pressure to attitude change (when other routes for the reduction of dissonance are excluded experimentally). Such nonobvious predictions have been the stock in trade of dissonance theorists.

Nowhere in research on dissonance theory is the amount of dissonance independently assessed, and the impression that cognitive elements can be isolated, weighed, and counted is wrong. Festinger and his followers compensate for the weakness of the theory in this respect (the lack of coordinating definitions to link it with social reality) by great ingenuity in the creation of special experimental situations where the presumed balance of elements is such that pre-

---

[2] The foregoing paragraph is adapted from Smith, 1968a, p. 463.

dictions can be generated. The theory is thus ill adapted to application in the interpretation of social behavior outside the laboratory.

Much of the ingenuity of Festingerian experimentation goes into "conning" the experimental subject into taking a stand or engaging in a specified behavior while under the impression that he has a free choice. The predictions of the theory mostly concern what happens after this behavior because of the cognitive discrepancies that it gives rise to. The elaborate manipulations employed to set up situations in which the theory can be tested are themselves more a matter of artistry than of theory. This whole line of research has tended to substitute experimental ingenuity for theoretical explicitness.

Several years ago I was taken to task by some of my colleagues for the following appraisal of dissonance theory: "The conjecture may be ventured that, in the long run, dissonance theory will turn out to have made sense of certain paradoxical feedback effects of a person's behavior upon his attitudes but to have said little that is important about the main themes governing the formation of attitudes and the direction of behavior. Or it may become incorporated in a more comprehensive theory that deals with these themes. The lure of the paradoxical 'nonobvious prediction' can deflect attention from the main story, which may be 'obvious' but needs to be formulated and specified" (Smith, 1968a, p. 464). I now feel comfortable in standing by this assessment. There is some solid residue from the flood of research oriented to dissonance theory, but it is clearly no longer at the cutting edge of apparent advance in social psychology. Attention has turned elsewhere.

Paradoxically, the consistency theories, dissonance theory among them, are poles apart from the cognitive theory of Asch (1952), which, Gestalt-wise, exaggerated the rationality of human judgments. (Asch claims that even if people have to decide and act on inadequate or distorted information, they still can be counted on to behave rationally in the world as they see it. The kind of irrationality brought to light by Freud embarrassed him, and he could only treat it residually.) Consistency theory has turned out to be mainly a theory of rationalization, not of rationality. In its alternative versions, it gives a good account of the strain toward a simple complacent view of oneself and the world, which, we can agree, is

all too characteristic of political attitudes. It has much less to say
about the circumstances in which some people, some of the time,
come to attend to uncomfortably insistent facts and even to seek
them out—though both Rosenberg and Abelson (1960), and
Heider (1958) before them, had the promising thought that we
move toward views that are more complex cognitively because simpler ones make trouble for us, either in our commerce with reality
or in keeping our own inner peace.

An additional cognitively oriented approach to attitude
change remains to be considered. This approach—the application
of psychological theories of judgment (Sherif and Hovland, 1961;
Sherif, Sherif, and Nebergall, 1965)—has, I think, more direct applicability to political attitudes and behavior than the consistency
theories, though it is less fully developed and tested in research. According to this approach, a person's attitude on a controversial issue
corresponds to the range of discriminable opinion positions that he
finds acceptable. The person's *latitude of acceptance* is typically narrower than the accompanying *latitude of rejection* when he is highly
ego-involved with the issue or when his position is extreme. In re-
sponding to a persuasive communication that advocates a particular
position on the issue, he first locates it on a subjective pro-con scale
of favorability with respect to the issue. The persuasive effect of the
communication on the recipient will depend heavily on the distance
between the recipient's own stand and where he locates the position
advocated by the communication on his scale of judgment. Maximal
persuasive effects are to be expected when the position advocated in
the communication falls within the recipient's latitude of acceptance
but near its boundary. (If the position advocated falls centrally in
the person's latitude of acceptance, he agrees with it, but there is
no occasion for persuasion.) Under these conditions, the recipient
is likely to minimize its judged distance from his own position (assimilation effect) and to be open to its influence. When the position
of the communication falls within his latitude of rejection, he is
likely to exaggerate its judged distance from his own stand (contrast
effect) and to resist influence. On issues that do not ego-involve the
recipient, relatively broad latitudes of acceptance may be expected.
Under these circumstances the more the position of the communication differs from that of the recipient, the greater the persuasive

effect, within broad limits. High ego involvement, however, is accompanied by narrow latitudes of acceptance. With high ego involvement, therefore, contrast effects are likely to magnify the perceived discrepancy between the positions of the communication and
the recipient. A more discrepant communication would thus be expected to be less effective.[3]

An additional concept drawn by Sherif from the psychology
of judgment concerns the *anchoring* of judgments to particularly
strong or salient reference points. If I know that a particular weight
is heavy, I am likely to judge any lesser weight as light. So with
opinions: depending on which ones define a radical position on my
subjective scale, my judgments of what is liberal will vary. The extreme or end stimuli in any continuum of judgment are especially
likely to serve as anchors when a person has had little experience
with an ordered stimulus series on the particular dimension, when
the potential range of stimulus values is unknown, or when no explicit standards for judgment are provided (Kiesler, Collins, and
Miller, 1969, pp. 241–242).

There are problems with the theory, and data from the fairly
substantial body of research that it has stimulated are not entirely
consistent with it. On the whole, however, principles of social judgment are directly suggestive about important phenomena of political
life. In observing the radical protest politics of the late 1960s, for
example, I often thought that a constructive political consequence
of dramatizing an uncompromisingly pure and extreme position—
say, on the Vietnam war—is to establish a new extreme "end
anchor" in people's scales of political judgment. The extreme position will not initially attract many supporters, and when it is pro-
moted without benefit of invitation to reasonable compromise, it is
hardly designed to do so. But to the extent that it catches the
public eye sufficiently to anchor a new end point on people's subjective scale, it may lead people to redefine what they regard as a
moderate position and thus contribute to shifting the grounds of
political debate.

Another group of theories, personality-oriented theories of
attitudes, were low in prestige during the boom years of laboratory

[3] This paragraph is adapted from Smith, 1968a, p. 462.

experimentalism, if only because individual differences in personality cannot themselves be manipulated as independent variables. (But the empirically oriented Yale program nonetheless paid attention to personality variables as facilitating, limiting, or interacting with the independent variables of persuasive communication; see Hovland and Janis, 1959.) Before surveying the theories that guided such research as did go on, we need to clear up a confusion that I think prevails in references to personality factors in political psychology.

For most writers outside of psychology, personality has come to connote the realm of deep motivational dynamics typified by Freudian psychoanalysis. When researchers announce, with disappointment or with satisfaction, that they have tried and failed to show the relevance of personality factors to some class of outcomes in political and social life, attempts to show the effects of variables in this realm are usually at issue. A less restrictive conception of personality is also possible, and I think has much to recommend it.

According to this view, personality is the overall organization of a person's dispositions. From this perspective, attitudes themselves are important components of personality and also may be regarded as influenced by the encompassing personality system in which they are embedded. Social psychologists have focused mostly on relatively superficial attitudes, leaving the more central ones to clinicians (like attitudes toward the self and complementary attitudes toward the world, such as hopefulness and trust or suspiciousness and despair). But there is nothing inherent to the concept of attitude that pushes it outside the realm of personality or even toward its periphery.

Researchers of many persuasions have drawn upon psychoanalytic theory for hypotheses about the motivational sources of attitude formation and change. Although Sarnoff (1960) has attempted the most direct and explicit application to the theory of social attitudes, the most substantial impact has undoubtedly come via the theory of the authoritarian personality (Adorno and others, 1950). The prejudiced person, and by implication the proto-fascist, uses his attitudes to maintain a rigid and defensive posture; bolsters his vulnerable self-esteem by identifying with the strong and rejecting the weak; and resolves his own uncertainties and keeps his unacceptable impulses in check (while giving them covert expression) by cleaving moralistically to a world of clear-cut alternatives, one in which the safe areas of conventional respectability seem bounded by unknown dangers and conspiracies. This is a special theory of a particular type of political-social orientation that I would myself place in a broader framework of functional theory (see below). The theory is better than much of the research that has been adduced to support or to refute it. It is still very much alive and relevant.

Christie's concept of Machiavellianism (Christie and Geis, 1970) occupies a similar position—intermediate between attitudes, ideology, and personality—though its sources are not psychoanalytic. Scores on the Mach scale, drawn in part from Machiavelli's writings, tap an orientation of manipulativeness and cynicism about human nature that turns out to have behavioral consequences in accord with expectations in contrived experimental situations. The dimension has obvious relevance to political behavior.

A theoretical approach to attitudes and attitude change that has yet to be elaborated would draw upon conceptions of the self. The data upon which such a theory could build come not from the laboratory, with its pallid ego involvements (Sherif and Cantril, 1947), but from the engagements of self in life crises—including the crises artificially provoked by the Chinese communists in brainwashing and "thought reform" (Lifton, 1961; Schein, Schneier, and Barker, 1961) and in psychotherapy. Laboratory studies of attitude change have perforce been confined to attitudes that do not make too much difference to people, and the theories to which they have given rise may well be correspondingly limited.

In successful cases of brainwashing, a person's deep-seated convictions are attacked and their social supports withdrawn to achieve a profound reorientation of attitudes. The metaphor of "death and rebirth" comes naturally here, as in the case of religious conversion. If attitudes that have become central constituents of the self are to be changed, the person's very sense of identity must be challenged; guilt is evoked, confessed, and expiated. The person is then given practice in performing the roles of his prescribed new identity and is supported in this identity by a new set of social relationships. Erikson (1958) has given a strikingly similar account of Martin Luther's transformation from a young layman into a monk. The parallels between attitude change in self-involving life situations and in psychotherapy (in faith healing and brainwashing as well) have been noted in a provocative and readable book (Frank, 1972).

The most systematic recent attempt to formulate the common ingredients of these "self-reconstitution" processes is by Sarbin and Adler (1970–1971), whose conception of the self is embedded in the more general perspective of social role theory. They note the following common themes: the enactment of symbolic death and rebirth, the importance of the group or the "other" as a source of role demands and a model for identification, the use of ritual behavior, reliance on proprioceptive stimuli to manipulate "core anchorages" of the self, and the prominence of "trigger" events that enhance the process of conversion. In the cases they examined, they observe that "three central processes appear to be at work: (1) a physical and/or psychological assault (symbolic death); (2) surrender and despair (becoming a nonperson); and (3) a working through, active mastery, reeducation, or adaptation process (the rebirth experience)" (pp. 614–615). Unfortunately, largely because of the emphasis on laboratory studies of attitudes, these important processes have not been treated in most formal presentations of attitude theory. Among the academically based contributions that can be drawn upon to extend this view of fundamental, self-involving attitude change is Rokeach's (1960, 1968) structural treatment of personal belief and value systems, in which (among other distinctions) he contrasts a central region of primitive beliefs about the self and world with a peripheral region comprising beliefs received on authority.

A final set of personality-oriented theories to be considered has come to be known as the *functional* approach, because their angle of access is concerned with the functions that opinions and attitudes serve in the ongoing economy of personality. During the era dominated by laboratory experiments, functional theory did not enjoy much prestige among experimental social psychologists, although the variant proposed by Katz and Stotland (1959) generated its share of research. We have already noted that personality-oriented theories did not fit the experimentalist mold of focusing on independent variables that could be manipulated. The laboratory era was also a time of formalization, of miniature theories that seemed to lend themselves to definitive test. In contrast, functional theory attempted to create a coherently eclectic framework in which, for example, the defensive processes highlighted by psychoanalysis have an appropriate place—but only a place, not an exclusive billing.

From the standpoint of aspirants to hard science, another drawback inheres in any functional approach: it is admittedly only a way station en route to a more detailed causal analysis. Only from a dubious teleological standpoint can functions be regarded as explanations. In his focus on the adaptive transactions of the human organism, the functional theorist rests his pragmatic case on the de facto teleology of the adaptive process. He insists that although functions are not causes, an analysis of how a person's opinions and attitudes are useful to him is bound to be relevant to a causal understanding of their acquisition, maintenance, and change. In the social psychology of attitudes, he would argue, we may need to go through the naturalistic functionalism of Darwin before it makes sense for us to aspire to the causal models of Watson and Crick. Psychology has a bad habit of aping the most advanced models of the hard sciences, whether it is ready for them or not.

If we are concerned with understanding the personal basis of political attitudes and their contribution to political behavior, some of the features of the functional approach that put off the experimentalists may even be appealing. This may explain why the schema advanced in *Opinions and Personality* (Smith, Bruner, and White, 1956) may have had more currency among political scientists than it has had in psychology. Greenstein's *Personality and Politics* (1969), which featured it saliently, surely has much to do with its currency in his discipline.

Functional Approach[4]

The functionalist conceptual map presented in Figure 1 is an outgrowth of my attempts to apply the approach developed in *Opinions and Personality* to the analysis of various problems involving social attitudes and behavior—in particular, McCarthyism, civil

[4] This section is adapted from Smith, 1968e.

liberties, and anti-Semitism. I have also found it useful in teaching. It is not a theory that can be confirmed or falsified but rather a declaration of intellectual strategy to be judged as profitable or sterile rather than as true or false. As a framework, it provides a roost for verifiable assertions. My main claim for it is that it may help to counterbalance the normal human tendency to stress the exclusive importance of the variables or theories that one is momentarily captured by. A second claim is that such an armchair "path analysis" of relationships between types of variables can undercut prevalent disputes between partial accounts regarded by their proponents as mutually exclusive but perhaps better regarded as complemenary.

For the moment, disregard the tangle of arrows in the fine structure of the map and look only at the five major panels identified by Roman numerals. In keeping with the psychological focus of the map, Personality Processes and Dispositions (panel III) occupy the center of the stage. Because we are used to reading them from left to right, I have put the payoff in Political Behavior (panel V) at the extreme right. Imagine that panel to include any politically relevant actions that we may be interested in: voting, information-seeking, influence attempts, administrative decision-making, or even question-answering. Our observational data come from this panel and the other peripheral ones; only by reconstruction and inference do we arrive at the contents of panel III.

Starting with Political Behavior (panel V), the arrows (marked A and B) that link it with Personality Processes and Dispositions (panel III) and with the Situation as Immediate Antecedent of Action (panel IV) represent Lewin's methodological premise: All social behavior is to be analyzed as a joint resultant of characteristics of the person, on the one hand, and of his psychological situation, on the other. To specify the contribution of either requires taking the other into account. To take this feature of the map seriously is to regard the old quarrel between psychologists and sociologists about the relative importance of personal dispositions versus situations as silly and outmoded: the two classes of determinants are jointly indispensable. Depending on the behavioral outcome in question and historical contingencies, one or the other may control more of the variance; one or the other may also be stra-

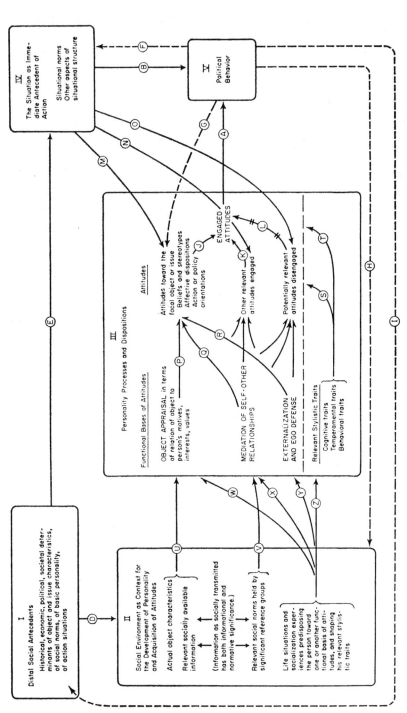

FIGURE 1. A functional map: political attitudes in their personal and social context. Adapted from Smith (1968b).

tegically more accessible if we are interested in influencing the behavior. Thus, changing the law (panel IV) may be a better way of
reducing racist behavior than attempting to change personality—
even if one grants the correctness of the theory of authoritarianism.

Causal antecedents can be traced back from each of the
two panels that show immediate determinants of action. From Personality (panel III) a cluster of arrows leads us to panel II, Social
Environment as Context for the Development of Personality and
Acquisition of Attitudes. Both the environment of socialization
(panel II) and the immediate situation of action (panel IV) have
their own more distal antecedents, represented in panel I. Historical,
economic, and institutional factors have their impact on individual
behavior—both by shaping the contexts in which socialization occurs and attitudes are learned (arrow D) and as sources of the features of the immediate situations in which action takes place (arrow
E).

The broken arrows from panel V reflect the consequences of
political behavior, which may alter the situation in which it occurs
(arrow F), and cumulate across the many actions of many persons
to modify the social environments that shape and support the attitudes of each (arrow H), in the longer run constituting history and
shaping institutions (arrow I). Arrow G, leading back from behavior to personal dispositions in panel III, represents the effects
that self-committing behavior can have on attitudes. This is the
phenomenon so much emphasized by Festinger (1957), which
stands in its own right independently of dissonance theory. A political actor who adopts a position for expedient reasons may be convinced by his own rhetoric.

With the broad framework of the map clarified, we can now
turn to the details. Consider first panel III, Personality Processes and
Dispositions, working from right to left within the panel. We are
concerned here with the inferred dispositions that the person brings
to any situation that he encounters, and with their motivational
basis. The problem is a dual one: to formulate how a person's attitudes come to bear on his political behavior and how these attitudes arise and are sustained in relation to their part in his ongoing
psychological economy.

A first point that the map suggests is that we cannot take for granted just which of a person's attitudes will become engaged as a codeterminant of his behavior in a political situation. Political scientists are probably less naïve than psychologists about this. A citizen's vote for one or another presidential candidate depends, as we know (Campbell and others, 1960), not only on his focal attitude toward that candidate but also on attitudes toward alternative candidates, toward party, and toward issues. As arrows M, N, and O are intended to indicate, the situation plays a dual role. It engages with certain of the person's attitudes and leaves in abeyance others that might potentially be engaged; and it serves as a codeterminant of behavior, together with the engaged attitudes. An example: On the floor of Congress, certain of a congressman's attitudes become engaged with the issue under discussion—different ones, very likely, from those that would be engaged in his discussion of the same issue with an important constituent. But what he says in either situation (and saying is behaving) will depend not only on his engaged attitudes but on what seems appropriate and instrumentally effective, given the norms and contingencies of each situation.

These complex relationships give us no reason to suppose that people's political behavior should correspond to their attitudes on a single focal issue in any simple way. There are other technical aspects to the problem of the relation between attitudes and behavior (Fishbein, 1967); if the foregoing analysis makes sense, however, much of the puzzlement of sociologists and psychologists about the lack of clear correspondence between attitudes and behavior is pointless.

Moving to the left of panel III, we turn to the problem of how attitudes are formed and sustained. Three functions of attitudes are proposed, slightly modified from Smith, Bruner, and White (1956).

Under *object appraisal* we recognize the ways in which a person's attitudes serve him by sizing up significant aspects of the world in terms of their relevance to his motives, interests, and values. All attitudes, not just prejudice, involve an element of prejudgment: they are useful to the person in part because they prepare him for his encounters with reality, enabling him to avoid the confusion and inefficiency of appraising each new situation afresh.

A person's attitudes not only embody a provisional appraisal of what for him is significant reality but also serve to *mediate* the kinds of *relationships* with others and the kind of conception of self that he wants to maintain. Is it important to the decision-maker to think of himself as a liberal Democrat? If so, his adopting a liberal position on an issue may contribute to his self-regard as well as to maintaining his standing with his political fellows.

Finally comes the class of functions to which psychoanalytic depth psychology has given the closest attention, here labeled *externalization and ego defense,* which underlies the theory of the authoritarian personality (Adorno and others, 1950). Here there is a covert agenda: the person's attitude is really less concerned with the avowed object than with containing some inner conflict that is analogically linked with it. McClosky's (1967) data suggest a substantial ingredient of externalization in isolationist attitudes. Not only do isolationists tend to score high on scales of hostility, paranoia, misanthropy, and authoritarianism—content that suggests unfinished intrapsychic business—but they also show more contempt than others for weakness and more intolerance of human frailty. As McClosky notes, it may be logically inconsistent for an isolationist simultaneously to fear the demonic power of others and to scorn them for their weaknesses. The psychological consistency lies in the realm of externalization.

The arrows P, Q, and R raise the functional question about the motivation underlying any attitude. Different topics may be biased toward one or another function (think of the fluoridation issue, for example), and on the same topic people will differ in the balance of the functional mix on which their attitudes are based.

We have by now traced through enough of the map to place on it the distinctions drawn by Kelman (1958) in a widely cited article on three processes of opinion change. *Compliance* in overt behavior for the sake of rewards or punishments represents the impact of arrow B—the predominance of situational pressures over one's own attitude in the resultant behavior. This is really not a case of opinion change but of social influence on behavior. *Identification,* which "can be said to occur when an individual accepts influence because he wants to establish or maintain a satisfying self-defining relationship to another person or group" (p. 53), corresponds in my terms to influence governed by *mediation of self-other relationships. Internalization* "can be said to occur when an individual accepts influence because the content of the induced behavior—the ideas and actions of which it is composed—is intrinsically rewarding. He adopts the induced behavior because it is congruent with his value system. He may consider it useful for the solution of a problem or find it congenial to his needs" (p. 53). This formulation closely parallels my conception of object appraisal. As Kelman notes, the conditions and consequences of social influence are describably different for the three cases. The function of externalization and ego defense understandably falls outside his scheme, since it does not lend itself so obviously to deliberate social influence (his scheme really pertains more germanely to social influence than to opinion change). Attitudes strongly grounded in this function are likely to be held rigidly, but if they do change, the change is likely to be saltatory and irrational, to another attitude that is dynamically equivalent for the person, as in the conversion of a true-believing Communist to a true-believing Catholic.

Returning to the map, arrows S and T, near the bottom of panel III, reflect a different kind of relationship, which falls outside a strictly functional analysis. A person's attitudes and the way they engage with particular political situations bear the mark of his stylistic traits of personality as well as of the purposes that they serve him. Intelligence or stupidity, incisiveness or vagueness, zest or apathy, optimism or pessimism, decisiveness or hesitation—cognitive, temperamental, and behavioral traits like these have their own history and may perhaps partly be residues of the person's previous motivational conflicts, but their immediate relevance for his political attitudes and behavior is hardly motivational.

As we turn to panel II at the left of the map, we now have a basis for identifying aspects of the person's social environment that are relevant to the development, maintenance, and change of his political attitudes. To the extent that object appraisal is involved, he should be responsive to the information that his environment provides about the attitudinal object or issue (arrow U). The actual facts about it will be important in this connection only insofar as they affect the information that is socially available to him. The quantity and quality of this information will obviously vary widely from issue to issue and across the various niches that people occupy in society.

The information about a topic that reaches a person has a

dual relevance, as the internal arrows in panel II are intended to suggest: it feeds into his processes of object appraisal, and it also carries a second-order message about the social norms that prevail. When discussion of birth control began to percolate through Catholic channels, new grist was provided for object appraisal; and, in addition, the important news was conveyed that these previously taboo topics had become moot and discussable. As arrow V indicates, the second motivational basis of attitudes—the mediation of self-other relationships—may then lead to a state of affairs in which it becomes safe to think in new ways. These relationships link reference-group theory (Merton, 1957, pp. 255–386; Kelley, 1952) to the functional analysis of attitude formation and change.

A person's life situation and socialization experiences may also predispose him—in general or in a particular topical domain—toward one or another of the functional bases of attitudes (arrows W, X, and Y). What makes the rational man, in which the first function predominates? A good guess is that part of the story is rearing by loving and confident parents who give reasons for their discipline. In the shorter run, environments that sustain self-esteem and allay anxiety should also favor object appraisal. Research by the Witkin group (1962) on field dependence-independence and Miller and Swanson's work (1958, 1960) on child-rearing and personality in entrepreneurial and bureaucratic families contain suggestions about the sources of primary orientation to the second function, mediation of self-other relationships. As for externalization and ego defense, I would guess that conditions that subject the developing person to arbitrary authority, that deflate self-esteem, that arouse vague anxiety, that provoke hostility but block its direct expression are likely sources.

In order to provide a useful simplification, any map leaves out complexities that it does not attempt to handle. This one assumes the basic processes of motivation, perception, and learning rather than spelling them out. Thus, the threefold functional classification sorts out the ways in which a person's attitudes are rooted in his underlying motives, whatever they may be, without spelling out a conception of human motivation. As for perception, the map ignores the perceptual screening processes that intervene between the environmental facts (panel II) and what the person makes of them (panel III); likewise, between the immediate situation as it might appear to an objective observer (panel IV) and how the person defines it for himself. In regard to learning, the present formulation makes the broad functionalist assumption (compatible with either a reinforcement or a cognitive theory of learning) that in general people acquire attitudes that are useful to them. But it ignores the details of the learning process and the persistence of learned structures beyond their original point of usefulness. It also ignores incidental learning, according to which a person may acquire much of the content of his political attitudes in an unfocused, only mildly attentive effort to make sense of his world. At the time of learning there may be little or no real payoff in object appraisal or mediation of self-other relations; yet should the occasion arise, the basis for resonance to certain political positions rather than others has been laid.

Political Attitudes and the Model of Political Man

The functional view of political attitudes, as I have just illustrated it, fits a view of man as a political actor who is guided in part by rational considerations of how to advance his values and interests according to his lights, in part by the social imperative to locate himself in relation to significant others, and in part by irrational byproducts of his symbolic ways of handling his inner conflicts. The quasi-teleological phrasing embedded in the functionalist approach is in keeping with the view of man as an actor or agent, not as a mechanism or robot, which it seems to me is essential if the realm of politics is to retain its legitimate human meaning. But is the search for *determinants* of political attitudes and behavior, for which my map provides a scaffolding, compatible with the conception of man as a political actor?

V. O. Key (1966), the salty master analyst of American politics, thought not. He saw the new empirical analyses of electoral behavior as adding up "to a conception of voting not as a civic decision but as an almost purely deterministic act" (p. 6), and summarized his own counteracting view thus: "In American presidential campaigns of recent decades the portrait that develops from the data is not one of an electorate straitjacketed by social determinants or moved by subconscious urges triggered by devilishly skillful propagandists. It is rather one of an electorate moved by concern about central and relevant questions of public policy, of governmental performance, and of executive personality (p. 8).

"[There is] at least a modicum of evidence for the view that those who switch [by crossing party lines from one presidential election to another] do so to support governmental policies or outlooks with which they agree, not because of subtle psychological or sociological peculiarities" (p. 104). I am in no position to assess the extent to which Key's assertion at the end of the first quotation accords with the full data available, although there is apparently room for legitimate disagreement (see Sears, 1969). My concern is rather with Key's assumption that any account of political behavior in terms of social or psychological determinants is incompatible with the respectful treatment of "civic decisions." This seems to me to misunderstand the purport of sociological and psychological analysis.

Nobody has claimed that "sociological peculiarities" or "social determinants" exert their influence by any mysterious process of "strait-jacketing" the electorate. Their influence lies rather in the fact that common experience and common social position yield similar perceptions of interest, and over time lead to the emergence of norms that reflect these perceptions. "Civic decision" is channeled, not abolished. It would be the less rational if it did *not* reflect social determinants.

Similarly with psychological determination, which is not to be equated solely with subconscious urges—the realm of externalization and ego defense. (Note, however, the political rationality in the aggregate is entirely compatible with the influence of subconscious urges as long as they are divergent or randomly distributed in the electorate. It is when blocs of voters start externalizing in tandem that a democracy is in trouble—for instance, from McCarthyism.) Decisions governed by object appraisal and the mediation of self-other relations remain decisions, potentially rational ones, even when their psychological determinants are displayed.

Skinner (1971), the humanists, and on this occasion Key (1966) appear to agree on philosophical or "metapsychological" premises according to which the scientific search for determinants of human behavior is incompatible with human freedom, dignity, and responsibility. These premises have recently been given a searching examination by Chein (1972), who makes a strong case that human freedom as we know it (of which political freedom is a special instance) depends on causal relations of the sort that science explicates, far from being incompatible with them. These abstract considerations need concern us here only insofar as they legitimize the scientific treatment of man as an agent.

Empirically, it is obvious that some people enjoy more freedom than others, whether we are concerned with political freedom (as cherished in normative political theory) or with inner freedom (to which psychological analysis is appropriate). Political man may be more an agent or less. A political psychology that seeks to contribute, as did Key, to a democratic politics that enhances human values should be particularly interested in the psychological determinants of political agency. Recent research and theory have made a promising start in identifying one set of these determinants, the sense of political effectiveness—a concept that lies at the boundary of the psychology of attitudes and of broader features of personality. I cross this boundary with the justification of "hot pursuit," because my own theoretical interests have veered sharply in this direction from the traditional area of attitude psychology.

Almond and Verba (1963) show that a sense of political efficacy on the part of the citizens appears as a central aspect of the "civic culture" of more effective democracies. Somewhat earlier, Douvan and Walker (1956) provided survey evidence that the sense of effectiveness in public affairs is at least loosely related to people's general feelings of competence. We appear to be dealing here with highly generalized *attitudes toward self and world* that are important partly because they tend to be self-confirming. A person who feels ineffective in politics guarantees his ineffectiveness by failing to participate. Conversely, a person who feels effective is more likely to participate in ways that actually make him so. The extent to which people's sense of effectiveness is generalized, the extent to which it is specific to particular types of situations or realms of concern, is of course an important empirical issue.

The work on political effectiveness seems to deal with a special case of much the same variable that Rotter (1966) studied under the concept "locus of control." With a rather crude pencil-and-paper scale that has since come to be widely used (called the I-E scale, for internal-external), Rotter found that people show consistent differences in whether they regard their significant outcomes as under internal control (resulting from their own skill and ability) or under external control (resulting from fate or chance). Their standing on this variable is related to whether they take an active or a passive stance in various contrived situations. From a different theoretical starting point, De Charms (1968) arrived at approximately the same distinction, between people who regard themselves as *origins* of social causation and those who regard themselves as *pawns*—and by virtue of this attitude act in ways to perpetuate their being so in fact. He is currently working with schoolchildren on methods for increasing their sense of being an origin.

Much work remains to be done to clarify concepts and measures in this area. Psychological research has unfortunately tended to freeze on the I-E scale because of its availability, much as it did on the F scale of authoritarianism two decades ago. Nevertheless, the line of investigation opened up seems likely to add to the empirical base for understanding, in a causal framework, how people can become more self-determining personally and politically. Since fundamental attitudes toward the self are involved, this research focus makes contact with the subtype of attitude-change theory that, in an earlier section, I noted as especially needing further elaboration and development: theories hinging on the self as a psychological construct. I am currently very much interested in both matters, so I am keenly aware that the functionalist map presented in Figure 1 has no convenient place to represent them.

A next agenda item, then, might call for refocusing the functionalist map to relate the psychology of attitudes more cogently to the acts of political actors (in keeping, in this respect, with the proposals for the study of politics made long ago by Lasswell and Kaplan, 1950). In the new focus, a kind of personality variable would be highlighted that differs from the unconscious motives of orthodox psychoanalytic theory and the stylistic variables of psychoanalytic ego psychology: attitudinal orientations that are constitutive of the self as actor and as reflexive object. Origin versus pawn is a good example. Perhaps in this new conceptual setting, the artificial barriers between a social psychology of attitudes and a personality psychology of motives and mechanisms may be dissolved. Such a development is fervently to be desired if we aspire to a scientifically powerful and humanly relevant political psychology.

Chapter Four

•••••••••••••••••••••••
•••••••••••••••••••••••
•••••••••••••••••••••••

ACTIVISM AND
APATHY IN
CONTEMPORARY
ADOLESCENTS

Jeanne H. Block, Norma Haan,

M. Brewster Smith

•••••••••••••••••••••••
•••••••••••••••••••••••
•••••••••••••••••••••••

*I*n the early 1970s, it is still too
early to gain an adequate historical perspective on the wave of political protest and of countercultural disengagement that swept
American campuses during the 1960s, or on the altered mood that
appears to be supplanting the protest—no replica of the apathetic,
conforming, success-oriented mentality about which complaint was
frequently voiced during the Eisenhower era of the 1950s. A large
research literature on political and social protest in the 1960s had
just been synthesized into some coherence (see Sampson and Korn,
1970; Lipset and Schaflander, 1971; and Horn and Knott, 1971)
when the scene changed. The nature of the change itself is a matter

for debate; surely the public's perception of the change toward peace and quiet on the campus has been heightened by journalistic selection and exaggeration in the same way its perception of the 1960's disruption was heightened.

In revising a chapter written before the campus conflicts reached their peak, we are thus faced with puzzles about both past and present, and with a plenitude of theories and conjectures, many of which are already inadequate. We can be sure that explanations of what happened in America in the 1960s that ignore the world-wide sweep of student alienation and protest—explanations that focus only on the civil-rights struggle, the Vietnam war, and the draft—cannot be complete. Accounts that interpret the campus crises of the 1960s in broad sociohistorical terms as a watershed in the history of youth in modern postindustrial society (for example, the revolutionary and counterrevolutionary views of protesting students discussed by Keniston, 1971) also run into trouble in the face of subsequent developments. At this point in emerging history, we must be modest in our aspirations. While we avail ourselves of find-ings that suggest what may become the trends of the 1970s, we are mainly concerned with what has been learned about the political and social orientations of campus youth in the 1960s—a period that captured the attention of social scientists and the public alike.

Political and social protest in the 1960s, as previously, was carried out by a minority of students. But this committed and pro-testing minority was distinctive in comparison with both the socially unconcerned, conforming majority (who held the center of the stage relatively unchallenged in the Eisenhower years) and the ac-tivist minority of the Depression 1930s. Ethos and action—sincerity, authenticity, purity of gesture—seemed in the 1960s to count for more than achievement and success (goals of the 1950s) or ideo-logical correctness and consistency (values in the 1930s). The reac-tions of young people to American political and social institutions have some genuinely new elements. This chapter attempts to identify the nature of student protest in the 1960s, to provide a coherent conceptualization of the several varieties of activism and apathy, and to summarize the results of major empirical studies regarding the origins, correlates, and consequences of societal involvement or uninvolvement. We begin with a brief historical excursion to compare activism during the Great Depression and in the Affluent Society.

Activism in the Thirties and in the Sixties

In both the Depression era and the 1960s, student radicalism arose from the background of an immediately preceding period in which political apathy, concern for security, and passive conformity were pronounced. These complacent periods, in turn, followed the two most calamitous wars in history. During the Depression, large numbers of young people were actively involved in radical organizations. The American Student Union, an amalgamation encompassing most radical student groups of the time, claimed a membership of one hundred thousand students in a college population that then numbered one and a half million (Lipset, 1966). Student protests of that time were oriented around two themes: radical revision of the social and economic order, and pacifism. Many of the activities in which radical students then participated were similar to those of today. They organized associations of the unemployed, picketed, demonstrated, signed the Oxford Pledge refusing to bear arms for the United States, and designated Army Day as an annual day of protest on which rallies were held and strikes conducted in the cause of peace. It has been estimated that more than two hundred thousand students took part in the antiwar parades of that period (Lipset, 1966).

As of 1966 the combined memberships of the Student Nonviolent Coordinating Committee, the Congress of Racial Equality, Students for a Democratic Society, and the Student Peace Union were estimated between only twelve thousand and fifty thousand students in a college population of six million (Munk, 1965; Peterson, 1966; Braungart, 1966). For activists of the 1960s' college generation, civil rights and peace were the two consuming issues. Each of the activities of the 1930s has a counterpart in recent protests: community organization of the poor in urban ghettos, picketing, demonstrating, burning draft cards, anti-Vietnam days of protest, and peace marches. By the time of the reaction to the United States invasion of Cambodia, and the subsequent killing of students at Kent State and Jackson State universities by National Guard troops and state police in the spring of 1970, destructive and violent actions had become more common. But even in the peak year 1969–1970, only about 8 percent of United States four-year colleges and universities experienced protests in which property was damaged, and only about 5 percent saw protests in which there was physical violence. Arrests were reported in connection with incidents on 12 percent of the campuses (Astin, 1971).

In their status as minorities of their student generation, in their antiwar commitments, and in some of the strategies of protest employed, these two generations of student activists—separated by thirty years—share important features. There are also significant differences which distinguish the younger generation's preferred modes of protest and which have led to different reactions on the part of the adult community.

The Depression years were a time when dissent was flavored and polarized in one way or another by Marxist ideology. Ideology and theory were often so important that differences of opinion within a particular organization could not be resolved. As a result, many splinter groups were formed, each homogeneous ideologically. In contrast, the radical youth groups of the 1960s began as relatively nondoctrinaire; they were oriented to specific issues or particular injustices. Concerned as they were with immediate moral tasks, they were not inhibited by ideological dogma from cooperating with groups whose values might be widely different from their own. The largest radical student organizations in the 1930s were campus derivatives of adult political organizations of the so-called Old Left whose programs were determined and dominated by the older membership. In contrast, most radical student organizations of the 1960s' college generation had no affiliation with adult-sponsored organizations and operated autonomously. But factionalism and ideology developed in the later 1960s, with a splintering of the movement reminiscent of the earlier generation.

Still another difference between these two generations is that protest in the 1960s occurred at a time when, for large segments of the population, material affluence and financial security were at unprecedented levels. In this time of affluence, the leaders of youthful revolt came primarily from families in the upper economic and educational strata; as children they were financially secure, had enjoyed material comforts and educational opportunities, and could look forward to successful careers in high-status professions. Protest was more understandable and acceptable to society in the 1930s, when poverty, unemployment, hunger, disenchantment, and fear were rife. Greater countenance was given to the radical causes of that time by the New Deal government itself, which was modifying its doctrines and policies along liberal lines to accord with economic and social realities. In the 1930s, then, student radicalism was closer to the mainstream of opinion than it appears to have been in the 1960s.

The most dramatic difference, however, between the student activists in the 1930s and those in the 1960s is not in ideologic emphasis but in strategy, specifically in the exercise of civil disobedience. Activist students of the 1960s learned their most valued technique from the civil-rights demonstrators in the South, who successfully used tactics of civil disobedience to fight segregation of buses, restaurants, parks, and other public facilities. In the 1960s, student activists extended the use of civil disobedience, especially sit-ins, into other areas of dissent. Ordinary citizens find civil disobedience disconcerting. The tactics employed by activists in the 1960s estranged many in the adult world who, as the activists saw it, valued security, image, and conformity but who, in their own eyes, valued order, due process, and civility. Estrangement turned to indignant opposition, not only in the adult world but also on the part of many previously sympathetic students, when destructive violence became an explicit tactic of certain extremist groups, such as the Weatherman faction of SDS. Many observers felt that in resorting to violence, the youthful extremists had discarded the movement's most potent moral weapon.

The attention drawn by young activists—in public anxiety, in controversial articles, and in research—has been disproportionate to their actual numbers, since a rather small minority of students on relatively few campuses were centrally involved in protest. They spoke for many not so articulate as themselves, as was shown on the Berkeley campus during the legendary sit-in at Sproul Hall that initiated the epoch of campus protest. During the Berkeley free-speech rebellion, for every student sitting in, there were twenty-one sympathetic students who approved—either mildly or strongly—of the

Free Speech Movement (FSM) (Gales, 1966). The university, particularly the selective campus that aspires to intellectual leadership, provides one of the few institutional bases in American society for cultural criticism and social renewal. What happens on campuses, therefore, matters much, particularly when it is realized that the most selective universities were the scenes of greatest student unrest and protest. In the campus microcosm, as in the larger world, it takes only a minority to set the spirit of an age.

Scope of Student Activism

Almost all research studies of social action and protest among youth have limited their inquiry to the college population. The findings we cite, therefore, do not deal with younger adolescents nor do they reflect the majority of young people in the late teens who do not continue their education. The studies of Coleman (1961, 1965) and of Musgrove (1965) indicate that in the United States, and in England, secondary-school youth for the most part have not been conscientious critics of society. Held off by adult society from full participation, teen-agers have participated instead in a youth culture that is, in good part, an exploitative adult creation. Aspects of the youth culture might be seen as implicitly critical of the adult world of square, respectable values. But even though conscientious protest spread to many high schools by the late 1960s and the downward spread of drug use had become a national problem, the phenomena with which we are concerned primarily involve college students, not teen-agers. Note, also, that we do not discuss the important but very different wave of black and Chicano campus protest that began after the political protests discussed here. Minority activists were concerned with gaining opportunities that the white activists could take for granted for themselves, as well as with distinctive symbolic issues of the ethnic identity.

The earliest thorough study assaying the scope of organized student protest is that of Peterson (1966), who surveyed deans of students in all regionally accredited four-year colleges in the United States in the fall of 1965. Peterson found that local issues of civil rights were most apt to provoke student protest. Complaints about food service and parietal rules governing personal conduct were cited as the next most frequent causes of student dissent. The Vietnam war ranked next, while educational reforms and issues of academic freedom were the categories least often cited as student concerns. Only the off-campus issues of civil rights, the Vietnam war, and disarmament showed variation in protest by type of institution. Private secular universities and liberal arts colleges and large public universities tended to report student protests involving these issues more frequently while public liberal arts colleges, religiously sponsored institutions, and technical and teachers colleges reported little student activity in these spheres. A positive relationship was found between institutional quality as indexed by the proportion of faculty with doctorates and the frequency of protest over off-campus issues. Colleges in the South reported substantially less student protest over off-campus issues: civil rights and American foreign and military policies. In Peterson's study, only one in four deans reported the presence of any radical student groups on their campuses, and only 6 of the 849 colleges included estimated the number of student radicals as exceeding 5 percent.

Peterson (1968), Bayer and Astin (1969, 1971), and Astin (1971) carry the account up to the beginning of the 1970s. In 1970–1971, about 20 percent of United States campuses of all kinds and sizes experienced violent or disruptive protest—this in a year commonly regarded as "quiet" on the campus. (Data collected on the same basis for 1968–1969 gave a comparable figure of 22 percent.) But in the private universities that had been the primary scene of protest, the percentage experiencing severe (violent or disruptive) protests dropped from 70 to 52 percent over this two-year period. In general, the relationship between institutional selectivity or quality and campus size, on the one hand, and severe protest, on the other, seemed to be flattening out. By 1970–1971, protests focused on war-related issues occurred at 46 percent of the institutions where any protests took place, on issues concerning services to students at 51 percent, on minority-group issues at 19 percent, on student-power issues at 62 percent, and on ecology-pollution issues at 16 percent. The data for "severe" protests are much the same with the exception of minority-group student issues, which were more frequently involved (Bayer and Astin, 1971).

Peterson (1966) and Braungart (1966) agree in estimating

the number of organized students actively engaged in social protest at fewer than 1 percent of the total college-student population. However, when the definition of activism is broadened to include politically unaffiliated students participating in social protest, a far larger percentage of students is included. In a national sample of college students polled by *Newsweek* magazine (1965), 18 percent said they had participated in picket lines, presumably for civil rights. Katz and Sanford, in their research on the Stanford and Berkeley campuses, concluded that the number of socially involved students totaled about 15 percent of the student body (see Katz and others, 1968).

What, then, of the majority of students on the campuses of the early 1970s? The most suggestive picture of the changing scene is given by Yankelovich (1972) and is based on interview surveys of representative cross sections of the national college population conducted from 1968 to 1971. Yankelovich finds that, although political protest declined over this period, disaffiliation from the dominant cultural values—or attraction to the values of the counterculture (see Roszak, 1969)—continued to increase. Changing cultural values, in regard to marriage, authority, religion, work, sexual morality, and other aspects of the Puritan ethic became more marked year by year, while political beliefs moved away from the radical peak of 1970. "For example, students in 1971 were less critical of our major institutions—the two-party system, business, the universities, the unions, the Supreme Court, and so forth—than they were in the previous year. . . . Three out of four [now] believe that desirable social change can best be effected within the system. In 1970, two-thirds of the student body thought that student radicalism would continue to grow. A year later a majority believed it was leveling off or declining" (Yankelovich, 1972, p. 7). But for the 11 percent who remained identified with the New Left in 1971, the life-styles of the counterculture and of radical politics continued to go together.

The prevailing mood as it emerged from the Yankelovich surveys was increasingly focused on private concerns. While six out of ten thought things were going badly in the country and three out of ten thought they might prefer to live in another country, students described themselves as confused about the future (55 percent) but personally happy (50 percent). Their key self-ascribed values were love and friendship. In 1971, for the first time, a majority (not a minority) would welcome more acceptance of sexual freedom, and a minority (not a majority) would welcome more emphasis on technological improvements. For 43 percent there was some appeal to the idea of living off the land for at least a year or so; over a third expressed interest in living in a commune for at least a short term. Were we witnessing the early stages of a profound cultural change, as Reich (1970) claimed in his book entitled *The Greening of America?* Or was the mood rather a protective response to prolonged political frustration? As we write, we can only be confident in noting that the momentum of change in values seemed to be continuing as the wave of activist political protest faded.

Although the common concerns of young people center around a search for personal identity, this search takes many different forms. Some direct themselves quite determinedly toward future goals and the achievement of adult roles and status; others take a tortuous, circuitous path as they attempt to challenge the values of a society whose goals do not conform to their sense of humanity or insistence upon justice. In the next section of this chapter, we explore the development of activism and apathy in terms of the tasks of adolescence, the parental values that have been inculcated, and some sociomoral discrepancies that affect youth as they seek to establish an authentic place for themselves in a complex and sometimes compromising adult world.

Development of Political-Social Sensitivity

Constructing a firm sense of identity and fashioning a set of values consistent with the self, consonant with one's history, and worthy of commitment are tasks of the adolescent (Erikson, 1963). The young person entering adolescence has not only to respond to the changes occurring in his physical state and stature but also to encompass a rapidly expanding world as his psychological life-space and his actual geographic environment enlarge in diverse ways. New, extended perceptions of the world, complex new cognitive skills, and different, intense affects emerge and require integration during adolescence.

The scope of the physical environment enlarges because newly acquired competencies and mobility permit the early adolescent to range beyond the boundaries of his immediate neighborhood into the larger, outlying world. Junior and senior high schools widen the range of his encounters with students and teachers and confront him with subject matter, leaving room for opinion and interpretation. The greater freedom to discover and explore presents the middle-class adolescent with a diversity of situations, people, and ideas from which he was earlier insulated (geographically or by parental prohibition). The adolescent must digest these new perceptions and awarenesses in a way that is consonant with his own sense of emerging integrity; however, marked discrepancies with his own earlier values and attitudes and those of the significant people in his childhood are likely because he is confronted with the contemporary values of a world that has dramatically shifted during his and his parents' lifetimes.

The adolescent period is marked not only by a broadening of experiences and a heightening of awareness but also by an increased capacity for dealing with cognitive complexity so that hypothetical, reflective, abstractive, future-oriented thinking becomes possible. According to Piaget, most children prior to the age of eleven conceive of themselves in concrete, definitional, empirical given terms and have not yet developed abstract notions of self or ideals. Between the ages of thirteen and fifteen, a new affective component enters; the adolescent becomes able to experience feelings about himself in relation to abstract ideals (Piaget and Weil, 1951). The development of an ideal concept is possible only when the individual is capable of future-oriented reflective thinking, thinking about thoughts, and when he is able to differentiate between the real and what could possibly be true (Inhelder and Piaget, 1958). With the development during adolescence of propositional, hypothetical thinking it becomes possible to articulate a set of ideals based upon what could be real for one's self and one's society and to evaluate oneself relative to those ideals.

As the young person becomes capable of hypothetical thinking and begins to anticipate the character and qualities of his own and his generation's future within the society, he may find it wanting. He begins to think in terms of daring possibilities, often dedicating himself to bringing about changes in societal values and institutions. Inhelder and Piaget (1958) call this developmental juncture the *idealistic crisis* and suggest that commitment to concrete cognitive attainment by taking a job or starting professional training turns the idealistic reformer to the realities of the adult world, leading him away from the dangers of purely formalistic, hypothetical thought.

The cognitive capabilities emerging during adolescence are accompanied, influenced, and sometimes exaggerated by other future-oriented necessities. The adolescent aspires to define himself as a person who knows himself, not only in terms of what he is but in terms of what he is not. Individuation of one's self cannot occur in an unpeopled vacuum, and the future adult and citizen-to-be frequently casts his self-examination in terms of comparative similarities and contrasts between himself and his family and between himself and his society.

This scrutiny of self in relationship to historically significant mentors and previously unquestioned and unexamined social institutions is a daring maneuver emotionally and is not handled with skill or grace by many adolescents. Some do not even venture to probe at all. Some may parry the hazards and gambles that self-definition entails by avoidance, either by not thinking or only thinking concretely of the next best thing to do—with little occasion for criticism of self or society—defining their roles and goals without serious self-examination.

Questioning adolescents, however, are in a stage—aptly described by Erikson (1963, 1964) in rich detail—that involves a central and essential preoccupation with establishing a sense of *fidelity*. Fidelity concerns the articulation of ideals, interpersonal and social values, and qualities of particular human relationships worth the devotion of one's self. In constituting a sense of fidelity, the adolescent wonders whether he can trust himself to behave reliably, that is, predictably and consistently. He tests to see whether he can esteem himself in terms of his own humanity, veracity, courage, or other components of his ego-ideal. If he is to persuade himself to enter his society as a full-time participant, he must examine his past, his forebears, and his society and its institutions to determine what they imply for himself and his generation. His scrutiny involves at least a three-sided question: Can I find fidelity within myself; can I find it in my parents in spite of our generational differences; and can I find it in my society? Adolescence is thus a time for examination and testing of self, parents, and society. If all goes well between the adolescent and his elders, the emergent adult knows who he is and who he is not; he has made differentiated, informed commitments to some aspects of his society and selected the causes that he will continue to support.

Constituting a sense of fidelity is both an internal matter for one's self and an external matter for one's society, one's parents, and one's own generation. The adolescent's choice in committing himself to the making of his own generation's history depends upon the tolerance of his society for dissent and also upon the adaptive strength of his personality for dealing with dissonance. Some societies and some parents cannot afford, and will not allow, the scrutiny involved in establishing fidelity. Some adolescents cannot pose the questions, protecting themselves with the shared code of peer-group uniformism (Blos, 1962) or conformity. Other young people pose their questions in a nonnegotiable manner so that the answers are merely self-fulfilling prophecies. In these instances, growth may be impaired since, as Erikson (1964) suggests, fidelity is a matter acutely relevant to the ego's adaptive strength—essential for continued growth and greater personality differentiation. Young people who cannot manage this difficult task constructively, either because their own resources are insufficient or because their social predicament is too formidable, not only foreclose their own potentialities for growth but also deprive society of one of its major sources of creative change: the push from each new generation to make society more responsive to its needs.

In the favorable case, the outcome in late adolescence is a shift in emphasis from experiencing, questioning, and experimenting to integrating. In Erikson's terms, such a resolution involves the development of a *historical perspective* that relates to an understanding of the irreversibility of events and the significant cause-and-effect relationships in society. Adolescent ideals become tempered by the knowledge of the intransigencies of reality. The adolescent adjusts to outer reality as he recognizes aspects of his own self and life that cannot be changed or helped. The realistic integration comprised in such a historical perspective does not merely represent compromise with the world as it has always been. Rather, the maturing person's efforts to effect social change become more differentiated as they are directed toward making society more responsive to the needs of each new generation of youth.

The development of political and social sensitivity is, for the individual adolescent, a derivative of his confrontation with life and of the disparities and contradictions that he notices, and has to integrate, between society as it is and its professed values and ideals. The adolescent's reactions to the actual societal context may, however, take a variety of forms, which we now consider.

Adolescent Reaction to Societal Context

To avoid the terminological confusion that seems to prevail in much discussion of adolescent political-social behavior, we introduce some conceptual distinctions. Young people engaged in protest against contemporary social institutions have been variously termed *protesters, rebels, radicals, activists, demonstrators, beatniks,* or young people engaged in *pro–social action.* These terms obviously vary in the extent to which they are pejorative. They also confuse degree of social involvement with acceptance or rejection of social institutions, ideological orientation, and the pro- or anti-social nature of the protest. Similarly, in the descriptions of uninvolved youth, important differences are obscured when such labels as *alienation, lack of commitment, passivity, disaffiliation,* and *resignation* are used interchangeably. Two dimensions seem useful to us in conceptualizing the political stances and social reactivity of the adolescent. The first dimension is the degree of involvement with contemporary political-social issues. At one extreme we find uninvolved, socially indifferent, or apathetic youth, while at the other end of the continuum we see involved, active, dedicated young persons with a sense of instrumentality. In the political-social sphere this dimension is reflected in the degree to which an individual feels that he can make a difference, that he can be an instrument of change in his society.

The second dimension is the degree to which the adolescent accepts or rejects the traditional values and the institutional authority of the society. At one end of this dimension we encounter the young person who accepts the prevailing values of society and conforms readily to its institutions. At the other extreme is the young person who rejects traditional societal values and flouts legitimate authority.

How involvement or uninvolvement is conjoined with acceptance or rejection of traditional values and authority has widely different implications for the quality of adolescent behavior. Before we attempt to coordinate these two dimensions, the reader should note that we are maintaining ideological orientations as a conceptually independent dimension. Although there has been a tendency to equate social involvement and political activism with liberal politics, we have been impressed by the existence of an active protest group with a conservative political philosophy. The continuing presence of such individuals requires that activism be defined independently of political ideology if we are to extricate the correlates of activism per se from those of liberalism per se.

In the discussion that follows, we talk of adolescent political-social behaviors in terms of typologies for reasons of expository convenience. It should be understood, however, that continua are presumed.

One group of young people, politically apathetic youth, is distinguished by its lack of political-social involvement and its readiness to accept the societal status quo. Judging from the studies of Katz and others (1968) on the 1960s' college generation, this group represents the majority of contemporary youth. These young people have identified with and accepted the values of their parents, which are largely within the mainstream of societal opinion. They have tended to handle whatever conflicts that have arisen from perceived discrepancies between their own and the larger world by minimizing the discrepancy and by retreating to their own small portions of society in which career, success, marriage, family, and financial security are the overriding considerations. They tend to accept the status quo, perhaps with a pessimistic attitude about the possibility of change. Focusing primarily on their own individual lives, these young people are little concerned with the long-term problems of society. We may describe these young people as *politically apathetic*. The Yankelovich (1972) data suggest that both the apathetic majority and the activist minority have recently yielded ground to the next group to be considered.

A second group, alienated youth, rejects the traditional values of society, rebels against institutional authority, and does not participate in the political-social arena. Unlike the youth described above, these young people do not accept the prevailing leitmotifs of the culture. They reject its values, refuse its roles, and elect to escape from the culture by opting out. This was the beat or hippie position, well described by a Berkeley student in the campus newspaper: " 'If you radicals see the disgusting nature of present society and see how unlikely it is that anything you do will change it, why waste your time trying? We agree with you that no sensitive human being wants to be a part of the society, but why worry about changing it at all? All that will happen is that you yourselves will waste your youth in an impossible struggle that may well leave ugly blemishes on your soul. Give up the struggle, try to love as much as possible, take a few trips and forget about it all' " (Lerner, 1966). (The quotation marks are Lerner's: This is Lerner's characterization of the hippie position, not his own.)

Young people with this outlook have much in common with those described by Keniston (1965), who studied alienated Harvard students in the late 1950s. Keniston's alienated students had an approach to life that was primarily egocentric and aesthetically oriented. They concerned themselves with a search for adventure, the creation of experiences, and the pleasures of sentience and unmediated responsivity. The alienated are relatively unideological. They live in the present, and their personal present may have little continuity with their personal history. They value their individuality and freedom, and distrust commitments that imply submission of the self to long-range, compromising goals. Their regard for self-expression, their pessimistic evaluation of society, their concern with existential experience, and their patent refusals to accept the hypocrisies they project into adulthood combine to produce an adolescent subculture bent on escape from the conventional society and deeply involved with experiencing. It is not surprising that consciousness-expanding drugs and other sources of mystical experience are sought by many of these adolescents who feel estranged from society and judge issue-oriented protests to be meaningless. We confine the term *alienated youth* to include young people who are both uninvolved and rejecting of societal values.

Individualistic youth compose a group of young men and women who are involved with political-social issues and accept the traditional American values and authority structure. Their political-social commitments are directed to maintain the status quo or even to reestablish an era of unhampered individualism. Their activities include petitioning, letter-writing campaigns, active support of conservative candidates and policies, and techniques of counterprotest as they seek to reinforce the positions of traditional institutional authority. Although participants in demonstrations or members of picket lines, these young people confine their activities to legal forms of protest and reject the tactics of civil disobedience.

This group is not ideologically homogeneous. Some present-day conservatives have been influenced crucially by the writings of Ayn Rand (1957, 1964) in which individualism and autonomy are stressed. These young people may endorse seemingly radical causes requiring only that they be consistent with individualistic principles. Less extreme student groups, influenced by the politics and morals of the conservative position, direct their energies toward maintaining the traditional values that they see as responsible for America's growth. Both conformity and the strong political involvement of these active conservatives are suggested in the term *obedient rebels* given them by Schiff (1964). We call them *individualists*.

As we move to another point along the acceptance-rejection continuum, we encounter a cluster of adolescents, constructivist youth, that overlaps with the activists still to be considered. These actively committed adolescents occupy an intermediate position on acceptance and rejection of authority but are highly involved with political-social problems. They devote themselves to restitutive work in volunteer activities: in mental hospitals, in work with physically handicapped, in tutoring children from urban ghettos, and so on. Enlistment in the Peace Corps, Vista, or Teacher Corps also represents a kind of commitment to effect social change in ways that involve working *within* the existing framework of society. Although these young people may have formulated an ideological position for themselves, they show little homogeneity except in their common altruistic concerns. They lack the zeal of the revolutionary but feel committed to work constructively to alleviate the ills of society. They are prepared to undergo discomfort, physical hardship, isolation, or even physical danger in order to contribute to the betterment of the human condition. They differ from the activists and dissenters primarily in that they tend to be task-oriented, do not categorically reject authority, and work in ways that do not necessarily challenge the institutions of society. Young people falling in this group we will call the *constructivists*.

Activist youth share with the constructivists a history of involvement in good works; but, unlike them, they have rejected major values of contemporary society and have dedicated themselves to fight, demonstrate, and protest actively against policies and institutions of mainstream American society that violate their sense of humane justice. Heterogeneous in ideology, they unite for action on common causes. Their rejection of authority extends to their selective willingness to engage in civil disobedience in the face of possible arrest and incarceration. These young people reject liberalism as misguided. They are not optimistic about the effects their protests will have on society. Although their protests seek to dramatize social issues, their behavior is based on a concern for personal integrity and authenticity. They feel compelled by their need for fidelity to speak out forcibly on issues they view as morally wrong; not to do so would be to participate in what for them is common hypocrisy. They deplore the dehumanizing forces of a technological society and reject authoritarianism and centralism in favor of a commitment to participatory democracy in which political power is placed in the hands of those affected by decisions. Unlike the apathetic, conforming adolescent for whom social concerns are irrelevant, a substantial part of the lives of the young activists is regulated and determined by the issues of current concern. Although sharing the disenchantment with American society and influences of existential philosophy that characterizes the alienated, the activists are more concerned with the existential *act* as a way of achieving integrity, whereas the alienated have been more concerned with existential *perception* as a route to a sense of oneness. This difference in orientation toward the outer or the inner world fundamentally separates what we here call the *activists* from the alienated.

A final group of active protesters, dissenters, must be

distinguished: dissenters share the preceding group's commitment to radical action but lack any history of involvement in constructive social effort. They are specialists in protest. As we will see, there are indications that the dissenters may arrive at their posture of antagonism by a psychological route that is quite different from that of the activists. As angry rebels, they may correspond more closely than the activists to popular conceptions.

Having made these conceptual distinctions, we are now ready to consider the findings of relevant research studies in these terms.

Research on Activism

Most studies have been concerned with the activists and dissenters, the involved, rejecting students—usually without making the distinction. This emphasis began with an interest in the participants in the FSM on the Berkeley campus and was impelled by the incidents of protest at other major universities. Most of the studies have been conducted on the elite university campuses of America where intellect, inquiry, and criticism are valued. Their findings are largely consistent but may not hold for other college environments. Quite other relationships might be expected in the case of minority-group protest. The research reviewed below, relevant to our five behavior types, far from exhausts the considerable volume of studies that has appeared in recent years.

Student Activists and Dissenters. Several investigators have studied student activists and dissenters at Berkeley. Watts and Whittaker (1966) collected biographical and questionnaire data from students who sat in at Sproul Hall, and examined the academic records of a sample of FSM participants. These researchers compare the academic status and questionnaire responses of FSM students with a sample of randomly selected students on the Berkeley campus. Heist (1965) compares a sample of students actually arrested in Sproul Hall with a randomly selected cross section of Berkeley students in terms of their backgrounds and responses to a personality inventory. His research focuses on the intellectual dispositions and academic history and achievement of his subjects. The present authors began a study a year after the FSM crisis erupted. This study contrasts a sample of arrested FSM students with a randomly selected sample of Berkeley undergraduates and with samples of politically active students representing different ideological positions who were on campus during the FSM crisis. The study was subsequently extended to Peace Corps volunteers and to comparison groups on another campus (San Francisco State College). Biographical information including political-social activities, descriptions of actual and ideal self, evaluation of ethical principles used in resolving moral dilemmas, and descriptions of the student's perceptions of their parents' child-rearing practices were obtained from each of the several hundred participants in the study (Haan, Smith, and Block, 1968; Block, Haan, and Smith, 1969; Smith, 1969a; Smith, Haan, and Block, 1970; Haan, 1972).

At the University of Chicago, Flacks (1967) compares activist with nonactivist students, defining activism by the extent and nature of participation in particular political-social causes. Some of the subsamples are matched on a number of social characteristics (socioeconomic class, sex, religion, and type of college attended). The research has been extended to include some parents of activist and nonactivist students as well.

At Pennsylvania State University, Westby and Braungart (1966) compared members of the Left (Students for Peace) and the Right (Young Americans for Freedom). Membership in either organization was the sole criterion for inclusion, and degree of participation in social or political causes was not taken into account.

Braungart (1966) extended the research on membership in extreme Left and Right student organizations by collecting questionnaire data from delegates to two national conventions, the Students for a Democratic Society and Young Americans for Freedom. The questionnaire data, obtained from more than three hundred activists, provides information about social, political, attitudinal, and other background factors that might relate to activism.

Solomon and Fishman (1964) obtained questionnaire responses from a large, randomly selected sample of participants in the 1962 Peace March on Washington. Interviews in depth were conducted with a small sample selected from the larger group to provide more information about personological characteristics of these young pickets for peace. Counterprotest demonstrators who were picketing in support of administration policies were also included in the research. Likewise, an intensive, qualitative study of participants in the Vietnam Summer of 1967 was reported in rich detail by Keniston (1968).

In a careful attempt to distinguish the correlates of activism from those of ideology, Kerpelman (1972) studied Left, middle-of-the-road and Right activists and nonactivists in three northeastern institutions (a small private liberal arts college, a medium-sized private university, and a large public university), focusing on measures of intelligence, personality, attitudes, and values. Activism was defined in terms of membership in specified organizations but validated in terms of a pencil-and-paper scale.

Let us now take into consideration the family background of student-activist youth. The origins of student activists were in the economically, educationally, and socially privileged strata of American society. Whether measured by family income, parental occupational prestige, socioeconomic indices, or the amount of parental education, the families of actively committed students were more advantaged than those of other college students (Braungart, 1966; Westby and Braungart, 1966; Flacks, 1967; Smith, Haan, and Block, 1970).

The parents of activist students themselves tended to be politically liberal (Solomon and Fishman, 1964; Flacks, 1967; Keniston, 1968). The radical positions of these youth can thus hardly be interpreted simply as a rebellion against parental values, as is required by Feuer's (1969) Oedipal theory of intergenerational conflict. Committed students may have chided their parents for failing to act in accordance with their political beliefs and may have accused the older generation of having sold out to the Establishment and the comforts of suburbia; however, the political values of parent and child had much in common and so it is essential to distinguish two facets in contemporary rebellion. Rejection of major *societal* values does not necessarily imply rebellion against *parental* attitudes. Although they placed themselves squarely in opposition to many of the prevailing views and practices of the culture, the activists identified with and accepted many of their parents' values (Block, 1972).

Many young people engaging in protest described themselves as nonreligious. In terms of parental religious traditions, a higher number of Jewish students were involved in protest than might have been expected. Different investigators estimate that from 20 to 37 percent of student activists were Jewish (Solomon and Fishman, 1964; Watts and Whittaker, 1966; Flacks, 1967; Smith, Haan, and Block, 1970). This overrepresentation of Jewish students in activist groups may relate to the great emphasis on intellectual values in the Jewish culture as well as to a historically determined identification with the oppressed.

When we consider academic achievement, not only did the parents of student activists achieve higher educational levels but the students themselves had strong intellectual orientation and superior academic records in their colleges and universities (Heist, 1965; Flacks, 1967). Heist found in his thorough studies of intellectual disposition and academic achievement among the FSM participants at Berkeley that the FSM sample scored higher than did the random sample. He found also that the cumulative grade-point averages of FSM participants, computed after the semester in which the FSM had preempted much student time and energy, exceeded the all-university undergraduate grade-point average. Heist concludes that the students arrested at Sproul Hall were well-qualified young people who were strongly committed to intellectual values and who mantained excellent academic records at a highly competitive university.

This view of activist students is challenged by Kerpelman (1972), who used two objective measures—a vocabulary test and a measure of academic ability—and found no significant differences between students who belonged to activist organizations of the Left or Right and those who did not. But the issue is not clearly drawn. Intellectual orientation and good academic performance are not identical with tested intelligence, and Kerpelman's organizational criteria of activism cannot be equated with the criteria employed in the studies cited in which participation in actual protest figures more largely.

Turning our attention to personality characteristics, questionnaire responses on the Omnibus Personality Inventory show that the FSM students at Berkeley presented themselves as intellectually committed, esthetically reactive, expressive young people who were independent and relatively free from their cultural and institutional past (Heist, 1965). Specifically, Heist found that FSM members received significantly higher scores on scales reflecting nonauthoritarian attitudes and independence of authority, skepticism about conventional religious beliefs and a tendency to reject them, and a tendency to express feelings and impulses directly. Heist also found that they scored higher on four intellectual dispositions: theoretical orientation, thinking introversion, estheticism, and complexity.

In our own study (Smith, Haan, and Block, 1970), the FSM men described themselves as significantly more critical, curious, idealistic, individualistic, impulsive, informed, moody, perceptive, rebellious, and restless than did those in the randomly selected sample. In contrast, self-description of males in the random sample indicated greater concern with conventionality and achievement, as suggested by their higher scores on the following adjectives: conventional, optimistic, practical, responsible, ambitious, reserved, foresightful, considerate, self-controlled, and orderly.

Essentially similar results were obtained when the FSM women were compared with women in the randomly selected sample. FSM women described themselves as significantly more informed, perceptive, loving, doubting, rebellious, and restless. In contrast, the women students in the random sample described themselves as significantly more conventional, ambitious, competitive, self-controlled, foresightful, orderly, responsible, and feminine.

These findings appear to be congruent with Heist's. The activists saw themselves as less conforming and conventional, admitted to restlessness and rebellion, valued knowledge and interpersonal perceptivity; and tended to be idealistic. At the same time, they were less concerned about achievement and success. No important differentiation in the picture results from applying our distinction between activists and dissenters.

Considering the value systems of activist students, we found in our study at Berkeley that FSM participants differed substantially from the randomly selected students as reflected in the adjectives with which they described their ego-ideals. The so-called Protestant ethic is spelled out strongly by the items more characteristic of the ego-ideals of the randomly selected students: ambitious, self-denying, conventional, competitive, self-controlled, foresightful, orderly, responsible and so on. In contrast, the FSM participants were more likely to proclaim values concerned with self-expression, intellectual orientation, and a sense of community with and responsibility for one's fellowman: curious, idealistic, altruistic, creative, impulsive, tolerant, perceptive, rebellious, empathic, responsive, restless, and so on. Again, there are no important differences between our activist and dissenter types.

Using a ranking procedure, Flacks (1967) found, similarly, that dedication to work for national and international betterment and interest in the world of ideas, art, and music were ranked as most important personal values for activist students. Those scoring low on activism tended to place marriage and family and career in the highest ranked positions of importance.

If the distinctive value perspective of student activists was much as one might expect, research on qualitative features of their moral reasoning reveals relationships that are less obvious. A major purpose of our Berkeley study was to throw light on these relationships (Haan, Smith, and Block, 1968; Smith, 1969a; Haan, 1972). We adapted the methods of Kohlberg (1963, 1964) to classify the quality of students' moral reasoning about a set of ethical dilemmas into three broad levels: *premoral* (characterized by egocentric, opportunistic thinking), *conventional* (by concern with stereotyped role expectations or with acceptance of established authority), and *postconventional* (by concern for the reciprocal necessities of the common welfare or for self-accepted abstract principles). Striking relationships emerged. The clearest contrast was between FSM arrestees and the comparable cross section. Among the cross section, 74 percent of the men and 90 percent of the women fell at the conventional level—as compared with only 22 percent and 34 percent of the arrestees. Substantially more of the arrestees reached the postconventional level (55 percent and 58 percent for men and women, respectively, as compared with 20 percent and 6 percent). But more of the arrestees also fell at the premoral level (23 percent and 8 percent versus 6 percent and 4 percent), which for college youth must be interpreted in Kohlberg's scheme as reflecting some kind of regression in moral thinking rather than retarded or arrested development. We suspect that participation in disruptive protest may follow from self-centered impulsiveness or opportunism as well as from commitment to principles. Similar comparisons be-

tween our pure types of political-social orientation make it clear
that participation in acts of public protest is the important dif-
ferentiating factor. Inactives, conventionalists (those who belonged
to fraternities or sororities and had not engaged in social-service
protest or activities), and constructivists differ little from one another in their distribution across the three Kohlberg levels, and
activists differ little from dissenters.

Research by Fishkin and Keniston (1972), undertaken in
May 1970 (the time of the Cambodia–Kent State crisis), shows
that radical versus conservative ideology as such is related to the
quality of moral thinking as indexed by the Kohlberg dilemmas.
While their data are based on a rather inadequate sample, they find
a strong association between political conservatism and conventional
moral reasoning, and an overall positive relationship between a
radicalism versus conservatism factor and both premoral and postconventional reasoning. The premoral students were especially
likely to endorse violent radical slogans; the postconventionals, to
disagree with conservative slogans (but not necessarily to agree with
radical ones, whether violent or peaceful). Since these relationships
strikingly parallel our own for the behavioral criterion of FSM arrest, they suggest that the behavioral relationships we observed may
be ideologically mediated.

The part played by parental child-rearing practices in producing student activists and dissenters has been the subject of much
controversy. Many young activists in contemporary America were
reared under the influence of Benjamin Spock (1946) who, as an
articulate pediatrician, led a revolt against the more authoritarian,
rigid, constraining child-rearing ideology characteristics of an earlier
generation of American parents. The Spock-oriented mothers of the
1940s substituted inductive reasoning for insistence upon blind
obedience, corrective discipline for punitive discipline, flexible responsiveness for rigid scheduling, and reasonable limits for arbitrary
prohibitions. It may be argued that the emergence of a dedicated
spontaneous generation concerned with humanitarian values and
personal authenticity is a triumph of Spockian philosophy and principles. Others have suggested that activism is the consequence of
excessive parental permissiveness, a failure to teach respect for authority, and an unfortunate submission to the needs and feelings of

the child. What do research data tell us about the relationship between activism and permissiveness?

The parents of activist students do appear to have been more permissive than those of nonactivist students. Parents of activists were described by their children as more lenient, less intrusive into the lives of their children, and milder disciplinarians than those of the nonactivists (Flacks, 1967). Confirmatory data were obtained from the parents themselves: parents of activists rated themselves as more permissive than did parents in other groups.

In our study (Block, Haan, and Smith, 1969; Smith, Haan, and Block, 1970), FSM participants as compared with the randomly selected sample described both parents as less authoritarian and more permissive. They perceived their parents as having a closer affective relationship with their children and as placing less emphasis on prohibitions, restrictions, and punishment.

The most characteristic parent-child relationship described by FSM students was, however, complex. While attributing closeness and warmth to the relationship, the FSM students also admitted conflict with parents. While subscribing to many of their parents' values and views, they were less likely than the randomly selected students to rate themselves as in agreement with their parents with respect to choice of occupation, religion, politics, and friends.

In this instance, our distinction between purer activist and dissenter types is helpful. Parents of the activists encouraged their children to be independent and responsible. Unlike the parents of conventionalists, those of the activists were described as encouraging the child's differentiation and self-expressiveness, with discipline per se being less critical. They were unaccepting of aggression. The picture is not one of laissez-faire permissiveness as the lay public understands the term, but of responsible, nonpunitive parenthood: Spock interpreted with sophistication. Parents of the dissenters, on the other hand, were described in terms that correspond more closely to the popular stereotype. They made rather minimal demands for independent, mature behavior and self-control. The overall picture is one of inconsistency between indulgence and intrusiveness, leading to a conflicted, unsatisfying relationship—a plausible dynamic basis for rebellion. And the evidence suggests that dissenters were indeed in greater rebellion against parental attitudes than were activists.

In conclusion, the studies that we have reviewed on student activists and dissenters yield quite consistent results. These position-taking young people tend to have been superior students from socially and educationally advantaged homes. To a large extent, their political values and social ideals were consonant with the values of their parents, who themselves were politically liberal. They were nonconventional in their moral judgments, whether from the basis of a principled postconventional morality or (to a lesser extent) from an opportunistic, premoral orientation. The activists described their parents as permissive and stressing a rational approach in their child-rearing practices. Perhaps because they had been reared in child-centered homes where communication and understanding were important, these young people came to value dialogue and to expect that social institutions, like their parents, would listen and be responsive to their concerns. Mostly, they felt supported by their parents as they challenged the values of modern society. A subgroup of dissenters, however, seems to have been carrying to the larger world a personal rebellion that had roots in their relations to their parents.

Individualists. Reviewing the research findings on individualist students actively engaged in conservative causes, we find inconsistencies. Fewer studies have concentrated on them, and the samples on which conclusions are based have sometimes been small. The groups have been defined in several ways: by actual participation in counterprotest demonstrations (Solomon and Fishman, 1964; Flacks, 1967), by membership in conservative activist organizations (Schiff, 1964; Westby and Braungart, 1966; Kerpelman, 1972), or by delegate status to national conventions of student conservative organizations (Braungart, 1966). There have been differences, also, in the ideological positions of the conservative groups studied. Schiff (1966) reports that students who were converted to conservative causes early in adolescence reflect primarily a search for meaning, while those converted later are rather seeking to escape from and to deny the possibility of real change as they encounter the adult world. Finally, some inconsistencies in findings may relate to the nature of the groups against which the individualist is contrasted—normative or activist.

A consideration of family background, apart from agreement that active conservative students tend to come from Republican families who are predominantly Protestant (Solomon and Fishman, 1964; Braungart, 1966; Westby and Braungart, 1966; Flacks, 1967), provides little consistency in findings; no conclusions can be presently drawn.

A consideration of personality characteristics reveals that few investigators have systematically assessed young people actively committed to conservative causes. There is some evidence that these students are more submissive to authority and tend to exert greater control over expressions of impulse and anxiety (Schiff, 1964). Interestingly, and contrary to stereotype, no evidence of greater prejudice or ethnocentrism was found by Schiff in his evaluations of student conservatives. We found at Berkeley that the individualists (as contrasted with the random sample) described themselves in ways that emphasized their independence: unwilling to compromise, egocentric, and unconventional—traits highly prized in Rand's (1957, 1964) individualistic philosophy that influenced many conservative activists at Berkeley.

On the basis of his study, Kerpelman (1972) concludes that Right activists (and nonactivists) were the highest of his comparison groups on a factor identified as authoritarianism (Left activists were lowest). Right activists resembled Left activists in being high on a second major factor, autonomy. All activists—Left, Middle, and Right—were found to need less support and nurturance, to value leadership more, to be more socially ascendant and assertive, and to be more sociable than their ideological counterparts who were not politically active. (Remember Kerpelman's organizational criterion of activism.) In Kerpelman's study, there were no differences between groups classified independently by activism and ideology in regard to measures of emotional stability or responsibility and restraint.

In considering value systems, as reflected in distinctive characterizations of self-ideals, we find that individualists studied at Berkeley were oriented to matters of personal integrity and individualism. These students ascribed less value to interpersonal relationships and were less oriented to altruistic or humanistic values than were other groups. But the sample was small. Flacks (1967) found that his counterprotesters ranked marriage and family and career as first and second in order of personal importance, while giving low ranks to interest in the arts, abstract ideas, or involvement in improving world conditions.

Finally, let us consider the child-rearing practices of individualists' parents. These parents appear to have expected much of their children and to have placed high value on achievement and characterological goodness, according to our results and those of Schiff (1964). When parental expectations were not fulfilled, the mothers of conservative activists tended to react with anger and disappointment, while their children responded to the pressures with feelings of resentment and failure. Particularly for the males in the conservative sample, there was an emphasis on the mother's use of guilt-arousing techniques of control. The mother-son relationship was described as more impersonal, less affectionate, and less appreciative than that depicted by the randomly selected sample. The father-son relationship appeared to differ little from that typical of the random sample. However, our sample was small, and these findings obviously need corroboration.

Overall, we know less about the individualists than about the activist group, and the information is less consistent. Any conclusions about active conservatives must be very tentative. One apparently clear finding is that greater parental pressure in the direction of achievement exists in child-rearing that relies on arbitrary authority and is relatively lacking in emotional warmth. The values expressed by the conservative students reflect an emphasis on individualism, integrity, and consistency. The nature of the conservative movement itself may satisfy the adolescent's needs for structure, certainty, and reliance on authority.

Alienated Youth. We find that relatively little systematic research, beyond the intensive study of Harvard students conducted on a small scale by Keniston (1965) in the 1950s, is stimulated by alienated, estranged, politically apathetic adolescents. This is in part because the alienated, by inclination and conviction, are antipathetic to quantitative research. On the basis of psychological-test responses, Keniston selected twelve disaffected and disaffiliated Harvard undergraduates who manifested the alienated syndrome—rejecting the dominant values, roles, and institutions of contemporary American society—and studied them intensively over a period of three years. He became well acquainted with these young men and has provided an incisive portrayal of them and of their cultural and familial heritages, with an insightful analysis of the social context that predisposes young people toward alienation. His analysis remains relevant.

Of course, Keniston describes the alienated syndrome in a very atypical group of young people, upper-middle-class students at one of the most prestigious private universities. The fact that most of these young people were able to remain students for the three years of the research indicates that their rejection of traditional American achievement values was discriminating rather than total.

The alienated young man, according to Keniston, regards his mother as a talented woman whose career has been sacrificed to marriage and family. He expresses a special sympathy for his mother's unrealized potentials and identifies with her unhappiness. His desire for a close, dependent relationship with his mother is countered, however, by his resentment of her domination, possessiveness, and neuroticism. The father image portrayed by the alienated Harvard students is of an inhibited, constricted, cold, withdrawn man oriented to success, status, and security. Fathers of the alienated are pictured as men who, in their youth, had visionary dreams and idealistic hopes. Under the stress of parental and societal pressures for achievement, the fathers of the alienated abandon these dreams and, as their sons see it, sell out their noble aspirations to the demands of the marketplace. Keniston's alienated young men were not overtly hostile toward their fathers but were condescending and accorded them little respect.

In early childhood, the alienated described themselves as shy and reserved; they were oriented to the intellectual world of books and ideas. The adolescence of the alienated was marked by turmoil accompanied by strong negative feelings about sexuality. During mid-adolescence, these alienated-to-become began questioning the values of their parents and of society at large. It was not until later adolescence, however, that they overtly rejected parental, community, and cultural values.

The rejections of the alienated are many. They refuse to orient themselves and their lives toward long-range goals because of an inherent pessimism about the future. They reject the Puritan virtues of self-control, self-denial, order, responsibility, insisting on the values of spontaneity, expression, intense confrontation with experience, and personal freedom. They reject the conventional adult role with its attendant responsibilities, inevitable compromises, and the expectation of adult sexuality. Their positive values are in experiencing—deeply, freely, and appreciatively.

In a subsequent essay, Keniston (1971) distinguishes between two types of alienation, the activist (similar to our conception) and the disaffiliate. The disaffiliate is nonpolitical, culturally alienated, and rejects societal offerings and values. The demonstrations of disaffiliates, according to Keniston, are private rebellions manifested in beatnickism, bohemianism, or psychedelic withdrawal from the mainstream of public life. Keniston finds little political participation in this group but occasional peripheral involvement in protest movements. The disaffiliate's rejection of American society is based less on idealism and outraged indignation, Keniston postulates, than upon temperamental opposition to the requirements and rewards of American society—and to his father who epitomizes this society for him. The disaffiliate is estranged from both family and society.

Estrangement from family and friends was also found by Watts and Whittaker (1968; see also Whittaker and Watts, 1969), who studied disaffiliated nonstudents living on the fringes of the Berkeley campus. These investigators recruited their research volunteers from the coffeeshops and bookstores adjacent to the university. The group included a heterogeneous range extending from students temporarily out of school in order to work for one semester, to others who never were students and were unemployed. Nevertheless, the sample did not differ from Berkeley students in socioeconomic background. For this sample, rejection of contemporary society, personal isolation, estrangement from family, and experimentation with drugs were more frequent than in the contrast sample of Berkeley students. The nonstudent sample was equal to the contrast sample, or better, on a vocabulary index on intelligence. On the Omnibus Personality Inventory, both males and females (whose profiles were closely similar) were very high in scores for psychological complexity and impulse expression, strong in intellectual orientation and in aestheticism, low in authoritarianism, and high in socioemotional maladjustment, in comparison with the student sample.

The importance of distinguishing subtypes within the alienated student syndrome is demonstrated in a study by Block (1972), who identifies two patterns of alienation that differ in their personal and familial concomitants. In a study focusing explicitly on the question of generational continuity-discontinuity, Block compares two groups of Berkeley students: students actively rejecting societal institutions and values as well as parental value orientations—the discontinuous individuals—and students actively rejecting societal institutions and values but accepting the basic value orientation of their parents—the continuous individuals. Comparisons of the two groups revealed that the continuous group described themselves and asserted personal values for themselves that might be considered, comparatively, more straight, for example, responsible, practical, informed, foresightful, while the discontinuous group proclaimed a counterculture orientation, for example, rebellious, free, artistic, playful, loving. Differences in socialization emphases, replicated in a second study that included the parents of continuous and discontinuous students, revealed that parents of the continuous students were described as more "responsibly responsive." They encouraged individuation, reflectivity, assumption of responsibility, and discussion of issues and problems. These parents also indicated a feeling of greater satisfaction in their parental roles. Parents of the discontinuous students displayed a greater adherence to authoritarian child-rearing orientations. They placed greater emphasis on achievement, conventionality, and control and attempted both to circumscribe and prestructure the experiences of their young. Generational continuity was found to be associated, also, with greater agreement between parents with respect to their child-rearing values—a factor that might be expected to contribute to a more consistent, coherent learning matrix for the growing child.

In summary, the alienated, like the activist, is engaged in a repudiation of traditional societal values. He differs from the activist, however, in a passive pessimism, in keeping with which he concerns himself with the extension and intensification of subjective experience rather than with active protest. Another basic difference between the alienated and the activist is in their attitudes toward parents and family. The activist tends to identify with many of the values of his parents. The alienated, however, has developed a disparate set of values, inconsistent with those of his parents, that are likely to elicit disapproval and strain communications.

Constructivists. Young people directing their energies to constructive programs of action within existing societal institutions have not been the object of much research. Gelineau and Kantor (1964) assessed a number of Harvard and Radcliffe student volunteers in a large public mental hospital and found them little different in social background from the typical Harvard or Radcliffe student. The only distinguishing features were that a larger number had attended public schools and a disproportionate number were from Jewish backgrounds while Catholics were somewhat underrepresented. Gelineau and Kantor found the volunteers intelligent, secular, sophisticated, idealistic, and valuing of creativity. They were motivated by their interest in human contact and by an altruistic desire to be helpful to others.

In a study of an early contingent of Peace Corps volunteers, Smith (1966a) suggested three main factors as motivating enlistment. A psycho-social moratorium (Erikson, 1959), providing time out for self-discovery and evaluation of life goals, was important to the volunteers. They required, however, that this moratorium be constructively earned by devotion to something intrinsically worthwhile. The opportunity in the Peace Corps for direct personal action toward good ends was an important motivational component. Opportunities for adventure and experience in foreign cultures was a third, but lesser, reason for the appeal of the Peace Corps. Volunteer service contributes to the adolescent's need to establish an identity for himself and to test his skills and competence in a way that does not directly confront or challenge authority. Altruism, in this context, provides a safe outlet for the expression of doubts about the adult society and a channel for the adolescent's idealistic desires to effect changes in society.

In our Berkeley studies, constructivists, especially the men, came from less affluent socioeconomic backgrounds than the activists and dissenters. The constructivist men were distinctive in describing themselves as responsible, practical, and tolerant. Females were distinctive only in calling themselves helpful. The constructivists' values, as indexed by traits they would distinctively like to have, emphasized being empathic and helpful (men) and optimistic and argumentative (women)—though the last trait was little chosen by any group and should therefore be discounted. We have already noted that constructivists did not differ appreciably from conventionalists and inactives in the quality of their moral reasoning, according to Kohlberg's scale. In regard to their reported experience of the parent-child relationship, which they evaluated positively, they resembled the conventionalists in emphasis on punishment and restriction of self-expression, though they reported less emphasis on achievement and competition. There was little suppression of physical aggression. Parental control relied on anxiety rather than on guilt. The family pattern seemed congruent with their altruism, which was achieved at the expense of spontaneous expressiveness.

Our survey of research findings does not include politically uninvolved young people who accept most of our prevailing societal values. Obviously, these are the large majority who provide the continuity in society that exasperates the activists and alienated who are attuned to its hypocrisies. We proceed now to consider briefly some of the factors predisposing to the activism of the 1960s and some explanations that have been offered for its emergence.

Sociocultural Factors Predisposing to Activism

The unpredicted change in the ethos of youth from the silent generation of the 1950s to the protesting student of the 1960s, followed by the equally unpredicted apparent decline of protest and disruption in the 1970s, has challenged sociologists and social psychologists for explanation. The traditional historical forces previously associated with the emergence of radical youth movements— limited occupational and economic opportunities, the breakdown of traditional authority under the impact of industrialization—seem an insufficient explanation for the protests of the 1960's. Several hypotheses that have been offered are summarized.

Sociological Explanations. Keniston (1965) posits that intensification of technological change in our country and in much of the modern world has been at the expense of human values. Our technological society stresses empiricism, pragmatism, efficiency, and production. The absence of articulate social goals and the deification of technological progress at the expense of social concerns dehumanizes society. The very rapidity of change makes the past irrelevant to the present, and the continuity with history that eases the task of identification and adaptation is weakened. The generational gap is widened by accelerating changes so that communication between generations becomes increasingly difficult. Patterns for the solution of today's problems cannot be found in the experiences of the past. The protest of youth against this process of dehumanization is a part of their struggle for identity and integrity. This line of reasoning has the merit of applying to the worldwide situation as well as to the United States and, insofar as alienation and protest are alternative responses to dehumanization, the recent decline of protest does not present special difficulties for its acceptance.

Psychosocial Factors. Feuer (1969), in a scholarly but tendentious historical analysis of youth movements that is colored by his early embitterment with student protest at Berkeley, combines a psychoanalytic view of inevitable underlying generational conflict (as a corollary of the Oedipus complex) with the hypothesis that romantic and destructive youth movements erupt when the adult generation has become "de-authoritized" for historical reasons. There is indeed good reason to believe that when the established generation is discredited, the grounds for protest or alienation are laid. But Feuer's theory ill accords with the evidence that many activists sought to realize parental values, far from rebelling against them, and it can hardly account for the collapse of the movement with the turn of the decade.

Bettelheim (1969), another caustic critic of the activists, saw paranoid trends in many of those whom he encountered clinically, and was perhaps unduly preoccupied with parallels with the youth movements that heralded Nazi Germany. But he suggests an underlying dynamic that warrants careful attention: the frustrations of modern young people in their prolonged dependent status and delayed adult responsibility, when they have little opportunity to deal with consequential matters of the real world. Certainly, this situation of youth is conducive to romantic activism, to apocalyptic politics— or to dropping out. How to involve the young more consequentially in the affairs of society, how to bridge the discontinuity between youth and adulthood that the American educational system has so much accentuated, is a serious problem for American society.

Flacks (1967) bases his interpretation of youth protest on an extension of Eisenstadt's (1956) and Parsons' (1963) analysis of the disjunction between the values and expectations of the traditional nuclear family and those prevailing in the occupational sphere of society. Although discrepancies between familial and societal values are inevitable in modern industrial society, Parsons suggests that these differences are lessening in middle-class America. Flacks proposes that within middle-class society there is a segment of well-educated families whose stress upon democratic, egalitarian principles, on permissiveness, and on values other than achievement does not accord with the prevailing values and expectations in the occupational sphere. Young people reared according to these precepts should find it difficult to accept the traditional social values that require submission to authority, competition, ambition, and self-control. Their questioning of the social norms, instigated by their parents, has been reinforced by their selectively chosen friends, by their experiences in progressive schools or camps, and by their reading. The customary rewards and incentives of the occupational sphere have only limited effectiveness for these young people who have already achieved status and affluence by virtue of their family origins. Flacks suggests that the abstract concern with democratic and egalitarian values of the parental generation, expressed in their child-centered approach to rearing, has become embodied in their children as personality traits. Adolescents who engaged in protest were thus not rebelling in a conventional sense but were expressing the values according to which they have been reared. Further, the nonauthoritarian stance of their parents released these young people to react to the problems and significant people of their time. This explanation, too, has no difficulty in accommodating the alternatives of protest and alienation.

Existentialist Attitude. The young people of today have been reared at a time characterized by the omnipresent and ominous pressure of the nuclear stalemate. Many cogently wonder, along with their elders, whether mankind will be able to get by by the skin of its teeth. As the voice of traditional religion wanes, these bleak uncertainties have made many youth responsive to the existentialists' call for individual commitment and responsibility—or absurd defiance. At first or second hand, the existentialist formulations of Sartre, Camus, and Kierkegaard have served to crystalize attitudes that differentiate thoughtful youth of the present generation.

The existentialist call to being, actualizing, or becoming appeals to many. In an age of mass society and impersonal technology, its emphasis upon an enlarged and acute sense of personal responsibility is refreshing. Sartre (1957) holds that man is responsible for himself, for his own individuality, and for all men. He emphasizes that the future will be as man decides it is to be. He exhorts man to involve himself in making the decisions that will determine his future.

If the existentialist posture in its version of human dignity repudiates the cosmic reassurances of traditional religion, it has equally little use for the rationalism of the scientific world view. In its romantic subjectivism, it offers no guidelines, no criteria for meaningful choice in a world of absurdity. All depends on inner conviction, on freely willed choice. What is chosen in full consciousness and freedom is authentic, and authenticity is a principal virtue. Depending on one's personal bent, one may seek authenticity in the intensification of inner experience and spontaneity (as do the alienated) or one may, like the activists, find meaning in the existential act of making a stand against injustice and hypocrisy. To the extent that youthful protesters conceive of their activism with a generally existentialist outlook, they feel no need for rationally elaborated or logically consistent theory. By the same token, they become the less accessible to rational dialogue with their elders. The alienated version of the existentialist posture is just as estranged from rational discourse.

Retreat from Protestant Ethic. With the increasing secularization of America, religion has declined as determinant of behavior. Psychoanalysis, existentialism, and the influence of the scientific method have encouraged the development of a more humanistic ethical system concerned with honesty, authenticity, and personal responsibility for one's acts. Freed from the taboos of the Victorian era and impelled by the dictates of a rational conscience, today's youth find that their struggles for authenticity often require dissent. At the same time, the consumption-oriented values of an affluent society have further eroded the foundations on which the traditional future-oriented achievement-centered ethos of Benjamin Franklin rested (Riesman, 1950).

Child-rearing Factors. Flacks has stressed the importance of permissive, democratic child-rearing practices in the development of the young activist. It is not only matters of respect for the child and encouragement of self-regulation with which we are concerned in this section but also with the very techniques used by parents who have rejected authoritarian methods of control. Such techniques encourage the development of empathy and concern for others. When categorical enforcement of arbitrary rules by implacable authority is abandoned in favor of more rational methods of discipline, several things happen. First, the reasons behind parental demands are explained to the child so that they no longer appear arbitrary. Second, these reasons are usually based on welfare concerns. The mother prohibits the child from actions, not because they are inherently bad but because they are potentially harmful to him and to others. Third, the child is encouraged to see the relationship between his own actions and their subsequent effects on other people. These other-oriented mechanisms of discipline are associated, along with affection, with the development of a humanistic conscience (Hoffman, 1964). The development of empathy and humanistic orientation makes it probable that a young person will concern himself with the plight of others. The relationship between activism and humanism is supported by our results on value systems reported earlier.

Child-training practices viewed in this way highlight the continuity between parent and child generations, explain to some extent the support accorded to protest by parents of activists, and rationalize the frustrations felt by activist youth when confronted by arbitrary authorities who refuse their invitation to dialogue.

But the considerable degree of discontinuity between generations, especially in matters of discipline in child-rearing, has left difficult problems concerning authority. Parents who try to raise their children at least partly in contrast to the way they themselves were raised do not have the assurance of established models, of having learned their own parental role from the reciprocal position of being a child. They are more likely than traditional parents to be uncertain and inconsistent and inept, even when they mean well. No wonder they depend upon Spock or his equivalent. Under these circumstances, it is not surprising that neither parents nor their children, nor modern society generally, have been able to keep consistently clear Erich Fromm's (1941) important distinction between rational authority and inhibiting or arbitrary authority. And it is not surprising that hang-ups about authority continue to plague contemporary youth. Thus, according to Yankelovich (1972, p. 33), "the major barrier students see standing in the way of securing desirable work is their attitude toward authority. No obstacle comes even close to this one, including political views [or] style of dress."

Summary

In this chapter we have discussed and examined the activist and the apathetic adolescent who raises his voice, or who does not raise his voice, in political and social protest. Our focus has been mainly on youth in the 1960s from the perspective of the different, but as yet confusing, scene of the early 1970s. The activist youth has voiced his dissatisfaction with contemporary society. This has produced tensions. Toward the end of the 1960s these tensions too often led to violence, to consequences that were destructive, however pure the motive. However, tensions between generations and between youth and society are inevitable because the older generation stands as gatekeeper to the opportunities and aspirations of the young and because the choices and commitments of youth have the power to either confirm or negate the values of their elders and of their society. If man and society are to change and grow, the adult world not only has to provide guidance for its youth but also must be able to hear and profit from youth's perceptions, indignations, and insights. The rejuvenations (Erikson, 1962) of society and the older generation come from vitalism, idealism, and dedication of the young.

Chapter Five

•••••••••••••••••••••
•••••••••••••••••••••
•••••••••••••••••••••

A SOCIO-PSYCHOLOGICAL VIEW OF FERTILITY

•••••••••••••••••••••
•••••••••••••••••••••
•••••••••••••••••••••

*I*n spite of the analytic fact that "the fertility of a population can be viewed as a resultant of many individual acts and decisions, made within a framework of biological and environmental constraints" (Smith, 1965b, p. 70), it has not been very profitably so viewed heretofore. Fertility has remained almost an unassailed supraindividual social fact in the Durkheimian sense, a social rate with social correlates that graciously yields to demographic analysis but stands mute and enigmatic in the face of psychological scrutiny.

Demographic analysis of census data has become ever more sophisticated, as techniques have been developed to disentangle how particular age cohorts contribute to the fertility of populations and to describe and project the age structure of populations through time. With increased technical competence has come attendant conceptual sophistication about the potentialities of cohort analysis for the study of social change (Ryder, 1965). Structured interviews of well-defined population samples have served to supplement the

95

census and to illuminate relationships that elude it, documenting the spread of contraceptive knowledge and use throughout American society, the narrowing of fertility differentials associated with socioeconomic status, and the persistence of religious and ethnic fertility differentials.

Typically such studies have found that answers by women of child-bearing age to questions about ideal family size are adequately predictive of subsequent cohort fertility, but most inadequately predictive at the individual level, a severe handicap for psychological analysis. The most diligent attempt to discover psychological determinants of differential fertility—the so-called Princeton study (Westoff and others, 1961, 1963)—drew a blank, perhaps because ideal family size was used as the dependent variable and because the psychological instruments were admittedly weak (Fawcett [1970] briefly reviews the major studies in this tradition; Hawthorne [1970] reviews the literature on fertility from a sociological perspective and also provides a good annotated bibliography.) A good deal can be said about the consequences for fertility of social status, social mobility, family structure, religious affiliation, and rural-urban residence and about gross contrasts in fertility between the industrialized countries and the rest of the world. Since it is individual men and women, not cohorts or social strata, who have babies, these social facts should have their psychological counterparts, and a sound psychological perspective on fertility should be an essential component in developing social strategies to bring the growth of population under control. Unfortunately, little that is well established can be said from the psychological standpoint.

For psychologists this unsatisfactory state of affairs should pose an irresistible challenge, given substantial variance in fertility left unaccounted for by demographic methods and also given the plausible conjecture that at least substantial components of the variance that is accounted for demographically should be traceable, in principle, to mediating processes and dispositions at the individual level. Yet, until very recently, few psychologists have risen to the challenge; many others must join in. The stakes are too high for us to accept the negative answer easily, especially when neither our theories nor our methods of measurement are in good enough order to make null results interesting or persuasive.

My part in the common endeavor is that of amicus curiae, not that of active investigator, so an even more modest stance befits me than the unsatisfactory research situation itself requires. In sketching some aspects of a sociopsychological view of fertility, my aim is to piece together scaffolding within which questions can be posed for research, rather than to present well-developed hypotheses ripe for empirical test. If the venture is worthwhile, it is because the psychological variables that were previously lying to hand may not have been the right ones, and some of the obvious questions from a psychological point of view remain to be pursued with proper diligence, or even to be asked. I argue that much descriptive work at the psychological level needs to be done before fancier theorizing and hypothesis-testing are warranted.

My task is made more difficult by the disorder of contemporary social psychology, a border area claimed by both psychology and sociology in which a congeries of perspectives, concepts, and partial theories compete with one another without synthesis, and in which there is disagreement about methods and data. The sociopsychological perspective cannot be represented consensually. In contrast with sociodemographic approaches, however, a sociopsychological approach implies attention to individual behavior viewed as an interactive product of personal dispositions and situational properties, the former seen as the developmental resultant of previous interactions.

A focus at the individual level does not coincide with a psychological approach, of course; physiological and sociocultural factors affecting the events from conception to parturition can also be examined as they bear upon the individual. Two very generally relevant accounting schemes at the individual level provide a framework for the analysis of psychological and other factors affecting fertility: the reproductive causal sequence and the life cycle. It is well to note them both at the outset.

As for the former, Davis and Blake (1956) point out that fertility change can be partitioned exhaustively among intercourse variables, conception variables, and gestation variables. Each step in the causal chain is the locus of nonpsychological influences; each step is also at least potentially influenced by such psychological factors as motives, attitudes, habits, intentions, and decisions. Such an abstract analytical scheme does not tell us how the terms of fertility-relevant action are defined for the behaving individual: thus, until the surprisingly radical shift in law and mores about abortion, gestation was a purely biological matter beyond the range of attitude and decision for many middle-class Americans. But the scheme reminds the psychologist to keep his search for the impact of psychological factors properly differentiated.

The relevance of the life cycle with its biologically and socially defined markers of puberty, adolescence, maturity, marriage, sequential childbearing, and middle age is as obvious to psychologists as it is to demographers. It is well to note that the psychological mediation of factors affecting fertility may differ systematically along the way as men and women move through the cycle; the timing with which people move through the cycle (age of marriage, age of first child, for example) is one of the important determinants of fertility for which psychological mediation may be sought.

In a now classic statement Garrett Hardin (1968) posed the problem of fertility control in a form that engaged productively with sociopsychological thinking. His parable of the commons dramatizes a structural feature that uncontrolled population growth shares with an interrelated parcel of contemporary social dilemmas, all of which hinge on the pressures that people are now bringing against an environment of limited resources. Hardin writes (p. 1244):

> The tragedy of the commons develops in this way. Picture a pasture open to all. It is to be expected that each herdsman will try to keep as many cattle as possible on the commons. Such an arrangement may work reasonably satisfactorily for centuries because tribal wars, poaching, and disease keep the number of both man and beast well below the "carrying capacity" of the land. Finally, however, comes the day of reckoning, that is, the day when the long-desired social stability becomes a reality. At this point, the inherent logic of the commons remorselessly generates tragedy.
>
> As a rational being each herdsman seeks to maximize his gain. Explicitly or implicitly, more or less consciously, he asks: "What is the utility to me of adding one more animal to my herd?" This utility has two components: (1) A positive com-

ponent, which is a function of the increment of one animal. Since the herdsman receives all the proceeds from the sale of the additional animal, the positive utility is nearly +1. (2) A negative component, which is a function of the additional over-grazing created by one more animal. But since the effects of overgrazing are shared by all the herdsmen, the negative utility for any particular decision-making herdsman is only a fraction of −1.

Adding together the component partial utilities, the rational herdsman concludes that the only sensible course for him to pursue is to add another animal to his herd. And another; and another. . . . But this is the conclusion reached by each and every rational herdsman sharing a commons. Therein is the tragedy. Each man is *locked in* to a system that compels him to increase his herd without limit—in a world that is limited. Ruin is the destination toward which all men rush, each pursuing his own best interest in a society that believes in the freedom of the commons. *Freedom in a commons brings ruin to all.*

Just as the private utility to an individual of adding one additional car to the freeway exceeds his private share in the public disutility of ever more tangled traffic and just as the private gain from discharging pollution in the air or waters (also a commons) exceeds the private component of the shared cost of a deteriorating environment when this cost is treated as an externality, so the individual share in the cost to all of a world clogged with people cannot balance the private gains to the behaving individual who wants more children (and people the world over presently want more children than are required for a stable population under existing conditions of health and mortality).

Hardin thus argues that the population crisis belongs to a class of problems for which there is no technical solution, in the sense of a solution that in principle is within the reach of science and technology. What is required, rather, is a political solution: "mutual coercion, mutually agreed upon," in Hardin's rendition of the Hobbesian social contract.

In a provocative and pessimistic rejoinder the political scientist Crowe (1969) accepts Hardin's statement of the problem but rejects as no longer feasible his conclusions for social policy. (He also chides Hardin for asserting what he says is a truism among social scientists: small matter, when so many social scientists still fail to see the structure of the problem as clearly.) In an increasingly "tribalized" world in which societies are fragmented into mutually alienated groups that diverge in ultimate values rather than in negotiable interests, how shall the social contract for political regulation be drawn? Matters are even more grim, says Crowe, because at the same time that the myth of value consensus has lost its force, the myth that the state holds a monopoly of coercive power has likewise been punctured by irreconcilable dissidents. If the population dilemma belongs to the class of problems that lack a technical solution, Crowe argues, these same problems now appear beyond the reach of political solution as well. Man's tragic predicament is deeper than Hardin supposed.

A temperamentally more sanguine and historically more sophisticated observer of the imperfections of modern government might take a less apocalyptic view than Crowe leaves us. But when ideological leaders of the black poor cry "genocide" at proposals for mild and voluntaristic programs of family planning, it should be easy to see what he is talking about. And one can hardly gainsay his complaint that little can be hoped for so long as scientists and technologists dump their insoluble problems on politics, while social scientists and politicians look to science and technology for magical solutions to the problems that they cannot solve—especially when precisely the same "insoluble" problems are at issue. We are in it together and had better cooperate.

Note, however, that when Hardin and Crowe write about problems that in principle lack a technical solution, they are talking about hard science and technology, and when Crowe writes about the lack of a political solution, he has in mind latter-day American politics. If we and our successors as American and world citizens are to grapple effectively with the potentially tragic problems— there is, of course, no guarantee that we will succeed—we cannot afford to accept either of these "givens."

The sense of impending catastrophe promulgated by apocalyptic writers finds an appreciative audience in many of the younger generation and may, after all, presage adaptive transformations in our political processes and institutions: faith in business as usual is waning. Facing the same ominous data, a more optimistic writer like Platt (1966) can envision the possibility that we stand on the threshold of "the step to man"; human life may shift to a new and more desirable level if we can only manage to navigate these treacherous waters.

As for the first given, the conception of science and technology surely must be broadened to include the social sciences, psychology among them. Hard science and politics-as-usual are not enough. And among the social sciences, the population problem is too important to be left to the demographers. As yet we have hardly begun the attempt to see if psychology and the social sciences can contribute to a solution that necessarily must have both technical and political ingredients.

If we follow Hardin, the incentives governing individual decisions about procreation produce actions that now cumulate to the disadvantage of all—this is the motivational structure of the population problem. In the sphere of fertility the "Unseen Hand" that Adam Smith imagined as guiding individually self-interested economic actions so that they cumulate to the common good is clearly not working, any more than it works in the other spheres that govern man's ecological balance or in the economy as such. The pragmatic problem that we face is thus how to restructure the dilemma of the commons so that individual decisions can dependably cumulate to social advantage, so that net growth in population is brought to a halt. Insofar as decisional processes are involved, an engineering of incentives and constraints in which deliberate social policy replaces the mythical Unseen Hand, would seem to be called for.

Of course, there are immense difficulties in the way of achieving an effective national population policy, let alone the effective international one that the facts require. These barriers also hinder the development of effective policy regarding any of the many matters that require comprehensive, long-term planning and implementation if the common good is to be advanced. Wildavsky (1964) is only one among many who have recently told us that the budgetary context of decision-making in government enforces incremental adjustments that are the antithesis of comprehensive and effective policy in response to short-term pinches of the shoe. But these difficulties surely cannot excuse our giving up the attempt to design social policy on the basis of improved causal understanding before the attempt is fairly begun. The recent rapid shift in national attention to issues of population and ecology should give us heart.

The decision-making framework in which Hardin presents the dilemma of the commons fits very well with thoughtways now prevalent among social psychologists. Indeed, a number of psychologists have worked with formal models of decision-making, an approach reviewed by Taylor (1965) and by Becker and McClintock (1967). More broadly, exchange theorists such as Thibaut and Kelley (1959) have productively adapted the cost-benefit approach of economics for the analysis of a variety of sociopsychological problems. But the analysis of behavioral alternatives in terms of their associated costs and gains, *as if* rational decision were involved, is much more widely shared. The fact that behavior is motivated and that motivation is governed by positive and negative incentives is an insight of commonsense psychology. The commons dilemma, as Hardin poses it, thus makes equal sense to the psychologist whose theoretical preferences turn him toward a cognitive theory of means and goals, to the stimulus-response behaviorist concerned with the shaping of behavior under the influence of the balance of reinforcements or rewards, and to the functional, personality-oriented psychologist who notes that people acquire and retain dispositions and behavior patterns that by and large work out for them adaptively in the balance of gratification. To insist that Hardin's phrasing of the dilemma should make sense to social psychologists of many stripes is not to minimize consequential differences that follow from these diverse preferences among strategies of theorizing. The point is, rather, that the practical dilemma is already shaped to present interesting theoretical problems for psychological research.

Research Questions

The remainder of this chapter suggests, at a more specific level, some of the research problems that social psychologists might concern themselves with if they take the commons dilemma seriously. For a starting point we may return to my statement, *"Insofar as decisional processes are involved* [italics added], an engineering of incentives and constraints would seem to be called for. . . ." A first empirical question thus has to do with the extent to which decisions are made in matters that affect fertility. A second concerns the terms in which decisions are made.

Whether or not having children is indeed a matter of decision surely varies with cultural group and with social stratum. At one extreme is the idealized case of the fatalistic traditionalist, for whom the appearance of offspring rests with the will of Allah; at the other, the voluntarism promulgated by the middle-class Planned Parenthood movement and fostered by the seemingly inevitable spread of a rational-technical orientation accompanying modern technology the world over. For the most part, as Rainwater (1960) has noted, the decision when it occurs is cast in negative terms—*not* to have (more) children, and failure to make a decision thus is likely to result in procreation. Even near the fatalistic pole, however, where the possibility of modern contraception does not exist in the range of choice, alternatives of delayed marriage, sexual abstinence, coitus interruptus, or abortion may have sufficient psychological reality to suggest the presence of child-bearing decisions. The involvement of decision would seem to be a matter of degree.

The second question is more complex and points to unexplored areas where careful descriptive socio-psychological research is needed. What are the terms in which decisions are made? And how do nondecisional factors in the technological and social context influence these terms and thus affect fertility? Moreover, what are the units of decision, and how do they come to bear upon fertility-relevant behavior? Do marital partners decide upon a wanted family size, or on an acceptable range, rather than upon the acceptability or desirability of a next pregnancy now? Are family decisions made in a short-run time perspective, like incrementalist government policy, or do some parents make their plans in a longer time perspective? Which parents? Which partner makes the decisions, and with what degree of real or assumed consensus? What alternatives are weighed, and what considerations are seen as relevant? It is easy enough to ask questions about these matters in KAP surveys of knowledge, attitudes, and practices about birth control and family planning, but it is not so simple to determine whether the answers reflect real decisions that strategically affect fecundity or essentially epiphenomenal pseudo-decisions of little real consequence. Close phenomenological inquiry followed up longitudinally is needed to throw further light on these questions.

Limits on the present rationality of decision-making that suggest openings for substantial change in the outcome of decisions, if the governing assumptions can be altered, can be identified through a careful mapping of what people take for granted as outside the range of decision or as setting the fixed terms of decision. A dramatic case in point is that of *pluralistic ignorance*. The term was originated in a discussion of normatively regulated behavior by Katz and Schanck (1938), who wrote: "People will stay in line because their fellows do, yet, if they only knew that their comrades wanted to kick over the traces too, the institutional conformity of the group would quickly vanish" (pp. 174–175). Such pluralistic ignorance was unearthed in the early Puerto Rican study by Hill, Stycos, and Back (1959), who found—contrary to the accepted tenet of cultural machismo that men are expected to want large families, especially of sons, as proof of their masculinity—that men were even more oriented toward small families than their wives. Since their wives were quite unaware of this fact, it was the false and vulnerable assumption that men want large families that must have figured in the women's decision processes.

What people take for granted can undergo rapid change. For many devout Catholics the papal interdiction of artificial contraception must once have settled the matter, removing the possibility of efficient contraception from consideration as an alternative. After disagreement with this dictum flared up among the priests and bishops of the post-Vatican II Church, however, the highly publicized controversy inevitably shifted the issues for decision on the part of the faithful. A dogma become moot no longer enjoys the privilege of automatically setting the terms of decision.

The same is true of legally enforced norms that formerly excluded abortion in America or relegated it to a risky and expensive underworld.[1] The first crack in the armor of state law seems to

---

[1] Since this chapter was written, my attention has been called to the provocative paper by Namboodiri and Pope, 1968, contrasting the implications of what they term the "economic" and the "normative" approaches to

have set in motion a process of rapid legal and normative change that has already made abortion figure in personal decisions on a scale that would have been unthinkable a few years ago. Was pluralistic ignorance involved in sustaining the former seemingly impregnable barriers? Or, as in the case of race relations, have we underestimated the responsiveness of the mores to legal initiative? Research is needed to capture some of the dynamics of the rapid change now in progress and thus add to our understanding of the malleability of the terms of reproductive decisions.

The impact of developments in contraceptive and abortifacient technology will also depend on how they affect the terms of individual decision-making. There is the obvious factor of risk that enters into the cost-benefit balance: when the perceived risk entailed by a contraceptive technique can be reduced, its acceptability is enhanced. Akin are the effects to be anticipated from reducing the bother, mess, or unwelcome side effects of contraception. Elsewhere (Smith, 1965b) I have stressed the psychological importance of differences between the various birth-control methods in how they package and structure the decision process. The existing methods can be ordered on a continuum from sterilization, through the loop and the pill, to the diaphragm and condom—according to the scope of the consequences governed by a single decision. I argue that only those methods in which a single decision commits the person to

---

the explanatory analysis of human fertility. To the extent that economic considerations of utility apply, the values involved in decisions affecting family size fall into a hierarchy of preferences; to the extent that moral norms supervene, choices are made without consideration of utilities. The paper provides appropriate references developing each point of view and argues that neither the economic nor the normative approach alone helps explain choice behavior in all situations: determination of the extent to which either applies is an empirical matter.

The approach taken in the present essay is, of course, broadly "economic"; it underplays the role of moral norms, which, as Namboodiri and Pope suggest, may figure more prominently in regard to family size in nonindustrial societies than in industrially advanced ones. It should be noted, however, that norms vary in their consensuality and in their moral force; utilitarian considerations may often result in contranormative behavior. As a result, in the longer run the content of what is normative may shift under utilitarian pressures. Something of the sort may be happening in the United States in regard to the issue of abortion. These considerations argue against a sharp separation of the utilitarian and the normative.

effective birth prevention over many occasions of intercourse hold much promise for population control; any method that requires a new decision to accompany each sexual act sets requirements too stringent to be effective in regulating behavior that is as impulsive and as private as sex. Moreover, the advantage should lie with methods that change the focus of decision from *contra*ception to *con*ception, so that pregnancy, not its prevention, requires active choice. Of presently available methods, only the imperfectly effective loop has this advantage for women who find it acceptable.

On these a priori psychological grounds, I set higher priority on improving the loop or on developing an implanted long-term pill that can be neutralized at will by taking a complementary pill than on investment in further psychological research, desirable as that is. For persons continually at risk of conception, such technological measures should create a context of decision in which unwanted pregnancies would be minimal. For persons only occasionally or unpredictably at risk—particularly the unmarried young—analogous considerations would give priority to the development of a safe, acceptable abortifacient for the morning after—a technological advance that would avoid the psychological and moral disadvantages of deliberately maintaining a constant state of readiness for sexual activity, as the regimen of the pill requires.

But convinced as I am of these armchair conclusions, research is clearly needed on how proposed new techniques actually do become involved in the motivational and decision processes of their users. Clinical tests of new methods should always include systematic study of these matters.

The effects on fertility of differences or changes in the social structure and institutional context are also likely to be mediated by their influence on the terms of behavioral decisions that affect procreation. Davis (1967) counts on such mediation in his controversy with proponents of voluntaristic planned parenthood. In Davis's view, support of family planning has misleadingly deflected potential support from more effective measures toward the control of population growth. He argues that only major social changes that entail the restructuring of incentives and the erosion of familistic values are adequate to change the fertility of a population. Planned parenthood, as Davis sees it, actually promotes rather than counteracts familistic values; moreover, it deals with trivial attitudes that cannot be expected to give leverage against the strong motives that underlie human fertility. One may differ with his verdict against the support of family planning (as I discuss the matter subsequently, I believe voluntaristic family planning and the programming of incentives are entirely compatible) yet accept his analysis of how social change can affect the motivational basis of fertility.

Plausible examples of these relationships are readily available. Thus the value of an additional child differs in an economy of farm or household industry versus one where prolonged education entails high costs and delays economic productivity until well after the capacity for independent adulthood has been reached. It likewise differs in a traditional society in which provision of sustenance to the aged and of ritual honor to the dead depends entirely on their progeny versus a secular society that provides for the social security of the aged. Corresponding differences in fertility rates follow. Yet it is difficult, indeed, to estimate in advance the net consequences for fertility of major social changes seen in process or contemplated as a matter of deliberate policy. There are no examples of success.

The structural changes now being fervently pressed by radical feminists would affect the terms of reproductive decisions as well as the values of parenthood. When few other options are socially available to women for creative self-realization, the values inherent in motherhood are likely to be seized upon and even magnified by default. If equal and adequate opportunities for women become available in what has previously been a man's world, however, motherhood—or at least compulsively repetitive motherhood—may less frequently be the most attractive alternative.

These conjectures need elaboration and testing in research. But I have carried the examples far enough to suggest that an adequate causal analysis, which is needed for the guidance of social policy, requires the joint application of sociological and psychological perspectives, which then become complementary rather than competitive. Controversies about which factors lend themselves most promisingly to strategic access are likely to be more illuminating, and less heated, than ones about the priority of social versus psychological causes, seen in the competitive terms of academic territoriality.

The loosely construed decision-making framework that I have found useful thus far must be still further qualified if it is not to become a Procrustean bed for the analysis of psychological factors in fertility. It is not always helpful to think of motivated human behavior in terms of decisions, even implicit ones. Behavior may be motivated and emitted without the weighing of alternatives. To try to compress the psychology of motivation into a decisional framework, with its implications of rationality, would surely be unwise. The quasi-rational component seems dependable enough, however, to make Hardin's analysis of the tragedy of the commons persuasive and to warrant the development of social strategies to shift the balance of incentives. In this connection it seems to me too bad that followers of B. F. Skinner's approach to the experimental analysis of behavior have not as yet turned their very considerable analytic and manipulative ingenuity to the population problem. Beginnings are made in a programmatic paper by Lipe (1971).

In the broader realm of motivational processes relevant to fertility, the social psychologist is accustomed to focusing on beliefs, attitudes, and values as dispositions that, jointly with the person's appraisal of his situation of action, enter into the determination of what he does. The psychoanalytically oriented psychologist will be alert to deeper motivations that are less directly expressed. The burden of much of the foregoing, for the social psychologist, is to suggest that we do not yet have adequately clear ideas about what beliefs, attitudes, and values engage with reproductively relevant behavior. Naturalistically conceived research in depth along the lines of Rainwater's (1960, 1965) is needed if we are to discern the relevant units of psychological organization.

Internal Versus External Control

People are not just bundles of beliefs, attitudes, and values that channel motives. These dispositions must be seen in the context of the organization of personality. An aspect of personality that shows special promise in the present context is the way that people differ in the degree to which they are psychologically organized to carry out a planful course of action. As we know, there is many a slip between intention and realization, between expressions of attitude and consequential behavior. Progress toward the conceptualization and measurement of personality differences in this respect should be relevant to family planning.

A recent socio-psychological approach giving considerable evidence of coming to grips with this problem deals with differences in the individual's capacity for self-determination in terms of his self-conceptions as "origin" or "pawn" of social causation (De Charms, 1968) or in terms of the individual's generalized expectations about outcomes of his actions as under internal or external control (Rotter, 1966; Lefcourt, 1966). As I have reinterpreted these convergent lines of research and theory (Chapter Eight), what seems to be involved is a cluster of self-attitudes that tend to function as a self-fulfilling prophecy. People who are convinced that they are origins, that their important outcomes are under their own control, behave to enhance the likelihood that their beliefs will be confirmed; so, unfortunately, do those who see themselves as pawns at the mercy of external forces. In his I-E scale (internal versus external control) J. B. Rotter has provided a convenient but rather crude and faulted measure of the variable, in terms of which there are validating indications that groups contrasting in actual social power differ as might be expected, and that the variable has behavioral consequences in line with our present interests.

More substantial clues are available that locus of control has a direct bearing on fertility-relevant behavior. In a study of undergraduates MacDonald (1970) reports that among the unmarried females who indicated that they had engaged in premarital coitus, substantially and significantly more of the respondents high in internal control than of those high in external control reported the use of some form of birth control. Essentially the same conceptual variable, differently approached, has been tapped by Williamson (1969) and others under the label *sense of efficacy*. In the context of a major study of modernization, Williamson finds his measure to be related to favorable attitudes toward birth control.

Still further supportive evidence has been reported by Keller, Sims, Henry, and Crawford (1970) in their suggestive intensive study of twenty lower-class Negro couples, half of whom were making effective use of contraceptives and half of whom were not. (The subgroups were well matched: all were of childbearing age with at least two children; all were informed about contraception and had contraceptive services available.) In a study presented as reestablishing the promise of a psychological approach to fertility, projective measures of feelings of efficacy, need for achievement (men only), and tendency to plan ahead were prominent among the measures that discriminated significantly between users and nonusers.

In contrast with the measures of personality traits that have proved so disappointing in previous research on fertility, where the rationale for expecting any relationship has tended to be vague and intuitive at best, personal control or sensed efficacy is a variable that fills a well-defined theoretical gap. Voluntaristic programs of family planning, whether or not they are thought of as steps toward the control of population growth, crucially depend on the planfulness of their participants. If we can develop adequate measures of people's propensity to take command of their own fate, we will have brought into view an important ingredient in the success or failure of the voluntaristic strategy. We may also have discovered a moderate variable that helps determine whether people act in terms of their expressed attitudes in matters of family planning.

The research priorities here seem clear enough. In the short run the Rotter scale, or one or another of the several short scales of survey items offered to tap the sense of efficacy, should be applied in newly undertaken studies of attitudes and practices about birth control and family planning. Taking into account the known deficiencies of existing scales, locus of control is sufficiently relevant to family planning behavior to justify setting even higher priority on the development of a theoretically and psychometrically more adequate measure from the pool of items now available.

Conceptualization and Strategy

The points I have chosen to emphasize are, I realize, a slim selection from the possible points of contact between social psychology and research on fertility and population. I have not dealt with the psychology of communication, persuasion, and attitude change

—central topics of social psychology—because I am reluctantly convinced that these useful areas of sociopsychological competence are unlikely to be the sites of major breakthroughs toward understanding what has eluded conventional demography. I have ignored the important area of small-group interaction as applied to communicative relationships in the family because it has been the preserve of social psychologists affiliated with sociology; I do not know enough about it.

In adopting a loose decision-making orientation as a point of departure for identifying research needs, I have risked presenting a rationalistic caricature of a realm of human behavior that is surely ridden with irrationality. In calling for research attention to limitations on rational decision, my preference for a cognitive theoretical approach has led me to stress factors in people's knowledge and beliefs, in their situations of action as they define them, that affect the terms of their decisions; I have slighted the barriers of habit and custom, less cognitively formulated, which also restrict people's options and which need research attention.

Underlying my selection of topics is a set of appraisals and value judgments that governs what I presently find most useful for learning about the social psychology of fertility; the purposes of this book are served best if I make these appraisals and value judgments explicit. I am personally persuaded by Hardin's analysis of the population problem as a tragedy of the commons and take seriously Crowe's elaborations of the difficulties that beset the search for a political solution. In these terms the problem is deadly serious: only the length of the period of grace left for us to find a solution seems open to debate. The world is limited; population will eventually cease to grow because of the mortality of war, famine, disease, and environmental fouling and depletion—or because the quality of life has fallen to such a miserable level that in Hardin's equation the individual utilities for having children, plus and minus, finally balance. The problem is so serious that even coercive measures must be considered. According to Hardin's analysis, jawboning and educational approaches will not by themselves suffice.

But here my commitment to the value of human freedom insists on recognition. The values embedded in my view of human potentiality call for the expansion, not the contraction, of the range of human choice. Freedom and self-determination seem to me to make more difference to the quality of life than even clean air and green land. How can we preserve the reality of choice, yet avoid the doom inherent in the common tragedy?

To put the question thus seems to me to point unmistakably toward a deliberate social policy of incentives for family limitation— incentives provided directly to the potential parents or produced indirectly via planned institutional changes that in turn modify the terms of reproductive decisions. A strategy of appropriately designed incentives would leave free choice to the individual—indeed, it would encourage planful choice—while it would steer the overall statistical outcome, as this outcome must be steered if we are to avoid catastrophe, by adjusting the nature or the value of the alternatives offered.

To further speculate, I see the strategy of direct incentives favored by Spengler (1969) as complementary to the reliance on major institutional change primarily stressed by Davis (1967). We are drastically inexperienced in the initiation and guidance of planned social change. Even if we can gird ourselves politically to bring change about, we still lack the competence to steer it to produce the desired effects on fertility. At best the feedback features of the social system inherently involve time lags that preclude accurate guidance. To achieve a desired target of stable population replacement, then, sensitive control over decision structures that a program of direct incentives could provide seems an essential component of an effective social plan.

These are admittedly Utopian speculations, but the seriousness of our predicament requires us to gain practice in Utopian thinking. At a more practical level, psychologists are already in a position to contribute to the design of antinatalistic incentives (Pohlman, 1973), which if they are to be ethically acceptable must rest upon a base of truly adequate income support. I would also note, with Chilman (1970), that other important human values besides stabilized population and freedom of choice are going to be deeply touched by any deliberate effort to limit population growth. Unanticipated and unwelcome side effects on the values presently realized in family life should be ferreted out imaginatively and monitored carefully.

To develop a policy of qualified voluntarism—voluntarism within a context of designed incentives—will require dependable and sophisticated knowledge about the terms in which people actually make the decisions that affect procreation and about the extent to which they make decisions at all. It is here that I have placed greatest emphasis in the present chapter. Developing such a policy also calls for knowledge of people's capacity for voluntary planning that is rational within a given incentive structure—the topic dealt with in the foregoing section.

In this bold—or rash—endeavor, what help may we reasonably expect from social psychology? Here I must return to my initial modest position. In the face of discouraging prior efforts, I hesitate to promise striking immediate gains from sociopsychological research in the control of additional variance in fertility. But the sort of empirical mapping of relevant dispositions, situations, and decisional processes that I have called for might reasonably be expected to yield a clearer understanding of the causal nexus that underlies demographic correlations. This understanding in turn should be relevant to the development of social policy.

From a strategic point of view, technology and other components of people's situations of action are more likely to be accessible to change than are people themselves. Special attention might therefore be given to how people interpret and react to proposed innovations in social incentives and in contraceptive-abortifacient technology. Fortunately the evaluation of social programs is at last becoming a subject of potential interest to competent and imaginative social psychologists.

Chapter Six

•••••••••••••••••••••
•••••••••••••••••••••••
•••••••••••••••••••••••

ETHICAL
IMPLICATIONS OF
POPULATION
POLICIES

•••••••••••••••••••••
•••••••••••••••••••••••
•••••••••••••••••••••••

*I*t is unfortunately a moot question whether our American governmental system is capable of developing and implementing a population policy, in the sense of a coherent legislative and administrative posture toward the attainment of explicit objectives concerning the growth, distribution, and structure of population. I have taken part in a discussion that included several eminent political scientists who ruled out the very possibility of policy in this sense, as unworthy of serious consideration; they could become interested only in latent or implicit policy, that is, the unintended consequences of governmental action—or in the effects of predicted population change on the processes of government. To me, this is rank and irresponsible defeatism. The need for explicit social policy in regard to population and a variety of related urgent issues is a principal challenge to our faltering governmental system. We have already gone too far in reaping the unintended and unwelcome consequences of implicit policy.

Any consideration of explicit population policy lands us squarely in the realm of political and ethical issues—political because competing interests are at stake, ethical because we have to assign priorities to competing values, to arrive at accommodations between competing standards or criteria of evaluation. Issues of political ethics—of who ought to get what, where, and when according to what substantive criteria or procedural rules—are central and exceedingly difficult.

As questions of sheer survival begin to surface, naked *Realpolitik*—the unenlightened self-interest of the already powerful or of those who aspire to power—is all too likely to eclipse humane ethics. In the ringing words of Mack the Knife (in Brecht's *Threepenny Opera*), *Erst kommt das Fressen, dann kommt die Morale:* The belly comes first; only then, ethics. We may be farther than we think along this ominous path, even in affluent and spacious America. For me, the handwriting began to trace itself on the wall when I read Hardin's (1971) guest editorial in *Science*. Hardin is of course well known for his classic analysis of the tragedy of the commons (1968), perhaps the most acute and eloquent analysis of our population dilemma. Three years later he writes (1971, p. 1297):

> If the world is one great commons, in which all food is shared equally, then we are lost. Those who breed faster will replace the rest. Sharing the food from national territories is operationally equivalent to sharing territories: in both cases a commons is established, and tragedy is the ultimate result. In the absence of breeding controls, a policy of "one mouth, one meal" ultimately produces one miserable world.
>
> In a less than perfect world, the allocation of rights based on territory must be defended if a ruinous breeding race is to be avoided. It is unlikely that civilization and dignity can survive everywhere; but better in a few places than in none. Fortunate minorities must act as the trustees of a civilization that is threatened by uninformed good intentions.

Erst kommt das Fressen—in spite of the fine words about civilization. What kind of civilization would it be? I am glad that

Minna Rees (1971), as President of the American Association for the Advancement of Science, subsequently called upon scientists and nonscientists to explore more humane alternatives. But the issue is joined, and it is very desirable that it be joined explicitly before we slip unknowingly behind the battlements of a tough-minded—and dehumanized—fortress America.

Ethical aspects of population policy are everybody's business. All the same, the professional philosopher has a special contribution to make—not in telling the rest of us what is right but in bringing to bear the cumulative sophistication of ethical inquiry to help us think clearly, consistently, and with the necessary degree of complexity about ethical issues. Here I can only advertise, not summarize, a splendid paper by Daniel Callahan (1971) on ethics and population limitation. Callahan provides philosophical duffers like me with the best brief guided tour I know through the technical alternatives currently available in ethical thinking, explains his own position—to me a sensible one (called a "mixed deontological theory"), and applies it to the succinct discussion of a set of important, concrete ethical issues concerning population limitation, as encountered by individuals, governments, and private organizations—more issues than I can possibly touch in this chapter.

The crux of Callahan's own ethical position is this: "One is obliged to act in such a way that the fundamental values of freedom, justice and security/survival are . . . respected and, in case of conflict, . . . one or more of these values can be limited if and only if it can be shown that such a course will serve to increase the balance of good over evil" (pp. 14–15). Further, Callahan states that "those choices of action ought to be preferred which give a primacy of place to the value of freedom of choice. If conditions appear to require a limitation of freedom, this should be done in such a way as to minimize the direct and indirect harmful consequences, and be just in the chosen means of limitation" (p. 23).

Let us accept this broad framework for present purposes, recognizing that others can be defended. The population crisis has injected considerations of security/survival into the ethics of population policy: that is what the crisis is about. Freedom and justice, on their part, sound like abstract values, far from the throbbing warmth of human concerns as they are experienced by nonphilosophers. But as abstractions they encompass precisely these concerns. Freedom is my right to pursue my values and goals, whatever they may be. It encompasses my other values as well as being a value on its own. Who is to decide how many children I should have? In the name of security/survival, we are beginning to be asked to consider coercive measures to limit population growth. When we ask who should bear the brunt of policies to limit population, justice or equity is involved. Men, women? The poor, the blacks? Americans, "underdeveloped foreigners"? These are hot issues, and they are going to get hotter.

I focus here on only two concrete ethical issues in the limitation of population: one centering on freedom, the other on justice. The first is examined usefully by Callahan; he does not touch on the second, and his principles give me no help at all.

In the context of freedom, the promulgation of voluntaristic family planning is ethically attractive. Intensive interviews by one of my students[1] have brought home vividly how, for lower-class or Catholic women, the new realization that one can decide how many babies to have (and the decision itself) can be the beginning of an active, self-choosing stance toward many aspects of life—a life as origin rather than pawn in De Charms' (1968) sense. Family planning is an ethical good. But as Davis (1967) argues persuasively, efficient birth control at the option of the individual is no substitute for population policy; given people's prevalent wishes for children, optional birth control will not limit population though it may reduce its rate of growth in countries where contraceptive information and technology have hitherto been inadequate. So, in the interests of security/survival, some compromise of freedom seems inevitable. The right to have as many children as one wishes must be limited. Or, which is not the same thing, one's wishes for children must be modified or manipulated. Exhortation will not do, both because it is usually ineffectual and because the ethically most responsible would suffer the greatest loss (inequity here!). Coercion in its more blatant forms is ethically unacceptable, a matter of last resort for which the burden of proof must be immense. In between lies the planned manipulation of incentives. (Strategies of incentive have

[1] The author is grateful to Virginia McDowell for these insights.

recently been discussed from a Skinnerian standpoint by Lipe [1971]. See also Pohlman [1971; 1973].)

In Chapter Five, I argued for "such a deliberate social policy of incentives for family limitation—incentives provided directly to the potential parents, or produced indirectly via planned institutional changes that in turn modify the terms of reproductive decisions. [Thus, planned changes in women's roles providing valued alternatives to child-rearing.] A strategy of appropriately designed incentives would leave free choice to the individual—indeed, it would encourage planful choice—while it would steer the overall statistical outcome, as this outcome must be steered if we are to avoid catastrophe, by adjusting the nature of the value of the alternatives offered." Designed incentives shape behavior, and thus limit freedom, but they preserve the reality of individual choice; indeed they depend upon it. Whereas Davis (1967) writes as though we had to decide between supporting Planned Parenthood versus a policy of incentives for limiting population, it seems to me that favoring both is rational and ethically responsible in our predicament.

Designing an appropriate structure of incentives to limit population growth is a technical matter in which psychology can help to contribute the empirical base, but the further ethical issues that are inherently involved should not be neglected. Any concrete proposal for a pattern of incentives (including that of leaving the happenstance status quo unaltered) raises questions of equity or justice, which in a democratic society are also bound to entail political issues. Positive or negative financial incentives bear inequitably on the poor. In a society that is far from solving its dilemmas of liberty and equality, I would myself find any scheme of monetary incentives unjust and, for the poor, unacceptably coercive, unless it could rest on a base of adequate income support. (In social policy, how often it turns out that to make headway on one problem, another equally difficult one must be attacked!)

Our pursuit of some of the ethical implications of an incentives strategy has thus turned our attention from freedom to justice among the ultimate ethical criteria. The issues to which I now turn are dilemmas of justice that arise when the unit of ethical consideration is supraindividual—nation, tribe, or ethnic group. Whatever our liberal intent and our actual readiness for altruistic accommodation, most of us are nationalists and racists in population matters. We do not really believe that "a man's a man for a' that." Most of us are bothered at the idea that the prevailing complexion of mankind might become other than our own; that some other country's posterity may populate the globe at the expense of ours. The comforts of our own kind matter more than the famine of the "others." (Happily, inexorable biological fact still protects us from parallel consequences of our sexism.) Maybe we should not be bothered by prospects that other genetic strains might replace our own genes—and it seems clear to me that by the highest ethical standards, indeed we should not be. But we *are* bothered, and as long as we find our identity in social categories of race or nation, they become relevant to considerations of equity. Which social category should have the right to breed seems to be an even tougher ethical and political question than which individuals, when the categories are ones with which we strongly identify.

Because of contingent features of our present situation that we have come to take for granted, the case is different in regard to nations and to ethnic groups. (The difference is more political than ethical, but in actuality, ethical decisions have to be made within the limits of the politically feasible.) The nuclear stalemate has essentially ruled out territorial conquest as a solution of one nation's population problem at the expense of others. And we have become habituated to the restrictive immigration policies of nation-states. Population policy in the realm of nations thus is considered within the framework of the territorial status quo. We only begin applying ethical considerations at this point—Callahan's paper is an example. *If* we grant the status quo of territoriality insulated against population flow, it follows that the impoverished countries of South America, Asia, and Africa should for their own best interest seek to limit their populations. If we aid them in discovering and furthering this interest, we contribute to solving the global problem with no sense of ethical conflict. But why should the status quo be regarded as a just allocation of the world's land among the world's people? Obviously it is not, but just as obviously, in the present collection of nation-states no other solution is identifiable and feasible, and the pressures of the population problem make a genuinely one-world solution increasingly unlikely. The best we can hope for realistically is that the glaring inequities be modulated by humanitarian concern.

It is because we are used to this situation that Hardin's (1971) proposal may seem more realistic than shocking. In the United States, with its previous stable condition of WASP domination and melting-pot ideology, we are *not* used to our emerging situation of ethnic pluralism—multiple racism, from another perspective. Unlike the case of nations, in that of ethnic groups the status quo does not provide us with a politically acceptable if ethically questionable formula. As the political scientist Crowe (1969) argues in a pessimistic rejoinder to Hardin's analysis of the tragedy of the commons, the Hobbesian social contract—"mutual coercion, mutually agreed upon," in Hardin's version—may be getting out of reach as a solution to the population problem in an increasingly "tribalized" society in which mutually alienated groups diverge in ultimate values rather than in negotiable interests. How can we agree on a just allocation of birthrights?

I have introduced the problem in a political context, but the ethical question seems even further from resolution, insofar as it asks for justice among the population claims of dissensual and unequal ethnic groups competing for resources in a common territory. The point was brought home to me by a Jewish friend who has five or six much-loved children. Far from sharing my qualms about having contributed four passengers to the load on Spaceship Earth, he expressed a deep moral commitment to help replenish the Jewish people after the Nazi holocaust. Why shouldn't the disadvantaged blacks at least have the right to increase? There is nothing ethically special about the status quo in relative numbers. When black ideologists charge well-meaning Waspish proponents of Planned Parenthood with genocidal intent, the point is overdrawn, but the underlying question of equity seems unanswerable. (See Darity, 1971.)

I see no possible ethical solution to the problem of population equity among groups and social categories when people find their identity in them and when power and perquisites are distributed unequally among them. Ethical thinking about population works pretty well for analyzing the decisions, the rights, and the obligations of interdependent individuals; however, it seems to break down when social categories are accorded supraindividual reality and value. Under the pressure of threats to survival, we will very likely arrive at political accommodations of one sort or another among ethnic interests, but these accommodations are likely to be the kind that prevail in Hobbes' "state of nature," reflecting the relative effectiveness of claims to power, rather than the result of ethical appraisal. Ethical consideration can hardly adjudicate between groups that fail to sense a common interest. Perhaps this is to say that we cannot expect to define, let alone attain, justice in the realm of population policy as long as severe injustice persists in relations between races and ethnic groups—or between classes and nations as well. According to Plato's extended metaphor of the *Republic*, justice is of a piece. But to recognize these difficulties should not inhibit us from seeking to reduce injustice where we find it.

I have tried to focus attention on some of the ethical problems that are implicated in any policy of incentives to population limitation and in policies affecting equity among nations and ethnic groups, at the expense of a host of other important issues that I might have discussed: among them, the definition and value of life as it affects policies toward abortion (cf. Knutson, 1967; 1973)', the rights of posterity as they compete with those of the presently living, and the values of a familistic society that are jeopardized by policies of zero population growth. But the problems I have talked about do seem to deserve top priority. Incentive schemes are the most practical and least unacceptable means by which the goal of zero population growth, which is essential eventually, can be attained. Psychology has a potentially important role to play in their development. And the problems of equity posed by nationalism, tribalism, and racism present the most obdurate barrier to agreement on population goals. The tough problem, when we try to make population policy explicit, is how to agree on the structure of an optimum population. At the moment, the problem appears to be beyond ethical or political solution. The crudity of our means for reducing population growth gives us some breathing time while we are still ethically and politically unable to specify our goals. At least we are beginning to agree that we want our population to grow more slowly.

PART II

●●●●●●●●●●●●●●●●●●
●●●●●●●●●●●●●●●●●●
●●●●●●●●●●●●●●●●●●

EMPHASIS:
PERSONOLOGICAL

●●●●●●●●●●●●●●●●●●
●●●●●●●●●●●●●●●●●●
●●●●●●●●●●●●●●●●●●

The four chapters that comprise this part, printed in the order in which they were written, present the recent sequential development of my version of a humanistic view of personality.

For historical and political reasons, psychologists seem to be stuck with the language of "mental health" when they want to look evaluatively at human functioning. This terminology is now an embarrassment conceptually and in interprofessional politics because of its medical connotations. Chapter Seven examines the social semantics of mental health in several sociohistorical contexts and argues for Robert White's concept of competence as best fitting the present public interest in human functioning. The chapter was written with the social priorities of President Johnson's abortive War on Poverty in mind. Since then, these priorities have been laid aside in a shameful interlude of not-so-benign neglect, and so I think the value perspective of the chapter remains relevant.

Chapter Eight extends the concept of competence more explicitly in the direction of self-theory. If the motivational basis of a competent, coping orientation is a cluster of core attitudes toward self and world that centers on self-respect and hope, attitudes that include expectations that tend to be self-fulfilling, it is only a small step to recognize that these attitudes provide a way of dealing psychologically with the perennial issue of self-determination, the goal of many recent social movements. From a psychological standpoint, self-determination or freedom is not a philosophical assumption but an empirical variable that is open to scientific inquiry in a causal context.

As I developed this argument, I became increasingly aware of its one-sidedness. In Rollo May's terms, there is Love as well as Will. As dimensions of human value, competence and self-determination focus on the instrumental, Promethean side of human potentiality and underplay the expressive side. For my own insights, they fall in the realm of the traditional male role and its hang-ups. I therefore welcomed the opportunity to address myself seriously to Maslow's central concept of self-actualization (Chapter Nine) as a corrective to this bias.

In an attempt to steer cautiously through the treacherous conceptual shoals that Maslow has bequeathed in his attractive but un–self-critical writings, I arrive at a defensible and useful interpretation of self-actualization, one that paradoxically can be described as more humanistic than Maslow's biologistic version. But my analysis leads squarely to the recognition that the meaning that we assign to the value-laden term self-actualization—and the ethical prescriptions that we draw from it—depends crucially on what we assume about the "self" that is to be "actualized." The final chapter in Part Two, Chapter Ten, is an initial attempt to sort out my thinking about the theory of the self, an unavoidable step in this line of value-relevant inquiry. A comprehensive theory of the self should indeed be the pinnacle of personality-and-social psychology from a humanistic-scientific perspective. This volume aspires to take only some first steps toward this goal, which are the more difficult because different approaches to the study and conceptualization of the self have hitherto been developed mostly in isolation from one another.

Chapter Seven

•••••••••••••••••••••
•••••••••••••••••••••
•••••••••••••••••••••

COMPETENCE AND "MENTAL HEALTH"

•••••••••••••••••••••
•••••••••••••••••••••
•••••••••••••••••••••

*T*he point of view to be developed rejects the model of somatic illness as irrelevant to the issues that have increasingly gained the center of the stage in contemporary concern with "mental health." We are captives, I think, of a metaphorical terminology that became current, for good reason, in social contexts different from those that we presently face. Our terminology makes a difference. It leads us to a continued preoccupation with symptoms and syndromes, to a strategic commitment to the search for disease entities, to the appraisal of human effectiveness in terms of the sum of a person's symptomlike liabilities with inadequate attention to the concurrent sum of his strengths.

The health-and-disease model also biases us toward a preemptive concern with the individual organism, so to speak in vitro, and, by extension, with intrapsychic processes. It predisposes us to neglect the context of structured social relations in which effectiveness or ineffectiveness is displayed, which contributes to their genesis, and which must be dealt with by programs of intervention that aim at increasing the balance of effectiveness.

I am obviously assuming that when we use the language of

124

mental health, we are talking about a range of effectiveness and ineffectiveness that strays far from the meaningful domain of the disease model. If we are to make headway with these present concerns, I think it is important to clear away the cobwebs of misplaced medical metaphors. I therefore seek to advance a way of conceiving effectiveness and ineffectiveness that seems more appropriate to present social tasks. As part of such a formulation, I stress the relevance of a concept of competence that is not just the opposite of having symptoms. The point of view to be developed may give little immediate help on the task of measurement (a focus of the symposium for which this chapter was prepared), but it claims a good deal of relevance to the prior question: What is worth measuring?

The route by which I have arrived at my present position has involved recurrent concern with "positive" mental health, and a generally frustrating series of attempts to deal with the value problems encountered if the term is given an empirical meaning that is defensibly relevant to research and practice (Smith, 1950, 1959, 1961, 1968c). My contribution can best be put in perspective if I view it as carrying an item of my private agenda a step forward.

Some Personal Agenda

I owe my initial and continued involvement with the difficult topic of positive mental health to Marie Jahoda, whose tolerance of ambiguity, push toward clarity, and good sense have encouraged me by example (Jahoda, 1950, 1958). Chairing the provocative seminar for the Joint Commission on Mental Illness and Health that she organized to assist her in preparing her admirable book (1958) further involved me in issues that had their own momentum. Working them through afterward carried me to the point of recognizing the necessarily value-laden nature of thinking about mental health, and the scientific (though not human) arbitrariness of decisions concerning which multiple criteria of mental health—for example, cognitive adequacy, personal integration, autonomy, positive self-attitudes, and the like—one elects to use as measuring sticks. I adopted the position that mental health, whether one likes the term or not, is at best a chapter heading, not a theoretical concept, under which various attempts to evaluate human personality can be grouped,

From this point of view, the boundaries of the chapter—just what is included in mental health—are hardly worth debating.

I argued that even though the choices that are involved in positing particular values as mental-health criteria cannot be decided on purely scientific grounds, psychologists and other behavioral scientists have a legitimate and possibly important role in the byplay through which private decision and social consensus on such matters of values must emerge, if they are to emerge at all. If the humanist, moralist, or social critic contributes to such an emerging consensus by sharpening our sensitivities and discrimination about possibilities in the realm of human values, the behavioral scientist can bring in facts about the causal contingencies in which choices of values are embedded. We may choose differently if we know the secondary consequences that our choices entail or if we know the antecedent conditions that are required for the effects to be realized that we think desirable. We actually know little about these matters—for example, about the long-term motivational consequences of an efficient conceptual Head Start for culturally deprived children—that the empirical contributions of behavioral scientists to these value-laden issues are urgently needed.

The danger of regarding mental health as more than a chapter heading is that it is easy to use the term as a cloak to hide one's own personal or professional value choices and thus give a spurious aura of scientific or medical respectability to recommendations that may follow. If scientists are to become involved in the controversy about values, and I thought they should, it is important that they keep their talk and thinking straight by maintaining a sharp and explicit distinction between their assertions about empirical relationships—where their distinctive role lies—and their claims for particular evaluative criteria—where they stand on much the same ground as everybody else. Thus, to revert to my Head Start example, perhaps in my personal scheme of values as a mental-health professional I give priority to "emotional adjustment" over "cognitive adequacy"; I would rather see children happy than bright and academically successful, if I were forced to choose. How easy to decry the risks to the mental health of children who, for example, are exposed to a program that exclusively features conceptual training! But how much more conducive to clarity and to the appropriate gathering and weighing of relevant facts if instead one specifies the particular valued psychological attributes, perhaps self-reliance or social poise, that are seen to be at risk. Perhaps the price in terms of competing values is one that people are quite willing to pay. At all events, if we avoid evoking mental health, we should all be more likely to know what we are talking about.

My argument, thus, was essentially a critical and negative one cautioning scientist-professionals in the mental-health fields from falling too readily into the role of a new priestcraft, in which some of the laity are ready enough to cast us. On the positive side, I favored research on value-relevant issues of personality development and functioning, but in so opting for science *and* values too, I was wide open to the charge of uttering pious and abstract platitudes. At any rate, if I thought I had put my own intellectual house in order by this sorting out of mental health as a special case of the problem of values in psychology (Smith, 1961), it was not to stay that way for long. Three things have stirred up the issues for me once again, and the personal agenda that I will pursue in this chapter attempts to cope with their consequences. First, I became involved with data, in the course of studying some highly effective young people in the Peace Corps. After such an experience, armchair considerations can hardly look the same. Second, like everyone else, I have been swept up into thinking through the implications of the new social programs under the aegis of Comprehensive Community Mental Health and the War Against Poverty. And finally, like many of my colleagues, I have been impressed by R. W. White's (1959) reappraisal of psychological theory and evidence in his discussions of the concept of competence. This chapter attempts to digest these recent developments and to accommodate my previous thinking about mental health.

Social Semantics of "Mental Illness" and "Mental Health"

Since my unwillingness to define "mental illness" and "mental health" has become a matter of principle rather than of mere preference, my first major task is to say why, as explicitly as I can. The crux of the matter is that conceptions of mental illness and health have been shaped by particular social contexts and purposes and that as these contexts and purposes have changed, usage has become increasingly inappropriate. The semantics of mental health rests primarily on pragmatics and much less on the intrinsic nature of the phenomena being dealt with. In relation to the purposes and opportunities that currently concern us, health terminology is an actual hindrance.

I realize that since part of the pragmatic context of current usage is the professional rivalry between medical and nonmedical professions that share a concern with human effectiveness and ineffectiveness, I run the risk of seeming to indulge in petty special pleading for the vested interests of psychologists. Indeed, the vested interests are real and had best be recognized. The language of health and disease, when it prevails, connotes an area of medical responsibility and preeminance. It fits the language habits and the professional interests of psychiatrists and other physicians better than it does those of the psychologists. It is, thus, hardly surprising that psychiatrists like it and psychologists do not. It is unbecoming to fuss about semantics if professional claims are the real issue. But if we are serious in the attempt to gain greater clarity in thinking about mental health, we should not buy amity at the cost of confusion. The social basis for evaluting human psychological functioning in terms of health and illness seems to me to have deep roots. Why, then, did we begin talking about mental health and illness, and why should we stop it now?

Mental Hospital. The answer must go back to the birth of institutional psychiatry, as part of the then-progressive movement under medical auspices that offered the insane asylum as a humane alternative for the care of grossly incapacitated, psychotic people. To regard the insane as sick was to regard them as human. It was to accept some responsibility for their care, and it was hoped, for their cure. If the insane asylum soon became a snake pit in which severe psychotics were put out of sight and mind where they did not disturb the equanimity of their saner fellows on the outside, that was, of course, not the express intent. The widely proclaimed slogan that "mental illness is an illness like any other" was at once a claim for humane care, an expression of hope, and a denial of the special stigma that still clung to the seriously disturbed. It was an important message adopted by the growing mental-hygiene movement for good reason. But it has remained a principal message of mental-health communication past its point of usefulness. And mental-health professionals have been so involved in purveying it to others that, in the process, they have almost convinced themselves.

The final report of the Joint Commission on Mental Illness and Health (1961, p. xviii) notes one respect in which mental illness and physical illness are unlike: "Mental illness is different from physical illness in the one fundamental aspect that it tends to disturb and repel others rather than evoke their sympathy and desire to help." But there are other more intrinsic differences, even if we limit our attention to the socially incapacitated psychotics who populated the custodial mental hospital. Though I cannot follow Szasz (1961) to all his conclusions, his critique of the concept of mental illness is hard to gainsay. With the important exceptions of brain disease and metabolic disorders, the patient with a "mental illness" is not sick in the same sense as one who suffers a physical complaint. The usage is metaphorical, not literal. Disordered and ineffective he is, but the disorder lies in his conduct of living; in his ways of symbolizing, thinking, and feeling; and in his relationships with self and others. Commonly what we call mental illness has an ingredient of deep moral failure, and that is what makes it so humanly poignant. It is no help to clear thinking to group these disabling human troubles with the physical illnesses. They are notably and perplexingly different.

The discovery and consequent rational treatment of a few clearcut disease entities that occurred in the mental-hospital population—general paresis is the most spectacular and, therefore, frequently cited case—tends to throw us off the track. The following quotation from Zubin's (1968, p. 71) contribution to the same symposium in which this chapter originally appeared is apropos: "Disease is usually defined in terms of etiology, structure, and symptomatology. In most mental disorders etiology is unknown, the structure of the organs of the patient as far as we know is unaffected, and symptomatology is the only available basis for the definition. Mental diseases whose etiology and structural defects become known are usually lost to psychopathology. Thus, disorders like general paresis, pellegra with psychosis, epilepsy, even PKU are now largely in the hands of other disciplines. Only the diseases of unknown origin remain in the field of psychopathology. Furthermore, there is also the question of whether mental disorders are in fact diseases or merely reaction patterns."

For his own purposes, Zubin elected to "bypass these philosophical dilemmas" with a working definition that, stripped down, equates mental disease with any progressive condition that leads to extreme reduction of efficiency and happiness. This is indeed to bypass the "philosophical" question of adequate definition: Zubin granted in effect that run-of-the-mill mental disorders have only the ingredients of misery and ineffectiveness in common with other illnesses that meet conventional medical criteria. This is essentially what Szasz had maintained. The label of mental illness adds nothing.

The social context of the mental hospital has further implications for our thinking about mental disorders. Since the inmates under medical care are by definition "sick," the ascription of sickness to them may "take": As sociologists are particularly fond of pointing out, the application of social definitions to people can be self-confirming. Ironically, a patient in remission may have to agree to his state of sickness before he can secure release.

Since mental patients are defined as sick with what for the most part are unknown illnesses, the biometric strategies favored by Zubin and others seek to create and process data in order to discover what these hidden disease entities may be. Against the unsatisfactory state of traditional psychiatric diagnosis, Zubin's tactics are sophisticated. If disease entities are there to be smoked out, as they still may be in the case of the schizophrenias, such an approach is likely to find them and to shed light on them. If, however, the theory of the existence of hidden diseases is wrong, or to the extent that it is wrong, these tactics may be relatively unproductive.

Of course common diagnostic practice has been far less satisfactory than Zubin's work. The real and imagined needs of medical administration over patient populations defined as sick have created a nomenclature of essentially administrative illnesses that have little apparent relationship to etiology, prognosis, or therapy. It may be the beginning of wisdom to regard many of the problems of diagnosis, the state of which few are content with, as artifacts of the historical social policy that has called these people sick, and, therefore, has had to find illnesses for them.

A final point needs to be made about the social context of institutional psychiatry as an influence on thinking about human effectiveness and ineffectiveness. So long as one stays within this context, the difficult problems of values that I mentioned earlier are unlikely to arise. This is because people who are disturbed or confused enough to be sent to the mental hospital are there because most other people are in agreement about their negatively valued condition. Values are involved, but we do not notice them because consensus is tacit and immediate. Hence, it is readily understandable that, as a hospital director, the psychiatrist Walter Barton (in Jahoda, 1958, pp. 111–119) had little sympathy with Jahoda's exploration of conceptions of positive mental health. Apart from custody, the task that he faced, quite simply and realistically, was to get as many of his patients as possible out of the mental hospital as soon as possible, for as long as possible. They were there because they were "sick." If they became capable of staying out, they were "well" in the sense that was relevant to his task. More searching criteria of effective functioning, criteria of the sort Jahoda reviewed, become relevant in other social contexts, but they have little to offer in the hospital setting.

Private Psychotherapeutic Practice. If the mental hospital launched psychiatry and bequeathed core notions of "mental illness," other social contexts have since taken the lead in the development of thought and practice in regard to mental disorders. The requirements of these social contexts have enriched and extended the meaning of mental health and illness, but by the same token, usage of these terms has strayed farther from the biological, adaptational base that still gives them some appropriateness in the hospital setting. The major setting to be considered is that of the private practitioner's consulting room, the home territory of psychoanalysis and the psychotherapies derived from it.

The contrasts with the hospital setting are, of course, immense. As we know, an entirely different clientele is served. Unlike the mental-hospital patients who are disproportionately poor and ill educated, those who seek psychotherapy tend to come from the middle classes, to have considerable verbal-symbolic skills, and to define their problems in psychological terms. (See Hollingshead and Redlich, 1958; Gurin and others, 1960.) They come with the milder sorts of problems, ones that are conventionally classified as neuroses, character disorders, and borderline conditions. And they come of their own choice, with their own notions of therapeutic objectives, rather than being sent because society cannot tolerate them. All these differences have a bearing on how the professionals concerned have tended to formulate what is wrong with their patients and how they have phrased the therapeutic goals of health that are to be achieved.

Under the influence of hospital psychiatry, the older text-books featured long catalogs of neurotic disease conditions: thus the lists of phobias compounded of Greco-Latin roots that still clutter the pages of psychiatric and psychological dictionaries. But the psychodynamic tradition that emerged in the consulting room for the most part swept these lists away. The problem of diagnosis was redefined as characterizing the balance of forces underlying the patient's life pattern rather than as a matter of fitting the patient into a disease pigeonhole. In this new framework, the symptoms and signs so dear to hospital psychiatry lost interest and status; they tended to be viewed as epiphenomena.

Although practitioners in this setting continued to think in the medical language of health and disease, there are many indications that these categories were incongruous to the tasks at hand. Were the patients in psychotherapy "sick"? Perhaps yes, in some obscure minimal sense of seeking help because they felt their happiness or effectiveness to be impaired. But those who did not seek help might have been even "sicker." If a person acknowledged his difficulties and sought therapy, this was regarded as a constructive sign. Here there could be no equivalent to the hospital wall as a de facto boundary between illness and health. As Bower (1963, p. 835) has put it, "Where living is equated with and therefore measured by degrees of illness rather than health, one can easily perceive the world as a giant hospital peopled by patients whose only health lies in discovering how sick they are."

Given a prosperous clientele that could afford prolonged self-exploration, decisions about the continuance or termination of therapy lost connection with conventional medical notions of health and illness. Anyone could benefit from a psychoanalysis. Was everyone, therefore, "sick"? The goals of therapy held by the therapist, which in successful relationships would be communicated to the patient, came to be phrased not as symptom relief or even as improved adaptation per se but in abstract terms of realignment or reconstruction of personality. The economics and social psychology of private practice led to the continuance of therapeutic relationships that patient and therapist rightly or collusively regarded as mutually beneficial, when illness in any medically definable sense was clearly out of the question.

Yet because of the medical auspices under which psychotherapeutic pioneering had been conducted, the language of health and illness continued to be used in presenting the problems of patients and the goals of therapists. Of course the very terminology of patient and treatment is cast in the same analogically medical framework. If the problems of living that bring people to seek professional help are illnesses, albeit mild ones not so severe as the psychoses, the notion of a continuum of mental illness and health emerges. The various abstract therapeutic goals that reflective therapists came to formulate for themselves were thus phrased as characterizations of psychological health. It is this reflective literature stemming from dynamic psychotherapy that Jahoda (1958) sorts out in her exposition.

The widespread, benign influence of the dynamic point of view has carried this expanded notion of mental health beyond the confines of the therapeutic relationship, for example, in child-rearing and in education. There may not be a consensus about the particular evaluative criteria suggested, but at one time there was consensus that whatever the criteria, they were criteria of mental health. Unlike the mental-hospital psychiatrist, but like the reflective parent and educator, the private psychotherapist could hardly do without such positively phrased goals. He could, however, readily spare the tenuous health analogy.

Changes in the problems that lead people to seek psychotherapy make the analogy even more tenuous. As Wheelis (1958) and others have pointed out, the presenting problems brought to therapy by middle-class patients tend increasingly to be those of the "sick soul," for example, malaise, meaninglessness, or a vague sense of missing out on the satisfactions of life rather than symptoms that mimic those of physical illness, as in the hysterias that provided the starting point for psychoanalysis. The trend in many quarters toward an existential rather than a biological-medical phrasing of the therapeutic task would seem to be a natural consequence.

Yet the private practice of psychotherapy is a luxury of the upper strata in an affluent society. The rather confused problems and goals that private practice has elicited appear rather precious when we consider the broader social problems of human ineffectiveness. The ferment during the Johnson administration of social concern and action to deal with the persisting hard-core human problems, which stand out embarassingly against the general affluence, provides a radically different context in which new formulations of effectiveness-ineffectiveness are called for and are indeed emerging.

Comprehensive Community "Mental Health." Free enterprise guarantees the continuance of one-to-one private psychotherapy. However, the public interest calls for the deliberate focusing of resources where the major pockets of human ineffectiveness lie. The methods used should reach the people who most need help if they are to become effective and should be compatible with the finite supply of professional manpower. The comprehensive community-mental-health approach, launched under the auspices of President Kennedy, and the War on Poverty proclaimed by President Johnson were intended to converge in a rational attack on these hard-core problems. The new context produced major changes in thinking about mental health—changes as great as those entailed by the shift of attention from the custodial mental hospital to the consulting room. (For analyses convergent with the views presented here, see Rae-Grant and others [1966] and Smith and Hobbs [1966].)

The hard-core problems that are the prime targets of these new programs are disproportionately those of poor people who have been excluded from or unresponsive to the cycle of expanding opportunity since the trough of the Depression. Prototypically, they are end products of vicious circles of social causation in which powerlessness, scant opportunity, and inadequate skill have led to low self-esteem, hopelessness and fatalism, life in a constricted present, and trained incapacity to take advantage of opportunities that become available. People caught in such a vicious circle readily fall into resentful passivity and dependence. For good reason they are unlikely to recognize or accept responsibility for their problems or to define their problems in psychological terms. Genuine problems of physical health abound, and psychological problems are likely to be translated into physical terms. Epidemiological studies have shown that such people contribute disproportionately to the mental-hospital load; yet these are also the people whom the traditional verbal psychotherapies are least likely to reach or help.

Such an analysis sees recalcitrant ineffectiveness embedded in the social or ecological systems in which people participate. The systems approach seems unavoidable here because manpower, relevant skills, and channels of access are largely unavailable to deal with this massive ineffectiveness on the model of individual health. Moreover, even if therapeutic efforts are momentarily successful in the individual case, the thwarting, self-defeating features in the social systems that prevail, if left untouched, are likely to undo the gains.

But the new emphasis on the systems context of human effectiveness and ineffectiveness has of course much wider applicability. Institutional psychiatry perceived its clientele as sick patients, who should be immured in hospitals where they could be cared for or treated. Psychoanalytic psychotherapy was also preoccupied with the internal system of personality and sought to treat personality in relative isolation through the minature social system of the transference relationship. The community approach sees psychological malfunction as arising in the context of the person's sphere of ordinary social participation and as best dealt with via the social systems in which the individual participates—that is, family, school, friendship, job, church and so forth. Whatever the contribution of genetic or other organic factors to the onset of a person's difficulty, the degree of his disturbance and the prospects for his recovery depend to a considerable extent on the nature of his participation, that is, on whether he finds in it sources of challenge and support or whether he is continually undermined, deflated, or provoked. Mental disorder is as much a failure within a person's system of social relations as it is an inner-personal difficulty. Though sophisticated students of physical health and disease are aware of the contribution of ecological factors to manifest pathology, the language of mental health, with its freight of meanings that inevitably focuses attention upon features of the encapsulated individual personality, seems ill suited to this emerging framework of discourse and social practice.

The perspective arising out of urgent public interests has

implications for characterizing the personal qualities that tend to lead a person into vicious or benign cycles of social participation. If the view of circular causation sketched above is approximately correct, symptoms, especially psychosomatic ones that abound among the poor, may occur as part of a loose package that reflects social defeat and in turn leads to further defeat—that is, a combination of low skill and knowledge, passivity, low self-respect, hopelessness, and the rest. On the other side of the coin, the person endowed with the complementary virtues—such as initiative, hope, and self-esteem—is set to participate in or to create social systems around himself that bring him further support and rewards. He can probably take some symptoms in his stride. At issue here are the personal essentials of productive social interaction, in the lack of which a person is likely to be mired in ineffectiveness. It seems fitting to use the language of Foote and Cottrell (1955), R. W. White (1959, 1963), and Rae-Grant, Gladwin, and Bower (1966) in discussing personal and social competence and its lack.

Social competence in a broad sense is multidimensional, like the more attractive versions of positive mental health, but it is not just another synonym for mental health or another label for virtue. The qualities that I have provisionally listed are singled out because they appear to involve the person in an active, productive orientation to his environment; in their lack he is likely to be at its mercy. If a person who is low in competence is in a supporting environment that makes few or benign demands on him, he may experience little distress or difficulty. High competence, on the other hand, appears compatible with some anxiety and with the symptoms it may cost a person to contain it.

Competence and "Mental Health" in the Peace Corps

I introduced the concept of competence by reference to the vicious circles that make it difficult to help the poor and socially ineffective. At the other end of the continuum of effectiveness[1] the concept appears equally relevant. That such is the case is suggested

---

[1] Effectiveness is a continuum by definition, whereas the debate about whether or not mental health–mental illness is a continuum cannot be resolved in the absence of a clear and defensible meaning for either term.

by data from my study of Peace Corps teachers (Smith, 1966a), with whom a colleague and I did very detailed tape-recorded interviews near the end of their first and second years of service in Ghana. From close study of selected interview transcripts in the light of our own field experience, we developed a set of descriptive items to characterize the personalities of the volunteers as they appeared through the job-focused interviews. These items were then used by judges other than ourselves in a Q-sort procedure to characterize each volunteer. Judges sorted the items from most to least characteristic of each volunteer. My colleague and I intercorrelated the resulting personal profiles of item ratings and factored the matrix of correlations to obtain patterns of personality as displayed overseas.

As might have been expected, the first principal component was a highly evaluative factor. Table 1 lists the items that were especially characteristic of volunteers who received high loadings. The items that defined what is uncharacteristic of these volunteers are given in Table 2. Inspection of the tables shows a pattern of self-confidence, high self-esteem, energy, responsibility, autonomy,

Table 1.

ITEMS WITH HIGH FACTOR SCORES ON SELF-CONFIDENT MATURITY

Item	Factor score
Generally self-confident	73
A genuinely dependable and responsible person	69
The values and principles which he holds directly affect what he does	65
Feels his own life is important, that it matters what he does with his life	65
Open to experience, ready to learn	62
Tolerant and understanding	61
Characteristically maintains a highly articulate intellectual formulation of his situation and problems	60

Table 2.

ITEMS WITH LOW FACTOR SCORES ON
SELF-CONFIDENT MATURITY

Item	Factor score
Feels a lack of worth; has low self-esteem	24
Basically a dependent person; characteristically leans upon others for support	33
Has had a characteristically high level of anxiety during the time in Ghana	33
Tends to expect little of life, pessimistic	33
Seems generally to lack energy, to operate at a markedly low key	35
Tends to be suspicious of others	35
Tends to give up easily when faced with setbacks	36
Would be unable to accept help from others when in need	37
When things go badly, would tend to let them drift	37
Tends to be preoccupied with matters of physical health	38
Irritable and overresponsive to petty annoyances	38
Engaged in "posturing" to self and others; concerned with maintaining "face"	39
Tends unrealistically to minimize or deny the difficulties that he faces	40

trust in others, persistence with flexibility, and hopeful realism that led us to name the factor "self-confident maturity." On another set of items relating to the Peace Corps role, volunteers who approximated this pattern were also described as highly committed to their jobs and competent in them and as constructively involved with their African experience. Their performance also tended to be rated highly by their Peace Corps supervisor. If we suppress some warranted skepticism that the coherence of the pattern may have partly resulted from a halo effect—that is, the raters attributing miscellaneous virtues to volunteers that they happened to get a good initial impression of—this factor seems to be a good first approximation to our concept of general competence.

We correlated several measures taken while the volunteers were still in training with our interview factor indices and with supervisors' ratings. Results for two of these indices are suggestive in the present connection.

One index was a rating of "predicted psychological effectiveness," pooled from the judgments of two psychiatrists who had rated each volunteer after a fifty-minute appraisal interview. Seven psychiatrists participated in the interviewing and rating. We had independent evidence that the psychiatrists based their predictions on estimates of the volunteers' mental health or absence of pathology. This was only natural in the absence of any real knowledge of the criterion situation, given the psychiatrists' main job of weeding out the seriously disturbed. For the volunteers who were sent overseas— a few did not go—these mental-health ratings correlated essentially zero with our criterion measures of competent performance.

In interesting contrast was the other index, our one modest predictive success. My colleague Raphael Ezekiel (1968) had devised a procedure in which the volunteers-in-training wrote three mock autobiographical essays: one on their immediate alternative plans if they should not be accepted by the Peace Corps, one covering the three years after their return from Peace Corps service, and a third covering their fortieth year. The essays were rated for *differentiation,* the extent to which the essays showed complex and detailed mapping of the future; *agency,* the extent to which the essays showed the self as the prime agent in determining the course of the person's future life; and *demand,* the extent to which the essays described a life viewed by the respondent as demanding long-term, continuing effort. The sum of these ratings correlated moderately (.41) with the overall administrative evaluation as of the second year.

Table 3 shows the Q-sort items, based on the overseas interviews, that were characteristic of the high-scoring volunteers. Apart from items that primarily show personal consistency from the time of essay writing until that of the interviews one and two years later

Table 3.

ITEMS THAT ARE CHARACTERISTIC OF VOLUNTEERS WITH HIGH SUM SCORES ON MOCK AUTOBIOGRAPHIES

Item	p[a]
Personality Q-Sort	
Envisions a challenging and demanding personal future	.05
Characteristically maintains a highly articulate intellectual formulation of his situation and problems	.05
Shows inventiveness, ingenuity	.05
Has developed a well-balanced, varied, and stable program for self of work, relaxation, relief or escape	.05
Devotes much of his energy to a deliberate program of self-improvement (creative activity, study, etc.)	.10
High in initiative; active rather than reactive	.10
Performance Q-Sort	
Elaborates his performance of teaching duties in nonroutine imaginative ways, invests self creatively in teaching job in and out of class	.01
Values his Peace Corps assignment as relevant to his career plans	.05
Actively employs self in useful, school-related activities outside of class	.10
Concerned with using his Peace Corps experience to test himself	.10

[a] By t-test comparing extreme thirds of the distribution.

(the first two in the personality sort and the career item in the performance sort), the picture of inventiveness, initiative, job-elaboration and self-testing or responsiveness to challenge indicates that the procedure indeed tapped qualities that contribute to a more than routine performance. Ezekiel's interpretation of his measures is highly relevant to the conception of competence with which we are concerned. The volunteer's readiness to commit himself to demanding tasks and to take the initiative in bringing about well-cognized futures that he desires, as crudely indexed by the essays, provides a motivational basis for his response to the Peace Corps assignment with commitment, initiative, and effort.

Personal Agenda: Reprise

I now return to the personal agenda that I presented at the start of this chapter and assess what progress I have made. I started the enterprise skeptical of mental health except as a general rubric under which a variety of evaluative appraisals of personality might be made. I lacked rational grounds for selecting one basis of appraisal over another. Exploration of the social semantics of mental-health terminology, which has occupied much of this chapter, has made my dissatisfaction with the health-and-illness framework more explicit. As the focal or salient context has shifted from the custodial mental hospital to clinical psychotherapy, and incipiently to community-centered programs, the metaphor of health and illness has made progressively less sense as a framework for formulating the problems with which so-called mental-health professionals must deal.

Attention to the social contexts in which problems of human effectiveness and ineffectiveness have been encountered has not only served a critical function but has also served a constructive one. The social context that is currently exigent provides the basis that I previously lacked for selecting alternative conceptualizations. That the public interest is prominent in our present focal concerns, as it was not when private practice psychotherapy represented the forefront of progress, makes me more comfortable about the basis of choice.

We have seen that the community-centered approach to human effectiveness, whether under auspices of mental health or of poverty, requires emphasis on two relatively novel concepts. One is that human ineffectiveness or fulfillment cannot be usefully conceived or dealt with as a property of the isolated individual. It is, rather, a characteristic of behavior that a person shows as a participant in the small interpersonal systems that frame his daily life. Where there is ineffectiveness, look for vicious circles in his personal involvements; where there is fulfillment, look for benign ones. The second concept, that of social competence, summarizes a person's own contribution to whether these circles are vicious or benign. (See Smith, 1968c, for a more detailed discussion.) His competence, in turn, must be regarded as in good part a resultant of his previous participation. The problem of how man can become more fully master of his fate, once a topic of ethical philosophy, has acquired new social urgency.

My digression concerning competence in the Peace Corps has two implications. One, the concept appears as relevant at the high end of the continuum of effectiveness as it is at the low. Second, the evaluation by criteria of social competence may sometimes be unrelated to evaluation by prevalent psychiatric and clinical psychological standards of mental health, which focus on the load of "symptoms" that a person carries. Initiative and commitment, symptoms and anxiety are terms which appear to come from different realms. Personal assets and liabilities on the two sides may not add or subtract in any simple way. There are implications here for public-health surveys in the appraisal of human assets and liabilities for the guidance of social programs.

Early in this chapter I mentioned my indebtedness to Robert White, as one of the sources of my personal agenda. His primary contribution in this connection, of course, has been to legitimize the concept of competence in dynamically oriented personality theory as well as in experimental and developmental psychology. Readers of his influential monograph (R. W. White, 1963) will recognize that he has also wrought manfully to bend psychoanalytic theory from the solipsistic concerns to which its consulting-room history predisposed it so that it could deal more adequately with man's transactions with reality. While my approach in this chapter has thrown competence into contrast with symptoms and with psychodynamics, place must be found for all three in a comprehensive account of human effectiveness. Surveys should attempt to develop indices in a framework of equal catholicity.

In such a broader framework, a person's strictly medical problems of bodily functioning have an obvious place, whether or not his psychological difficulties contribute to them. His anxiety, guilt, or unhappiness, and the behavioral quirks he develops in living with these unwelcome affects, also require attention but, from the point of view of the public interest, rather less attention than might be given them in private psychotherapy. The view I advocate would add to this mental-health mix, attention to a person's assets and deficits for constructive social participation. Broadening our attention to include competence and its lack should provide relevant information for guiding public efforts to deal with the actual social problems of human ineffectiveness. That the boundaries of the mental-health concept are stretched past breaking is of no consequence, since these boundaries have been imaginary all along.

Chapter Eight

•••••••••••••••••••••
•••••••••••••••••••••••
•••••••••••••••••••••••••

NORMALITY FOR AN ABNORMAL AGE

•••••••••••••••••••••••
•••••••••••••••••••••••
••••••••••••••••••••••

*P*sychiatry and clinical psychology need a theoretical and empirical grasp on normality for several reasons. For these clinical disciplines, the abnormal, the personally and socially deviant and problematic, is home base. Yet any conception of the abnormal requires, at least implicitly, a view of what is normal. If the view remains implicit, it may be based on assumptions that embody factual error and covert values; far better that the standard of comparison by which abnormality is identified be explicit and subject to empirical correction.

If the clinician needs a conception of normality as counterpoise to his preoccupation with the abnormal, as a comparative basis for establishing the meaning of abnormality, he has a distinguishable though related reason for concern with normality in his need to clarify his therapeutic goals. These goals will depend on many considerations: on his theories about psychological functioning, on the social context of his practice (for example, mental hospital versus consulting room versus community—see Chapter Seven), on his own values and ideals, and on pragmatic judgments about the kinds and degree of psychological change that can be achieved and

144

sustained. What he thinks and knows about normality will surely affect how his therapeutic goals are formulated.

Still a third reason for concern with normality is theoretical. The broad impact of psychoanalysis on psychology and other sciences of human behavior highlights a methodological assumption that has gained wide acceptance—that our understanding of the normal can be greatly advanced by a close look at the deviant, in whom processes that are hidden from observation in the normal person are prominently displayed for analytic dissection. Productive as this strategy undoubtedly has been, it has not been immune to challenge on principled grounds as potentially misleading (for example, Asch, 1952; Allport, 1961). Certainly, normal functioning deserves scrutiny in its own right, and, on the face of it, it is likely that the complementary methodological principle is equally justified: Good understanding of normal functioning should usefully modify our thinking about the abnormal. Such a principle, indeed, follows from the general systems approach that Grinker (1967a) espouses. Traffic in this methodological direction has dealt primarily in the currency of general and developmental psychology and of single-variable research; the potential contribution of holistic personality studies (paralleling the attention clinical research gives to abnormal "cases") and of multivariate research has been exemplified (for example, R. W. White, 1952; Heath, 1965) but far from realized.

But the meanings of normality are elusive. A useful catalog of current usage has recently been provided by Offer and Sabshin under Grinker's sponsorship (Offer and Sabshin, 1966; Sabshin, 1967). The authors distinguish four functional perspectives on normality: normality as health, normality as Utopia, normality as average, and normality as process.

Normality as health in effect is a residual category left over after identified cases of illness or malfunction are excluded: people who are not sick, and that is most of us, are normal. This, as Sabshin (1967) observes, is the traditional medical-psychiatric approach. It fits our accustomed patterns of thought and practice and research and so remains widely prevalent in spite of telling objections that have been raised by many recent critics. Thus, Szasz (1961) and other more temperate critics among whom I count myself (Chapter Seven) object to the medical characterization of much psychological malfunctioning, rejecting the term *illness* as metaphoric and unwarranted in this application. Other critics, notably Clausen (1968), point to the slippery criteria by which the psychiatric case is identified in practice and in epidemiological research. The seeming solidity of the cases to which normality is residual in this approach dissolves on close inspection. Jahoda (1958), in her classic review of concepts of positive mental health, rejects "absence of mental disease" as a criterion of mental health (read "normality" in the present context) on the grounds that what is regarded as mental disease is subject to wide cultural variation and that our conceptual framework should be kept open to the possibility that man's resources of strength and areas of vulnerability and malfunction may vary in some independence of one another. That is, we should not decide arbitrarily that health and illness can usefully be represented as opposite ends of a single dimension. For all these reasons I will henceforth ignore this first perspective on normality as an obstacle to clear thinking. What is pragmatically useful in the approach can be reformulated in one or another of the three remaining ones.

By *normality as Utopia* Offer and Sabshin designate the approaches that treat normality as an ideal, or set of ideals, of optimal functioning. In this usage, nobody is completely normal. The facets of ideal normality that have been proposed in thoughtful discussions of psychotherapeutic goals by psychoanalysts of various persuasions, by humanistic-existential therapists, and by others have been well cataloged by Jahoda (1958), whose book is firmly planted in this perspective and which demonstrates that to be Utopian in the sense of positing idealized evaluative criteria is fully compatible with an empirical orientation. Elsewhere (Smith, 1961), I have argued that clarity about the evaluative nature of such Utopian criteria has the merit of avoiding the surreptitious advocacy of values in scientific-professional disguise. The conditions and consequences of placement on any particular evaluative dimension, however, are entirely an empirical matter, knowledge about which may affect the choices we make as we assign relative priority to competing values.

Normality as average is the straightforward statistical notion, useful, indeed unavoidable, for descriptive purposes. When, as in the case of psychiatric research, the tedious work of conducting normative studies to define the normal in this sense has largely been skimped, pioneer efforts such as Grinker's (1963) description of the "homoclites" and Offer's of suburban adolescent boys (Offer, 1969) can provide a useful corrective to untested assumptions about what is in fact prevalent in human dispositions and behavior. More systematic studies in this vein are being undertaken by the National Health Survey of the National Center for Health Statistics. (See Sells, 1968.)

The trouble with this approach to normality lies not in its proper descriptive use but in its ready misuse, its confusion with the other meanings of normality. What is prevalent need not be biologically healthy or desirable in terms of other evaluative criteria. All too often it is not. And depending on the intrinsic nature of the dimensions or variables on which one is averaging, the ideal, Utopian norm may lie near the midpoint of the scale (for example, flexibility as intermediate between rigid overcontrol and impulsive undercontrol) or it may just as well be located near one end or the other (for example, intelligence, capacity for intimacy, mendacity). The judgment of what is healthy or desirable—or important—does not follow from the descriptive statistics.

Normality as process is the most elusive category because it hinges on the development of scientific theories, which are still primitive. Offer and Sabshin classify conceptions of normality as processes tending toward adaptation, whether in the perspective of individual development or of evolutionary or sociocultural processes. As Grinker has long argued (Grinker, 1967a, 1967b), general systems theory provides a widely applicable abstract framework within which, in principle, it is possible to identify processes that promote the maintenance and growth of the system (organism, personality—or society; the framework is very abstract) and processes that comprise decompensation and regression. To the extent that our empirically based theory can be carried forward to fill in this abstract paradigm, we will have attained evaluative criteria of normality that rest on a solid empirical footing. They will still be evaluative, and the value choice involved will still remain optional, like all value choices (the saint or martyr or rebel may set other values higher than those of system growth and maintenance). But evaluative criteria rooted in a well-matured systems theory should have an intrinsic connection with empirical fact that our present criteria largely lack. (See Smith, 1959.)

For the present, the process approach to normality is best represented by various attempts to conceptualize and study effective coping behavior (for example, Murphy, 1962; Haan, 1963; Hamburg and Adams, 1967). Short of the full development of a systems theory of personality, there will be wide agreement that active coping processes will in one way or another be part of an adequate formulation. The more we understand about them the better.

In his collaborative study of mentally healthy young males, Grinker half facetiously, half seriously, gave them the neologistic diagnostic label *homoclites* to legitimize them for psychiatric inquiry and put aside, for the nonce, intrusive problems of values (Grinker, Grinker, and Timberlake, 1962). This descriptive account of very ordinary young men is as a benchmark for comparison, not only with the abnormal as seen in clinical practice but also with the idealizations of normality held by highly educated and culturally sophisticated mental-health professionals. That Grinker's homoclites, undergraduates at the YMCA-related George Williams College with its tradition of muscular Christianity, were not statistically representative of the general population of young American men but were rather a fairly homogeneous group suitable for composite description adds to their stimulus value in provoking us to rethink our conceptions of normality.

Though the design of his study is rather primitive, Grinker's commentary on his findings is thoroughly sophisticated. In offering the homoclites as a version of average normality, he wastes little time in wonder at the contrasts they provide with the experience of psychiatry and psychoanalysis, though he vividly conveys the sense that acquaintance with them was eye-opening. From a critical standpoint, Grinker employs his homoclites to question the relevance of current Utopian views of normality, which may have arisen from a narrow cultural and experimental basis. He states (Grinker, 1963, pp. 128–129):

> The psychiatrist is educated, trained, and experienced in
> psychopathology and the treatment thereof. . . . In addition to
> knowing only patients, by virtue of his geographical location he

also sees mostly those engaged in the rat-race of city life. Finally, he is caught in his own middle-class perspective.

The ordinary person has simple and reasonable values. He wants to feel good, work well, love and be loved, play and enjoy life occasionally and have hope for the future. There are wide ranges and many permutations of these values. He settles for less than he originally hoped for, holding to Freud's adage that life is difficult but it is all we have.

What we as psychiatrists see to be the goal of American families includes: upward mobility regardless of intellectual, aptitudinal or social fit; doing and becoming which is operationally goal-changing rather than goal-seeking; permissiveness rather than boundary fixing of behavior, work, strict religious belief, and discipline; and child-rearing according to the latest fad based on current theory.

The difficulty is that these cultural values which Spiegel showed not to be entirely held by Irish-Americans or Italian-Americans are also not cherished by upper-lower or lower-middle class and later Protestant-American main-streeters in Kansas, Minnesota, or Illinois or in America as a whole.

Thus what is normality and what is mental illness is confused because of the value discrepancies among psychiatrists, people, and cultures.

Briefly stated, psychiatrists and other mental-health professionals may have applied out of their appropriate context Utopian versions of normality that are specific to particular subcultures, with resulting confusion.

In broadening the sociocultural base in which behavior is evaluated, Grinker's study contributes to a more adequate conception of "normality as average." But Grinker is admirably clear that homoclites, widely distributed throughout America as they undoubtedly are, represent only one kind of average normality—a relatively complacent type with limited ambitions better suited to maintaining a stable society behind the leaders, whomever they may be, than to giving leadership or to adapting in rapidly changing times. Within a broader adaptational frame of reference—normality as process—Grinker (1963, p. 131) speculates that the homoclites may have achieved their version of normality at the cost of "the limitation of patterned behavior suitable for a few roles and a restricted range of environments. . . . What prepares the developing boy for multiple roles and a wide range of environments *and* the behavioral and psychodynamic criteria of health, this study cannot answer."

Grinker's homoclites—and their conceptual descendents, Offer's modal adolescent boys in the suburbs (Offer, 1969)—are, one suspects, the psychiatric equivalent of President Nixon's "silent majority." I would not want to align myself with those observers who, in Grinker's words, "have developed a kind of moral judgment signifying intense anxiety when they imply the question, 'Should the homoclite exist at all?' " (Grinker, 1963, p. 129). Clearly homoclites do exist, and their version of the human condition also deserves respect, but just as I question the long-run viability of the prejudices and narrow goals that President Nixon finds and cultivates in his silent constituency, I underline Grinker's doubts about the adaptive limitations of his homoclites. They will no doubt always be with us, and they contribute stability and their own version of sanity to the social mix, but they are likely to find the modern flux increasingly baffling. They will make little contribution to solving our urgent social problems, which their reactions to bafflement are already complicating. We badly need to rear citizens to other, more flexible and autonomous forms of normality. I am calling for a particular Utopian version of normality as especially relevant to our present predicament. In the remainder of the chapter, I try to explicate these Utopian criteria and sketch some of the present basis for thinking that they can be grounded empirically—in my judgment, a major task of the coming years for research on psychological development and functioning in social contexts.

Grinker provides me with an advantageous point of departure in his psychiatric presidential address, from which I have been quoting, and lays the basis for confronting his homoclites from the adaptational perspective. Grinker (1963, pp. 130–131) writes: "The success of prediction regarding health depends on the possible relationship between person and environment. *The important question in the current fast-moving and changing social and cultural world is what stresses are, or will be, impinging on the individual* [italics mine]. With environments no longer stable even in the previously primitive cultures, the individual is required to make extremely rapid changes. Mental health thus depends less on stability but more on the flexibility of the individual."

The flexibility of the individual is indeed important and, as we have seen, raises serious questions about the viability of the homoclitic adaptation. Heinz Hartmann's "average expectable environment" (Hartmann, 1958) is becoming a will-o'-the-wisp—or a nightmare. But in the present, salient perspective of warranted concern over sheer human survival—surely the ultimate adaptational context—we are now compelled to frame an even more important set of questions: In the current fast-moving and changing social and cultural world, which in so many respects is becoming manifestly stressful, less livable, and may be speeding toward irretrievable disaster, how can individuals organized in society gain control over these stresses? How can people divert the ominous trends of population, pollution, escalating armament, and dehumanization of technology run rampant? How can they avert the disaster that looms so threateningly? And how—here the special competences of psychology and psychiatry become involved—can we rear and educate people who are capable of reconstructing their human situation rather than flexibly accommodating to the inevitable? How can we foster autonomy and realistic self-direction and political efficacy among people who have been reared to adjust—the socially oppressed and excluded, even the homoclites?

Earlier I argued that mental health is not a theoretical concept but merely a chapter heading for evaluations of human personality and that lists of mental-health criteria are inherently arbitrary, reflecting standards of evaluation that we embrace on essentially nonscientific grounds, though we may revise our standards in the light of empirical relationships. Subsequent consideration of the intrinsic requirements of different major contexts of mental-health practice—institutional psychiatry, the psychoanalytic consulting room, and the community as seen in the now-aborted War on Poverty—led me to back away from this rather unsatisfying relativism. (See Chapter Seven.) From the point of the public interest inherent in community psychology, the appropriate criterion seemed to be human effectiveness versus ineffectiveness. This was at least a relativism in a broader societal framework. I now proceed a step further. Just as the emerging sense of urgent human priorities is giving rise to an insistent demand for a rescaling of national priorities, so it seems to me to cut through academic relativism and point unequivocally to new priorities among Utopian criteria of normality, priorities that are called for by the hard adaptational facts. Whether it makes sense for psychologists and psychiatrists to respond to these urgencies depends, of course, on whether our conceptual equipment, our research and technical knowledge, can in fact be brought cogently to bear. My intent in what follows is to pursue related themes in research and theorizing far enough to suggest that such is indeed the case.

I draw the text for my Utopian message from Jacqueline Grennan Wexler—formerly Sister Jacqueline—who recently wrote (1969): "The question haunting society is whether or not the individual at all controls his own destiny." This is the question that underlies the adaptational issues I have just raised: Can man gain control over the societal processes that threaten to overwhelm him? The question is likely to evoke ambivalent feelings of hope and despair. In the light of our vastly increased knowledge and technological competence, what were once accepted as acts of God—fated natural calamities beyond the reach of human choice or control— are now displayed as failures of man, susceptible in principle to rational, planful attack. Yet the complexity of the problems that beset us and of the crowded urban society in which we live tends to leave us feeling more powerless than ever. The new potentialities for choice, for control over our destiny, do not produce the actuality.

It is also the question on which a remarkable diversity of contemporary reform movements converge. Whether the context be the new nationalism of the former colonial world, the strident claims for self-determination symbolized by Black Power and Student Power, or the efforts to break through the custodial tradition in prisons and mental hospitals, the focus now is on augmenting people's capacities to take charge of their own lives. Authoritarianism is in ill repute, and paternalism no longer seems a benign and acceptable policy.

Whether the individual can control his own destiny may indeed be the haunting question of our times, but is it one to which psychological science can contribute? In spite of recurrent discussions of autonomy as a psychological condition or variable (see, especially, Angyal, 1941; Riesman, Denney, and Glazer, 1950), psychology has largely been tongue-tied. Our metatheories and paradigms have not equipped us to deal with the problem coherently. We spot the timeworn paradoxes of free will lurking to bemuse us, and we throw up our hands in retreat.

In launching American psychology with its greatest classic, William James (1890) faced the problem directly but left it dramatically unresolved. His psychology is at once explicitly deterministic and voluntaristic. In the spirit of science, James adopted its deterministic methodological premise—the commitment to push the search for causes to the limits. But this did not shake his belief in human freedom, and his psychology could still include the "will" as a traditional chapter, long since read out of respectable academic psychology where it is replaced by "motivation."

Modern psychologies have typically chosen one or the other horn of James's dilemma. Both for behaviorism in its various versions and for psychoanalysis, free will is an illusion. Our experience of choice as human actors is denied validity. Models of man emerge that appear to be radically incompatible with the assumptions about human nature that underlie democratic political institutions. A reductionistic, mechanistic version of determinism—a determinism that becomes a dogmatic principle rather than a methodological commitment—can undergird programs for the manipulation and control of behavior; it does not provide a language in which we can talk meaningfully about personal or political freedom, about ethical or political responsibility, about personal or democratic choice.

The existential and humanistic doctrines that Maslow (1966) called *third force psychology* react against what its proponents regard as the dehumanizing tenets of both behaviorism and psychoanalysis. These proponents pick the other horn of the dilemma and opt for human freedom as a dogmatically given absolute. But in the process, they abandon the hard-won gains of deterministic science (Smith, 1966b). Grinker (1970) characterizes "this kind of existentialism"—the concern of third force psychology with an idealized, finalistic view of human potentiality—as "our modern delusionary system devised to alleviate the pain associated with the abandonment of certainty and meaning." I would not go so far; it seems to me that Maslow, Rogers, May, and Fromm have made suggestive contributions on matters of human import that have been neglected by behavioristic psychology and by psychoanalysis. But they are too ready to give up the advantages of inquiry that is governed by the rules of the scientific game—corrigibility and cumulativeness. Their view of man as a free agent is essentially nonempirical and therefore vulnerable.

If this must indeed be our choice, between a scientific deterministic psychology that disparages man and a humanistic voluntarism that idealizes him at the cost of discarding science, it is easy to see why so many of our students are fleeing from scientific psychology. But it is a Hobson's choice and an unnecessary one.

The convergent lines of thought and investigation that I discuss lead to a view of free will not as an illusory paradox (we have to act as though we have it, but we don't) or as a metaphysical postulate but as an empirical variable. In this view some people have more free will than others. The extent to which they enjoy freedom is subject to causal analysis. It can be changed, increased or decreased. And it has important consequences as well as causal antecedents. Our orienting question, of whether the individual at all controls his destiny, becomes an empirical one, within the bounds of psychological science. We will see that there are conceptual handholds for coming to grips with the question and also relevant though imperfect measures that are beginning to generate usable data. I am not conjuring up a speculative solution to a philosophical impasse; I am attempting rather to explicate and advertise some new ways of thinking, the full import of which has not been adequately recognized.

The empirical free will that I am talking about is not a matter of arbitrary fiat or chance. It does not hinge on a layman's naïve interpretation of Heisenberg's principle of indeterminacy. The indeterminate, which certainly provides no basis for a conception of ethical responsibility, is not what people have usually meant by freedom. What we mean by freedom, rather, is personal causation or self-determination, causal processes with ascertainable antecedents in which the self figures as an agent. The antonym of freedom is not determination but constraint. Freedom is limited by causal processes that bypass the self or constrain its options of choice; it is enhanced by processes that increase one's range of choice and one's resources for attaining what one has chosen.

It is time to begin fleshing in these abstractions. The best case study I know to exhibit self-determination as an empirical variable and to suggest some of the considerations that may bear on its deliberate nurture is Claude Brown's contemporary classic *Manchild in the Promised Land* (1965). Most often read for its shocking and realistic account of ghetto life, it is also a sophisticated psychological drama, the story of Brown's dawning realization that he could be the architect of his life.

Growing up in the Harlem culture of poverty, Claude Brown as we first encounter him is caught in a vicious circle. Life is a hopeless jungle. The most one can aspire to is successful predation in the street life and an early death. The self-sustaining dynamics of the culture of poverty have been described and illustrated by Oscar Lewis (1959, 1966) and by Chilman (1966); they appear vividly in the Harlem world of the young Claude. The critical missing ingredient is hope. In a realistically hopeless situation, people dependably reinvent a defensive fatalism. To hope is to be disappointed. Fatalism is at least a tenable posture toward a life situation that would otherwise be insupportable. One lives in a narrowly restricted present, and one gets one's kicks where and when one can. But the fatalistic adjustment is not just a private invention; it is a culturally transmitted solution to life's problems, a solution that does not solve the problems but makes life endurable. Storefront religion, cynical predation, and drug-induced oblivion are part of the culture; they do not have to be reinvented.

The culture of poverty is a trap, a vicious circle, because its hopeless prophecies are self-confirming. If you do not hope, you will not try, and if you do not try, you do not acquire the skills or take advantage of the opportunities that might make hope warranted— even under these difficult conditions. People enmeshed in the culture of poverty are very low in capacity for self-determination and low in exercising effective free will.

In Claude's case, there were mitigating features from the start that laid an essential basis for his subsequent escape. For reasons that he cannot explain, Claude was no ordinary street boy; at an early age he set out to become a first-class scrapper and hustler. Constitution and early experience had clearly endowed him with an ample supply of the motivation to have effects on his environment (R. W. White (1959) analyses such motivations in his discussion of the concept of competence). Because of his underlying hopelessness, however, Claude's deviantly channeled competence motivation seems heedless and self-destructive. During his early years Claude could realistically aspire to be a big man on the street, which he indeed became. Though he knew the street life as "nasty, brutish, and short," it did not occur to Claude that he could escape to a better life. His beliefs about self and world drastically limited his actual freedom of choice, beyond the severe limitations imposed by social realities.

The drama that unfolds concerns Claude's realization, at first faltering, then progressively firmer, that escape is possible, that there were steps he could take to bring it about, and that he could commit himself to take those steps. It is a story of many backslidings and of ultimate success—of a working through in real life of changes in Claude's self-concept that leave him, at the end, able to choose his life, not merely to adjust to the miserable realities that he was initially dealt.

As a case history, *Manchild in the Promised Land* is suggestive of causal factors in the progression toward greater self-determination and freedom. Close study would identify many clues about such factors; here I only suggest a few. Preeminent is the effect on Claude's self-concept of receiving the full respect and trust of impressive adult figures whom he could idealize. Two such figures play prominent roles in his story: Ernst Papanek of the Wiltwyck School (for delinquent children), and the Rev. William James. Brown makes it explicit that his experience of their seemingly unwarranted but also toughminded acceptance of him, respect for him, and confidence in him made a crucial difference in his feelings about himself; his account also illustrates how tentative and uncertain the process of change can be. The causal mechanism here might be labeled the *Quaker principle:* Treat a person with respect to make him worthy of respect.

One can also find evidence in Claude's story for the importance of successes—"reinforcements" in the current jargon—that added to his resources for coping. Claude's widely recognized accomplishments as a hustler were surely important in sustaining him through difficult times and in making it possible for him to revise his conception of what he could do with his life. When, finally, he could reject the street as a bad life in which he had nevertheless been successful on the street's own terms, neither Claude's delinquent friends nor he himself could accuse him of copping out from weakness or failure.

Fortuitous traumatic experiences may also have played their constructive part in saving Claude from two extreme hazards of the street life that could easily have undercut all the positive influences: After a particularly nasty initial experience with heroin, Claude had no further truck with it. It was no temptation, and his revulsion against the junkies' way of life, as it engulfed his brother and his close boyhood friends, helped to propel him from the streets where its use was so common and so visibly destructive. Claude's distaste for guns may have had a similar basis in traumatic experience. We learn that the necessity to carry a gun and to be prepared to use it was a main reason for his deliberate withdrawal from the life of a big-time hustler, just as Claude was rising to a level of conspicuous success.

The positive and negative import of social support is also evident. To choose a new life meant leaving Harlem and disengaging from old friends, finding new ones. No more than anyone else was Claude independent of his social environment, either early or late in the story. His achievement—a major one—was to become capable of choosing his environment. He could not have rebuilt his life within the old environment. Autonomy is never absolute.

Finally, Claude's life story evokes a feeling for the spiral, cumulative nature of the processes of change as they involve the self. When one is locked into a vicious circle of hopelessness and failure, the first steps out are very difficult, and backsliding is certain. This is what is meant by being locked in. But successes, insecure at first, cumulate in their effects. One gains in confidence. Eventually one comes to the point where one can profit even from failures, not be bowled over by them. Near the end of Claude's story, Claude appears to be in command of his life. The vicious circle has been transformed into a benign one, in which the consequences of his newfound self-direction will predictably tend to sustain him in his revised conception of himself and of what life can be. Claude's life may still contain neurotic conflicts, and even tragedies, but it will be his.

This sketchy account of a rich personal document makes it plain how self-determination can be conceived as a complex empirical variable that falls within the causal framework of a deterministic psychology. I now refer to some convergent strands of research that suggest the fruitfulness of self-determination in more systematic inquiry. The research suggests that what a person thinks and feels about himself makes a crucial difference to his effective freedom.

Rotter (1966; see also Lefcourt, 1966) under the ponderous heading "generalized expectancies for internal versus external control of reinforcement" has contributed a simple pencil-and-paper scale that lends itself to wide and, thus far, productive use. The scale captures imperfectly the distinction among people that I have been trying to draw.

Rotter devised his measure via a circuitous route. In the framework of his social learning theory of personality, he and his students had been doing experimental studies of the different dynamics of task performance when the performing person believes that his outcomes result from his own skill and effort as compared with when he believes that they are the product of fate or chance. Reinforcement is under internal control in the former instance, under external control in the latter—in the eyes of the experimental subject. It occurred to Rotter that he could supplement his experimental manipulations of internal versus external control to gain greater predictability if he were able to take into account individual differences in his subjects' expectancies about whether, in general, their outcomes were the product of their own skill and abilities or of fate and chance. Hence the I-E scale, made up of items paired for choice in which the respondent must choose between skill and ability versus fate and chance as the source of major kinds of outcomes in his life. The scale, once launched, has had a life of its own. Standardized on Ohio State students (who are more like homoclites, I imagine, than are students at more elite campuses), the measure yielded a single general factor.

As Rotter (1966, p. 25) summarized the findings that bear on the validity of the scale and hence on its interest for us, there is "strong support for the hypotheses that the individual who has a strong belief that he can control his own destiny is likely to (a) be more alert to those aspects of the environment which provide useful information for his future behavior, (b) take steps to improve his environmental position, (c) place greater value on skill or achievement reinforcements and be generally more concerned with his ability, particularly his failures, and (d) be resistive to subtle attempts to influence him." These are surely earmarks of a coping orientation.

The defects of the scale in its present form arise from its relation to Rotter's experimental setting, in which ability, skill, and effort are contrasted with fate and chance. The items in the scale pose the same forced choice. This might be an adequate choice if fatalists from the culture of poverty were to be contrasted, in a more innocent society than that of today, with believers in the Horatio Alger myth. But for alienated or dissident youth and for blacks imbued with the ideology of the Black Power movement, these are not the only alternatives. Perceived external control may not rest with fate but with "the Man" or the "system." And the perceived resources for personal control may reside not only in the individual himself but also, vicariously, in his identification with a charismatic leader or a powerful movement and, quite realistically, in the possibilities of joint action. Gurin, Gurin, Lao, and Beattie (1969) have shown that distinctions of this kind must be drawn when the I-E scale is applied to Negro samples. Not surprisingly, Negroes who blame the system are more likely to favor collective action. But in their measurements, most investigators have not freed themselves from Rotter's paired-choice format. However, the job of reconstructing an instrument capable of mapping out a complex of core beliefs about self and world seems now to have been done, after years of delay. (See Collins [in press], also Lefcourt [1972].) The generally intelligible relationships that Rotter's I-E scale has produced give much support to this approach. These relationships also indicate that people may be more able to give honest answers to questions concerning locus of control than to questions that bear on the delicate, ambivalent, and therefore highly elusive matter of self-esteem. (See Wylie [1961, 1968] for the difficulties encountered with self-esteem measures.)

Meanwhile, Richard De Charms (1968, pp. 273–274), whose theoretically elaborated account of personal causation is akin to my own, arrived at a distinction quite similar to Rotter's, between man as origin and as pawn.

> That man is the origin of his behavior means that he is constantly struggling against being confined and constrained by external forces, against being moved like a pawn into situations not of his own choosing. . . . Play that is forced becomes work; if one can choose his work without regard to external pressures and necessity, it takes on many of the aspects of play. . . . An origin is a person who perceives his behavior as determined by his own choosing; a pawn is a person who perceives his behavior as determined by external forces beyond his control. . . .

> The personal aspect is more important motivationally than objective facts. If the person feels he is an origin, that is more important in predicting his behavior than any objective indications of coercion. Conversely, if he considers himself a pawn, his behavior will be strongly influenced, despite any objective evidence that he is free. An origin has strong feelings of personal causation, a feeling that the locus for causation of effects in his environment lies within himself. The feedback that reinforces this feeling comes from changes in his environment that are attributable to personal behavior. This is the crux of personal causation, and it is a powerful motivational force directing future behavior. A pawn has a feeling that causal forces beyond his control, or personal forces residing in others, or in the physical environment, determine his behavior. This constitutes a strong feeling of powerlessness or ineffectiveness.

The research that De Charms (1968) reports creates origin-like and pawn-like situations experimentally and assimilates Rotter's I-E data for measurement of individual differences in the origin-pawn variable. In his subsequent research with school children, he has developed a system for scoring imaginative stories for the variable (still unpublished).

My own entry to this area stems from attempts to understand

my observations of the experience and performance of Peace Corps volunteers. In working over my data and those of my colleague Raphael Ezekiel (1968), I found myself turning to R. W. White's (1959) concept of competence in order to formulate what made the difference between able young men and women who rose to the challenge with full commitment and performed with corresponding effectiveness and equally able young people who responded to the same objective situations as frustrating, not challenging, and spent their energies on adjusting, not coping. (See Chapter Seven.) White's proposal of a biologically intrinsic motive to have effects on one's environment—effectance, he called it—is more modest and, I think, more tenable than De Charm's postulate (1968, p. 269) that "man's primary motivational propensity is to be effective in producing changes in his environment," but they are talking about the same human characteristic. Competence in dealing with the environment, in White's view, rests on this motivational foundation.

The more effective volunteers among a generally impressive group, who joined the Peace Corps when it was still unknown, seemed more than the others to have preserved this responsiveness to challenge with which most infants start life amply endowed. By this point in the volunteers' young adult lives, of course, this responsiveness was no longer the somewhat randomly directed effectance of infancy. Their readiness for engagement and commitment was very much integrated into their selves. Generalized attitudes toward the self, viewing the self as worthy of being taken seriously (self-respect) and capable of producing desired effects, seems to lie at the core of the motivational complex that involved the effective volunteers in benign circles of challenge, coping, accomplishment, and hope rather than vicious circles of passivity or frustration, defense, failure, and fatalism. This cluster of self-attitudes seemed to me the common thread linking White's competence, Rotter's internal control of reinforcement, and De Charm's sense of being an origin. I now propose it as a Utopian version of normality that is especially cogent to our present adaptive predicament. It permits us to translate Jacqueline Wexler's (1969) question into psychological terms with which we are becoming able to work.

Bits of evidence, often collected under seemingly unrelated labels, concerning family relations in childhood, educational practices, and kinds of life situations that contribute to people's ability to take charge of their own lives are beginning to emerge and to fall into place. I am not prepared to review them here. Rather, I call attention to a consequence that follows theoretically from the fact that the dispositions with which we are concerned are reflexive self-attitudes. To an important degree, the self is or becomes what one thinks it is; the self is the prime domain of the self-fulfilling prophecy (Merton, 1957). That is, what one believes about one's causal efficacy affects what one tries and what one does. We have seen evidence for this in the story of Claude Brown, in the correlates of Rotter's I-E measure, and in De Charm's observation that the feeling of being an origin creates origin-like actions. In the sphere of the self, the self-fulfilling prophecy is a prime causal mechanism. This is the basis for the Quaker principle, as illustrated in the transformation of Claude.

Of course there are many problems in this sketchy formulation that need to be clarified. What, for example, of the constraints of reality? Can illusory vicarious power create a sense of efficacy that lays the psychological basis for making it more realistic later on? What is the role of myth in compensating for but perpetuating the actual status of pawn ("opium of the people"), in helping pawns become origins? The heated discussions among liberal psychologists that are predictably evoked by the more romantic reconstructions of black history and the more unrestrained expressions of Black Power ideology make it evident that the answers are not clear.

To avoid misunderstanding, I close by making explicit the limited intent of this Chapter. I highlighted a Utopian version of normality, which contrasts strikingly with Grinker's homoclites, because I believe that this normality is attainable and important. I still agree with Jahoda (1958) that characterizing positive mental health—Utopian normality—requires multiple criteria. And in a day of women's liberation, I cannot help recognizing that there is a male bias to the criterion that I have selected for emphasis. The homoclites were males. Offer's adolescents are males, and my Promethean phrasing of competence is probably masculine-slanted. Within the female role, as modern culture presently defines it, there are ways in which women, too, can be origins—though the culture builds in highly probable pawn-like ingredients. We clearly need a new psychology of women, which encompasses the present cultural definitions—so different from those in Freud's day—and which also transcends them in seeking to identify enduringly distinctive directions of fulfillment that arise from the biology of sexual differentiation.

Culture aside, men will probably be moved to produce large and satisfying environmental effects—from a feminine point of view, often absurd ones, no doubt—and women more often predisposed to cultivate the values of human responsiveness and love that make the enterprise humane and worth the candle. But this assumption remains in doubt, and the range of individual differences in each sex is surely large. At any rate, the expressive-compassionate component of the feminine role and perhaps of the female biological bent need not impose pawnhood. As our present imprecise ideas about effectance and self-determination become elaborated in research, we may hope that the versions that apply to the two sexes will receive equal attention. We risk fatuity if we neglect sex differences in developing our Utopian criteria of normality, and we do injustice if we unthinkingly apply male-oriented standards to both sexes.

Note: Since completing this Chapter, I have been impressed and influenced by Steiner's, 1971, integrative review of a quite different, mainly experimental, literature of sociopsychological research under the rubric of "perceived freedom." There is much in his contribution that complements mine.

Chapter Nine

•••••••••••••••••••••
•••••••••••••••••••••••
••••••••••••••••••••••••

ON SELF-
ACTUALIZATION

•••••••••••••••••••••
•••••••••••••••••••••••
•••••••••••••••••••••••

Somewhere Abe Maslow observed that self-actualizing people manage to transcend their ambivalences. Over many years—essentially the full course of my life as a psychologist—I have been profoundly ambivalent about Maslow's contributions. There is much in his writings that appeals to me strongly. There is much else that sets my intellectual teeth on edge and makes me squirm in discomfort or withdraw in impatience or disagreement. When I am annoyed, I typically find that if I read on, in his great tolerance for ambiguity—indeed, his evident delight in the intellectually inchoate and disordered—Abe has anticipated my objections and said something sensible to mollify me (though usually not to put in order the problems that bothered me). My personal relationship with Abe was small but delightful; my intellectual relationship with his writings has been thoroughly ambivalent.

This chapter is an attempt to penetrate and transcend my ambivalence by focusing on a theme that is recurrent and central in Maslow's writings: self-actualization. It is a theme that he shares with other spokesmen of humanistic psychology (for example, Rogers, 1961), and it is central to the rationale of the personal growth movement (see Back, 1972) of Esalen-style centers and en-counter groups with which humanistic psychology is linked. I must come to terms with it, if I am to make headway in (see Chapter Thirteen) advancing a psychology that is both *humanistic* (germane to man's experience and distinctive concerns) and *scientific* in a sense that is more self-critical, more abstractive, and hence, I be-lieve, more potentially self-corrective and cumulative than Maslow's "Taoistic" version of science (Maslow, 1966; Smith, 1966b). As Maslow (1971) has noted, "The notion of self-actualization gets to be almost like a Rorschach inkblot" (p. 41)—a test of a psycholo-gist's fundamental conceptions of human nature.

I have been concerned with aspects of self-actualization since I wrote a sophomoric paper on Nietzsche, Ibsen, and Shaw that helped resolve my major adolescent identity crisis by formulating an ideal of authentic yea-saying selfhood that creates human meaning in an otherwise bleak and Godless universe (the Ibsen I examined was *Peer Gynt;* the Shaw, *Man and Superman*). Reading and re-reading Maslow for the present purpose, I realized with a shock how significant Nietzsche also must have been to him (for example, Mas-low, 1954, p. 201; 1971, p. 37). Not only does Maslow share Nietzsche's concern about a nontheological basis for human values but the Superman reappears for Maslow in the guise of the self-actualizing person. There are even echoes of Nietzsche in the aphor-istic style of Maslow's later, less self-censored writings.

Self-actualization, however we interpret it, is intrinsically concerned with values. For Maslow, the doctrine bridged the gulf between value and fact. Again and again I have been drawn to the problem of the psychological status of values—how to avoid the twin perils of ethnocentric (or theological) absolutism with its vul-nerable dogmas and of a relativism that undercuts the significance of human choice.

As I focused these persisting concerns in an attempt to clarify the nature and criteria of psychological well-being or positive mental health, I arrived at a skeptical view (see Chapter Seven) that never-theless seemed liberating (Smith, 1961)—that "mental health" is not a scientific concept but a chapter heading under which any and all evaluative perspectives on human personality can be placed. Pro-posed criteria of mental health—like the ability to love and work, realistic perception, integration, and active mastery—are values in terms of which personality may be appraised. Scientific psychology cannot settle *which* values people should live by, and, therefore, psychological arguments about criteria of mental health are fruitless. Nevertheless psychologists make a distinctive contribution to the discussion when they discover developmental and situational conditions under which particular values can be realized and consequences or side effects of pursuing particular values. This was not quite a relativistic position, since I assumed that people's value choices might converge in the light of such evidence and of human experience. My plea to those concerned with mental health was to be explicit about which values they had in mind and not to use the global concept as a cover to impose their own idiosyncratic values in the name of science. This plea still seems valid and, as I will shortly make clear, underlies a major bone that I have to pick with Maslow.

As it turned out, I could not remain comfortable with an uncommitted, skeptical position, since it gave me no help with my sociopolitical concerns for human betterment (a point where I feel a strong resonance with Maslow, who was also basically an optimistic reformist). In the moral atmosphere of the War on Poverty, it appeared that the public interest in mental-health criteria dictated a primary focus on human effectiveness as a successor to the gross value of not-illness (appropriate to the institutional psychiatry of an earlier day) or that of personal adjustment and fulfillment (appropriate to the private client in the consulting room). (See Chapter Seven.) I drew upon R. W. White's (1959) motivationally based concept of competence for the key to a reformulated conception of positive mental health that seemed adequate to the needs of the time.

Mulling over what seemed to me the requirements for survival at our critical junction in human history, my own direct experience with Peace Corps volunteers and college youth, and directly cogent research by Rotter (1966) and De Charms (1968), I came to refocus my thinking about "competence" upon processes of self-determination (see Chapter Eight). Some people more than others seem to be in charge of their lives—to be agents or origins of personal causation rather than pawns. The unprecedented human situation with its headlong trends toward multiple disaster sets a high premium upon agency, upon the rearing of people who will not passively take these trends for granted. A view of self-determination as an empirical variable in which people differ appealed to me as cutting through the philosophical deadlock between determinists and voluntarists in psychology. If, in the realm of the reflexive self, the self-fulfilling prophecy is a causal mechanism, people's causally rooted conceptions of themselves as origins or as pawns can make the crucial difference in whether they actively *live* their lives or merely suffer them. Many people who were previously not self-determining—blacks and Chicanos, former colonials, women, even students—were demanding self-determination as against external constraint, and achieving the inner basis of self-determination through redefinition of their identities. A scientific social psychology of personality could help to understand this humanly important process and perhaps to advance it.

These considerations still strike me as compelling. (They do not appear to fit very easily with Maslow's [1954] otherwise attractive hierarchical conception of human motivation. Events have shown that people who are still suffering from gross deficiency [D] motivation are capable of acting to promote self-determination for themselves and the groups with which they identify [though their leaders are unlikely to be dominated by D-motives]. Maslow's D-motive of respect is related to the quest for self-determination but does not seem to encompass it.) I have come to realize that a specialized focus upon self-determination, understandable and appropriate as it may be for minority activists or radical feminists, is a one-sided, biased perspective for the psychologist who is concerned with optimal human functioning. Even in the Chapter in which I developed these ideas (see Chapter Eight), I noted as an afterthought that they probably reflect a male bias.

The Promethean, instrumental, coping emphasis of competence and self-determination has a characteristic flavor of male aspirations and hang-ups (some self-analysis here!). It probably requires some modulation to fit the ways that females, on the average, will find suitable to living their lives as the cultural pressures that limit them are relaxed. Reflection on my own experiential sources of value and protracted discussions with Santa Cruz University of California students in seminar (a majority of whom had biases complementary to my instrumentalism) convinced me that the one-sidedness is fundamental. In the terms of May's (1969) provocative book, I had been focusing single-mindedly on will. What about love? Maslow had long been asserting the insufficiency of coping and competence as criteria of the "fully human." A long, close look at the inkblot of self-actualization, under which he dealt with the criterion problem, thus takes high priority on my agenda.

Among the many contexts in which Maslow discusses self-actualization, there are three major ones, which are closely interrelated. Initially, and throughout his subsequent writings, Maslow (1950) talked about *self-actualizing people* as rare specimens of psychological health who can be used as a kind of touchstone to explore human potentialities. Secondly, he refers repeatedly to *peak experiences* of transcendent value, which he finds common among self-actualizing people. For more ordinary humanity, these may be regarded as moments of self-actualization. And, thirdly, he refers to a self-actualizing *growth process* governed by "metamotives" that take over when deficiency motivation is satisfied. As a basis for subsequent discussion, I will characterize each of these nodes of meaning.

In a very modestly presented informal study (Maslow, 1950, 1954)—regrettably informal considering the speculative weight it was subsequently called upon to support—Maslow examined the characteristics that he discerned as shared among fifty-one public or historical figures, contemporaries, and carefully screened young people who seem to exemplify or to approach the ideal of psychological health. (Later [for example, Maslow, 1971, p. 34], Maslow preferred to substitute "full or diminished humanness" for the medical terminology of health and illness.) Maslow (1954, pp. 200–201) wrote that "the positive criterion for selection was positive evidence of self-actualization (SA), as yet a difficult syndrome to describe accurately. For the purposes of this discussion, it may be loosely described as the full use and exploitation of talents, capacities, potentialities, and so forth. Such people seem to be fulfilling themselves and to be doing the best that they are capable of doing, reminding us of Nietzsche's exhortation, 'Become what thou art!' "

The following, in brief, are the characteristics of Maslow's self-actualizing people: "superior perception of reality; increased acceptance of self, of others and of nature; increased spontaneity; increase in problem centering; increased detachment and desire for privacy; increased autonomy, and resistance to enculturation; greater freshness of appreciation, and richness of emotional reaction; higher frequency of peak experiences; increased identification with the human species; changed (the clinician would say, improved) interpersonal relations; more democratic character structure; greatly increased creativeness; certain changes in the value system" (Maslow, 1968, p. 26). Many of his later statements elaborate upon and add to the traits listed in this summary. Maslow is explicit: self-actualization in this defining sense is an uncommon achievement attained only in late maturity.

As just noted, Maslow found that his self-actualizers were especially likely to report transcendent, even ecstatic or mystical experiences that they regarded as imbued with the greatest intrinsic value, in which awareness of the self and its boundaries is eclipsed by immersion in larger meanings. Not all self-actualizers are "peakers," as Maslow later (1971) observed. Many people who fall short of attaining Maslow's criterion of self-actualization nevertheless have peak experiences—which Maslow suggests are transient moments of self-actualization, of "being." Because these moments involve a transcendence of the self, they also provide the link for him to "transpersonal" psychology.

Self-actualization can be viewed not only as a life achievement and as a momentary state but also as the normal process of psychological growth that occurs (in Maslow's [1954] theory of a hierarchy of motives) when a person's deficiency motives are satisfied and his defenses are not mobilized by present threats. "Self-actualization is not only an end state but also the process of actualizing one's potentialities at any time, in any amount" (Maslow, 1971, p. 47). Maslow (1968, p. 45) suggests that "growth takes place when the next step forward is subjectively more delightful, more joyous, more intrinsically satisfying than the previous gratification with which we have become familiar and even bored; that the only way we can ever know what is right for us is that it feels better subjectively than any alternative. The new experience validates *itself* rather than by any outside criterion. It is self-justifying, self-validating. . . . This is the way in which we discover the Self and answer the ultimate questions Who am I? What am I?" He continues, "Of course this formulation of growth-through-delight commits us to the necessary postulation that what tastes good is also, in the growth sense, 'better' for us. We rest here on the faith that if free choice is *really* free and if the chooser is not too sick or frightened to choose, he will choose wisely in a health and growthward direction, more often than not" (Maslow, 1968, p. 48).

It is here that Maslow espouses what the critic Kurt Back (1972, p. 110) identifies as the central model upon which the whole personal growth movement is based—"the model of a prisoner in a cage. Underlying most of the thought is the idea of man (or whatever the essential man is) as being imprisoned by different layers of circumstances which do not allow him to reach his full potentialities. Allied to this image is also the supposition that, if he could escape, everything would be good, and he would only use his potentialities for creative and beneficial results." With Back, I see problems in this faith that underlies the personal growth movement. I now consider, then, the difficulties that I encounter with Maslow's formulations.

Much as I would like to swallow the doctrine whole, the difficulties that make Maslow's doctrine of self-actualization stick in my craw touch upon central and perennial issues concerning human nature. Since I generally agree with him about which is the side of the Angels, since I entirely agree with him (and with Chein, 1972) in espousing an image of man as an actor, not a mechanism, and since most of the bones that I have to pick bear on other humanistic psychologies as much as Maslow's, I hope that a vigorous argument about points of disagreement may contribute to a reconstruction of humanistic psychology along lines that preserve the humanism but improve the chances for a rapprochement with science.

First I must note a petty methodological problem that seriously affects my reading of Maslow's study of self-actualizing people. Maslow is so modest about the study's inadequacies and technical flaws and so informal in reporting the study that it seems quite unfair to criticize—like turning a howitzer on a butterfly. But it is necessary, since the study provides the foundation for so much of what Maslow has to say about self-actualization.

The crucial flaw, one that I noted long ago (Smith, 1959) and so far as I am aware Maslow never acknowledged, has to do with the bootstrap operation by which he selected his "sample" of self-actualizing people. In effect, Maslow eliminated people with gross pathology—the Dostoevskis and Van Goghs—and selected people for whom, after close scrutiny, he had the highest admiration as human specimens. His empirical definition of psychological health or self-actualization thus rests, at root, on his own implicit values that underlie this global judgment. The array of characteristics that he reports must then be regarded not as an empirical description of the fully human (the value-laden facts that he claims to have established) but rather as an explication of his implicit conception of the fully human, of his orienting frame of human values. This is still interesting because of our respect for Maslow's discriminations of human quality, but it is not the factual foundation for humanistic values that he claims it to be.

The trouble is apparent when we look at the names of his seven cases of "fairly sure" or "highly probable" public and historical figures: Abe Lincoln in his last years, Thomas Jefferson, Albert Einstein, Eleanor Roosevelt, Jane Addams, William James, and Baruch Spinoza. Why not also George Washington in *his* later years, Casanova in his earlier years, Napoleon, Thomas Edison, or Lenin? All of these could equally be said to be making, in the phrasing of Maslow's criterion statement of self-actualization, "the full use . . . of talents, capacities, potentialities, . . . to be fulfilling themselves and to be doing the best they were capable of doing, reminding us of Nietzsche's exhortation, 'Become what thou art!' " In the inherent nature of the case, the dice are loaded toward Maslow's own values. I like them, but that is beside the point.

The methodological point shades into a theoretical one. How, indeed, are we to understand the "human potentialities" that become actualized? The term is most at home in an Aristotelian, finalistic conception, in which development is conceived as the realization of potentialities that are in some sense uniquely predetermined. As I subsequently suggest, that is not so bad a fit to the biological facts when we are dealing with the adapted products of long-term evolution (even though most biologists do not regard it as a viable theoretical formulation). Maslow (1968) stretches the biological analogy to human psychology, as in the following: "Man demonstrates *in his own nature* a pressure toward fuller and fuller Being, more and more perfect actualization of his humanness in exactly the same naturalistic, scientific sense [*sic*] that an acorn may be said to be 'pressing toward' being an oak tree, or that a tiger can be observed to 'push toward' being tigerish, or a horse toward being equine. . . . The environment does not give him potentialities or capacities; he *has* them in inchoate or embryonic form, just as he has embryonic arms and legs" (p. 160).

This will hardly do. Except for some universals of the human species such as language and symbolization, constructiveness, interdependence, and maybe reactive aggression that have an entrenched evolutionary status and probably fit the acorn-oak tree model as well as the plant itself does (which is to ignore the complex interactive processes of epigenesis), the young person has an extremely broad range of multiple potentialities. The course of life, including the choices of the emerging self, excludes some of them, sets limits on others, and elaborates upon still others. Vice and evil are as much in the range of human potentiality as virtue, specialization as much as well-rounded development. Our biology cannot be made to carry our ethics, as Maslow would have it.

I see that I am resorting to sheer assertions to counter Maslow's. But the burden of proof is upon him. The kinds of people that Maslow excludes from his self-actualizing sample and its consequent bias toward Maslovian values undermines his case for the *distinctive* humanness of the particular human potentialities that his sample exemplifies. These are among the attractive possibilities of human existence; its interest, its tragedy, and its glory lie in the fact that they are not built in but exist as possibilities among a range of very different possibilities, any of which can be regarded as an actualization of potentiality, though trivially so, when it occurs. In general, the doctrine of potentiality is more misleading than helpful (see also Chein, 1972).

The difficulties that I have just examined lead me to reject (unambivalently) a part of Maslow's doctrine. Now I come to a matter that remains a problem for me, though I think it can be clarified beyond the point where Maslow leaves it: How do our conceptions of the self affect our view of self-actualization?

Although conceptual attention to the self as actor, as reflexive object, and in its relations to other selves is a hallmark of humanistic psychology, theories about the self remain primitive and underdeveloped. Plausible fragments from P. Schilder, G. H. Mead, Carl Jung, E. H. Erikson, Gordon Allport, and others lie scattered and unintegrated. My own thinking about the self is not in good order, and Maslow's is mainly implicit. Yet one attractive meaning of self-actualization, as experience or action that is in deep accord with the self or carries forward its projects, depends entirely on what we assume about the self. Two radically contrasting versions of the self are current, with many variants. (See also Chapter Ten.)

One version can be identified with the Socratic dictum "The unexamined life is not worth living." Selfhood from this perspective inheres in the uniquely human gift of reflexive self-awareness. Actions actualize the self when they are done reflectively and responsibly to correspond to the values that comprise the core of self-accepted identity. Self-actualization is the cumulative product of such action and is accompanied by self-understanding.

Quite a contrary version of the self can be identified with Jung, who perceives selfhood as an "iceberg" according to which the true, essential self, the source of creativity, of authenticity and value, lies outside of awareness. One can aspire only partly to know and understand the self, but one can still be sensitive to and guided by the self's dictates. Self-actualizing experience, from this perspective, erupts for the prepared person if he is properly receptive to it—as in peak experiences. Action is likely to be self-actualizing if it is spontaneous and *un*reflective. Thus the term *self-actualization* can be employed to designate empirical phenomena and ethical prescriptions that are diametrically opposed. The growth movement in humanistic psychology, and Maslow with it, seems heavily committed to the iceberg version of the self.

I see no need to negotiate between these contrasting interpretations of selfhood, which I would rather understand as partial accounts of what it is to be human, that reflect competing realms of human value. Human nature *is* multipotential. A dazzling choice of options is available. There is no cosmic requirement, nor biological necessity, that our choices be well balanced. But they have consequences, all the same, in the inner world of experience and the outer world of practical affairs. I am sympathetic to what Maslow (1971, Appendix A) says, in a slightly different context, about Apollonian (orderly) and Dionysian (impulsive) versions of self-actualization.

As he puts it, the current Dionysian excesses of the encounter move-ment and the counterculture counterbalance the massive Apollonian emphasis of our technological society. But if I agree with this, I must also note that the major drift of Maslow's theoretical and quasi-empirical writings on self-actualization is Dionysian.

Maslow's Dionysian bias (an emphasis on the *diamonic*, in May's [1969] terms, though for May the diamonic carries more multivalent, potentially tragic overtones than the Dionysian in Mas-low's optimistic, rather sanguine version) has implications for the meaning of peak experiences as glimpses or criteria of self-actualiza-tion. Peak experiences belong on the nonrational, Dionysian side; if one grants the coreality of the more Apollonian forms of self-actuali-zation, their authority diminishes. In a purportedly general "psy-chology of being," it seems questionable to give as much weight as Maslow does to insights "validated" by the content of such experi-ences. Maslow notes that among his self-actualizing sample, Eleanor Roosevelt was a nonpeaker. Had his sample been drawn to follow his explicit criterion more faithfully, less according to his implicit value preferences, peak experiences would figure less prominently as a characteristic of self-actualization. In question, particularly, is the raising of mysticism to a status honored more than rationality, among the possible competing realms of value between which hu-man choice historically has oscillated.

For myself, I think I understand Maslow's peak experiences in love, nature, and music. These experiences contribute to the per-sonal richness and value of life, to the feeling that life is worthwhile and that one could die knowing that one had lived fully. These ex-periences remain great mysteries that make religion imaginable. I wish that a scientific psychology could encompass them; peak ex-periences surely reflect something unique to man and exceedingly important to him. It is to Maslow's great credit that he has brought them back into psychology. But the high value that I set upon these experiences does not persuade me to regard the "gut feel" as more enduringly valid than the considered thought, the passively eruptive as higher and truer than the actively sought. There are many varieties of human experience, religious and otherwise, all of which deserve respect and study. In a warranted pendulum swing against the prevailing emphasis in psychology, Maslow has opted for inspiration over perspiration, and, taken as a new, scientific gospel, his Dionysian bias is open to the charge of anti-intellectualism and romantic impulsivity. A pendulum swing should not be mistaken for the revelation of a higher truth.

Peak experiences transcend ordinary selfhood, which they temporarily obliterate. I can only applaud another of the senses in which Maslow employs the term *transcendence*. In an introduction to "being-values," Maslow (1971, p. 43) writes: "Self-actualizing people are, without one single exception, involved in a cause outside their own skin, in something outside themselves. They are devoted, working at something, something which is very precious to them— some calling or vocation in the old sense, the priestly sense . . . so that the work-joy dichotomy in them disappears." This, of course, is only a restatement of the Christian wisdom that he who would find his life must lose it—that happiness or fulfillment is a by-product that eludes direct pursuit. The observation has validity beyond Maslow's biased sample, and I conjecture that it will remain as an enduring truth about selfhood. It must be fitted into a conceptually articulated self-psychology.

Maslow's biologistic conception of man contrasts with the view of man as an historical human actor, which seems to me more appropriate for the consideration of self-actualization. In my earlier discussion of the doctrine of potentiality, I questioned Maslow's biologism, which projects a determinate course of self-actualization as rooted in man's biological nature. Here Maslow is faithful to his mentor, the holistic neurologist Goldstein (1939), who wrote: *"Normal behavior corresponds to a continual change of tension, of such a kind that over and again that state of tension is reached which enables and impels the organism to actualize itself in further activities, according to its nature. Thus, experiences with patients* teach us that we have to *assume only one drive, the drive of self-actualization* and that the goal of the drive is not a discharge of tension" (p. 197). Goldstein anticipated the current trend in motivational theory in his attack on the principle of tension-reduction. But his concept of self-actualization according to the *nature* of the organism seems to me to have limited applicability at the level of human action. What is the nature of the human organism or, better, of the human person? Perennial problems of philosophy and psychology are involved.

The member of subhuman animal species, stably adapted to a well-defined ecological niche as the result of long evolutionary process, has a nature, the fulfillment of which is likely to result in adaptation and the survival of the individual (at least until repro-duction). As a higher primate that also passed through a long evolu-tionary period of stable adaptation, man too has a biological na-ture—though what it is and what constraints it puts upon present human action are just now important controversial questions. The chances are that man's biological nature has to do with such prob-lematic matters as male enjoyment of hunting and a good fight, such essential safeguards as mothers' irresistible attraction to babies (embarrassing to the new feminists), and such important but moti-vationally neutral propensities as preprogrammed readiness to learn the elaborate symbol system of a human language. The "further reaches of human nature," in Maslow's phrase, are still beyond the reach of evolutionary processes: historical time is short.

Maslow's is a psychology for the affluent, postindustrial so-ciety. The eons of protohuman evolutionary history must all have been lived mainly at the lower deficiency levels (in Maslow's hier-archical theory of motivation) when life was indeed nasty, brutish, and short. Protopeople were in ecological equilibrium with their resources (which means the edge of hunger) and with their internal parasites (which does not mean health). How, indeed, could a bio-logical human nature of instinctoid metamotives of the kind Maslow regards as inherent in self-actualization be established in evolution? In his theory, these metamotives take over only when deficiency motives are satisfied.

These considerations raise questions of whether the "wis-dom of the body" (and of the untutored mind) is sufficient for the valid guidance of signicant human choice, as Maslow's faith would have it. Just as our gut reactions of pleasure may mislead us about saccharine and more dangerous drugs that had no part in our evo-lution, so these reactions may lead us astray or, what amounts to the same thing, into difficult and destructive conflicts in the human relations of an interdependent urban society. In evolutionary terms, these human relations are almost as new as saccharine.

The trouble is that Maslow's psychology is pseudobiologistic; it is inadequately humanistic in the sense long defended by spokesmen for the humanities. Maslow neglects the discontinuity in the biological record that came with language, culture, self-consciousness, and the accompanying moral order of society. What a humanist would regard as historical human action Maslow persists in regarding as the instinctoid expression of biological propensities. His misguided attempt to arrive at a naturalistic basis for human values rules out any serious consideration of the ethics and politics—and perhaps the aesthetics—of human action.

Darwin's principle of natural selection provides the equivalent of an Unseen Hand that gradually (though cruelly) shapes biological nature toward adaptiveness. In history and culture there is no Unseen Hand; there is human action. Human action can succeed or fail, it can be constructive or destructive of self and others, and, miraculously, it creates a variety of values and must choose among them. This is the essence of human hope, of human tragedy, of human dignity. "Becoming fully human" is a personal-cultural-historical adventure. The biological metaphor is ill suited to grasp the essence of this adventure, but a humanistic psychology should.

If an Unseen Hand is absent in human history, then self-actualization in the sense of growth process does not inevitably lead to the common good. "Doing what comes naturally" is not enough. The emphasis in Maslow's writings is on the fulfillment of the individual. Likewise, the encounter movement that draws upon his writings has become much more flagrantly individualistic.

Yet Maslow's (1971) own view is more complex. Not only do self-actualizing people tend to be altruists but their "basic needs can be fulfilled *only* by and through other human beings, that is, society" (p. 347). Further, societies differ in the extent to which they make it possible for people to transcend the conflict between selfishness and altruism. Maslow (1971, p. 202) adopts from Ruth Benedict the concept of synergy for this characteristic of societies according to which the social institutions either tend to make virtue pay or, instead, tend to structure social life as a zero-sum game. The concept plays a central role in Maslow's Utopian (or "Eupsy-chian") thinking.

There is a suggestive basis here for political and ethical analy-sis and empirical inquiry. In spite of Maslow's preoccupation with humane institutions and management in his later writings (see espe-cially Maslow, 1965), his thought was essentially unpolitical. He was an optimist about the extent to which Eupsychian arrangements could indeed provide the equivalent of an Unseen Hand. Maslow did not actually deny the irreducible reality of conflict, either in the unconscious psyche or in society, but he was not disposed to dwell upon it. An adequately humanistic psychology should come to terms squarely with conflict and tragedy in human life.

I have dealt severely with several aspects of Maslow's doc-trine of self-actualization because I think the doctrine deserves to be taken seriously. Now some efforts toward reconstruction are in order. For my own use, I should like to salvage the conception of self-actualization as *process*. I would interpret the process of self-actu-alization as characteristic of a person's actions or experiences when they are in congruence with his existing self (rather than dictated by external constraint or conformity or driven by inner compulsions that are alien to the self). Such actions or experiences feed back in their consequences to enrich the self, to express its values, or to further its enterprises. This is the crux of Maslow's concept. It is also a major part of his rationale for psychological growth. I think it important, and an adequate psychology of the self can build upon it. I would insist, however, upon an open conception of selfhood until our personological knowledge is more firmly based and better formulated—one with a place both for the creative depths of the iceberg theory and for the reflective commitments emphasized by a view that sets greater stock on rational consciousness. I would stress the many routes that are open to self-actualization (correspond-ing to the rich variety of human nature and its personal and cul-tural expressions). I would not expect, therefore, to find a single syndrome of virtues in the self-actualized people who are nearing the end of the journey.

Self-actualization, so conceived, seems a precious psycho-logical value, but it must be appreciated in the context of other psy-chological and social realities. Since I do not believe that self-actualizing action can dependably be counted upon to produce the common good (short of Eupsychia, which I fear would be as dull as Walden Two or the classless society), I see self-actualization as in necessary and desirable interplay with social norms and sanctions, on the one hand, and with internalized principles and perhaps even taboos, on the other. This interplay is essential if a degree of social and psychological order which people need and which does not "come naturally" is to be attained. For both individuals and societies the pendulum swings between order and expressiveness. Individual differences in personal priorities (Apollonian and Dionysian) are to be expected and valued.

Because social realities are at best imperfectly synergic in Maslow's sense, conflict will remain; there is need for politics. And because gut feeling and delight can be misleading guides to the common good (though valuable if fallible ones to individual self-actualization), ethics is needed as well. Neither ethics nor politics is bestowed upon man by any instinctoid biology, though workable versions of ethics and politics take into account his biological nature as well as his historically developing situation. Both ethics and politics are the emergent, historical creations of conscious actors who by their new human nature—a nature that is transformed in the dialectics of human action—are interdependent and must come to terms with one another. Ethics and politics involve human choices about difficult matters with uncertain outcomes.

A psychology is humanistic to the extent that it takes serious account of man as an experiencing actor. We know from man's history and from appreciative acquaintance with his cultural products that even a minimally adequate account must be very complex. Maslow's corpus of writing certainly goes far toward evoking this complexity. But some of his ideas about self-actualization seem to purvey a one-sided, though admirable, vision of human potentiality and to fall short of full justice to the distinctively human nature of the historical domain of human choice.

Chapter Ten

•••••••••••••••••••••
••••••••••••••••••••••
•••••••••••••••••••••••

THE ICEBERG AND THE MIRROR: PERSPECTIVES ON SELFHOOD

•••••••••••••••••••••
•••••••••••••••••••••
•••••••••••••••••••••

I still remember vividly how, some thirty-five years ago, my eye was caught and fascinated by the dust jacket of the book *Explorations in Personality* (Murray, 1938), carried by a knowing member of the self-ascribed in-group of students in the corridor outside Lewis Terman's Stanford class in personality. Under the title with its open invitation was a magic symbolic medallion of creatures of the ocean deep (among them, the portentous whale) and the inscription, Let not him who seeks cease until he finds, and when he finds he shall be astonished. What a contrast with any psychology that I thought I knew! One had to possess the book; one had to plunge in and devour it. Inside its covers, the variables teemed in Rabelaisian proliferation: also exciting new methods, and subjects with numinous pseudonyms. And the person of its principal author shone through the densely packed prose that struck sparks against itself. Obviously this was the work

180

of a benign and mighty Prospero with strange powers to induct us shipwrecked psychologists to a wondrous realm.

Now that he is eighty, we know Harry Murray much better, since, as he has taught us, the personality *is* the life, and by now Harry has displayed a large life indeed. I, for one, am still astonished. I feel especially privileged in the extent to which his life and work have touched mine.

The theme that I propose to introduce in this chapter, as my offering in Harry's honor, is not one that stems directly from his seminal studies of the person. But as we shall see, my theme bears closely on his concerns, and I think it belongs in the large agenda that Harry staked out for us: to create a psychology of the person that is at once humanistic *and* scientific. As part of that encompassing agenda, I attempt a small foray into the large undertaking of disentangling an articulate theory of the self from our present confusion.

The language of self and selfhood appeals to me, as it does to many others, because it connotes the distinctive feature of human personhood: man is at once subject and object ,"I" and "Me," and what makes him a time-binding human actor in personal and cultural history—not just a behaving organism—is precisely the symbolic interplay of the subjective and objective, of reflexive awareness and action. My preliminary view does not perceive the self as a substantive concept, a thing-like entity, nor does it identify the self with the person or personality, although an articulated theory of self requires a developed personality theory. I see the self, rather, as a perspective on personhood that highlights the interplay of the objective and subjective. The theory of self to which we subscribe, whether it be implicit or explicit or merely confused, inevitably embraces our metapsychology of core humanness. To formulate an explicit theory of the self, then, requires some sort of dialectic synthesis of the objective and phenomenological perspectives in psychology, focused on the emergence and transactions of personhood. No wonder that our concepts and theories of selfhood are in disarray.

The conceptual ingredients presently at hand for a theory of the self are fragmentary and await integration. In psychoanalysis, Freud's (1921) concept of the "ego ideal" was eclipsed by his more salient concept of "super-ego." Freud did not provide the full array of concepts that we need to discuss the interrelations of I and Me, but his elaboration of the concept of the unconscious permanently complicated the problem of relating the phenomenological and the functional aspects of selfhood. The body image, obviously an important ground of self-awareness, was stressed by the psychoanalyst Schilder (1935) and later by Fisher and Cleveland (1958) but remains a stray topic in personality theory—one that is quite ignored by the symbolic interactionist tradition stemming from Mead (1934). McDougall (1921) made the "self-regarding sentiment" the kingpin in his structural account of the mind, doing duty for what had formerly been treated as the will. But the clue was not picked up in the later social psychology of attitudes (which remained steadfastly devoted to peripheral dispositions) nor in the personality theory of Murray (1938), which in other respects is a marriage of the psychoanalytic (Freudian and Jungian) and McDougallian traditions. Rogers (1961) made the self-concept central in his research and in his theory of psychotherapy and personal growth, but in his bland optimism he ignored rather than solved or rendered obsolete the problems that Freud had posed. A massive and largely disappointing tradition of empirical research focuses on the self-concept (Wylie, 1961, 1968); the promising contributions of Rotter (1966) on locus of control and De Charms (1968) on origin versus pawn have still to be understood as enlarging and reorienting research on the topic. Erikson's (1959) elaboration of the connotations of identity remains to be clarified by more orderly theorists and has not been linked effectively with complementary concepts in the sphere of selfhood. On two occasions, G. W. Allport attempted an heroic sorting-out of concepts, once under the rubric of "ego" (1943) and again under that of "proprium" (1955), but each of these ventures amounted essentially to a catalog of the features or functions of selfhood. A difficult job still lies ahead if we are to put our best current thinking about selfhood into coherent order.

The mirror and the iceberg of my chapter title are intended to evoke two major conceptions of selfhood that compete for the terrain of a properly humanistic psychology. Let me add to this primary pair of images four others—the self as onion, as chooser, as knower, and as vacuum—and the roster of supposed human actors as presented by our competing metapsychologies is virtually complete.

First, the *self as mirror,* a metaphor that I draw from Charles Horton Cooley's (1902) "looking-glass self." (Other great names in this tradition of conceptualizing selfhood are William James [1890], James Mark Baldwin [1913], and George Herbert Mead [1934].) Symbolic interactionists in sociology have institutionalized the tradition and given it prominence in the stream of sociopsychological theorizing within their discipline. From this perspective, selfhood inheres in the uniquely human gift of reflexive self-awareness, and this, in turn, is the emergent outcome of social, communicative processes. We see ourselves as reflected in the responses of significant others; initially we see them in the god-like principal characters of the family drama. We come to acquire a coherent sense of selfhood through practice in role-taking: through adopting toward our own actions-in-process and toward our own attributes the perspectives of significant others, eventually articulating these perspectives to view the self "in the round" from the perspective of the "generalized other," in Mead's phrasing. We can then turn the mirror inward and use it for the critical guidance of our thought and action in the social world. Thus the self as Me. The I as actor and interlocutor of the Me is more mysterious, but, at least in Mead's version, it represents the spontaneity that characterizes reflective action and the results of inner dialogue. Selfhood in the mirror version, though it is seen as an emergent social product, does not have to be taken as a mere passive imprint of social definitions and pressures.

As I have already noted, the important agenda for theoretical development in this version of selfhood concerns the interplay between I and Me—between the causal-functional and the phenomenological perspectives, between self as actor and as reflexive object. Mead is of little help to us here, and philosophical pitfalls and empirical obscurities abound. It is understandable that symbolic interactionism and its descendent "ethnomethodology" have attracted a surge of interest from younger sociologists of humanistic or radical inclinations. The perspective, like that of Marx, and of Piaget in developmental psychology, takes man's distinctively human characteristics seriously. It sees man as an actor—in an interactive (for the Marxian, read dialectical) process in which these characteristics emerge and through which they are sustained. (Two experimental social psychologists, Duval and Wicklund [1972] have recently published a valiant attempt to contribute to the I-Me problem.)

For those who use the term, selfhood is a value-laden concept. If we hold that selfhood inheres in the inner mirror, we are predisposed to take as an ethical guide the Socratic dictum that "the unexamined life is not worth living." We are likely to interpret that ambiguous summum bonum self-actualization in a way quite different from that emphasized by Maslow. (See Chapter Nine.) Actions actualize the mirror self when they are done *reflectively* and responsibly to correspond to the value priorities that comprise the core of the person's self-accepted identity. That is, actions guided by self-awareness are self-actualizing. Self-actualization is the cumulative product of such actions and both requires and results in self-understanding.

Theorists of the *iceberg self* seem to live in a differently populated world, governed by incommeasurable values. Carl Jung (1953), a major source of inspiration to Murray, is the purest and most highly elaborated case of an approach to selfhood that is shared in degree by many humanistic psychologists. According to his view, the true, essential self lies mostly outside of awareness. For Jung, the submerged self has sources that transcend individual personality. Through a process of "individuation" ("becoming a person," in Rogers' [1961] phrase), the fortunate person gains touch with his potential for authenticity and creativity and escapes the charade of masks and personifications in which most of us are caught. For the purposes of a humanized psychology, Jung's respect for the religious ingredient of human experience is a strong point; for purposes of a scientific humanism, the extent to which Jung's doctrine seems to partake of religion rather than helping us to comprehend it is an embarrassment.

From the perspective of the self as iceberg, self-actualizing experience erupts for the prepared person if he is properly receptive —as in Maslow's peak experiences. Action is likely to be self-actualizing if it is spontaneous and *un*reflective. As Chapter Nine observed, the term *self-actualization* can be used for empirical phenomena and ethical prescriptions that are diametrically opposed! If the mirror version of selfhood fits the classical or Apollonian ethos, the iceberg version is romantic and Dionysian. (This characterization, I realize, does not do justice to Jung's complexities as a psychological theorist and ethical leader. Jung, too, seeks the complete man.)

Thus far I have used Mead and Jung to identify prototypical conceptions of the self. What are we to make of Freud? If conscious awareness is what shows above the surface, Freud certainly subscribes to an iceberg model. But his tripartite structural metaphor is of the *person*, not of the self. The bottom of the iceberg, the id or "it," is explicitly not-self—hence Freud's use of Groddeck's (1935) term *das Es*. And the closest counterpart in Freud to Mead's Me is not self either, but the superego, the internalized voice of social prohibitions and prescriptions—an alien voice. The locus of selfhood for Freud is wholly in the ego. Freud displays the values, the therapeutic goals, of the mirror theorist when he proclaims, "Where there was id, let ego be."

Freud's writings present us with a complex stimulus full of internal inconsistencies. In the context of our concerns in this volume, it is important for us to note, with Holt (1972), that both a humanistic and a mechanistic metapsychology can be extracted. What Freud himself viewed as the core of his metapsychology, the economic point of view focused on psychic energy or libido and its cathexes and transformations, now appears as a gratuitous importation from the mechanistic nineteenth century physics of Helmholz, whose law of the conservation of energy (the first law of thermodynamics) seemed in its day the epitome of the scientific. (Freud's later preoccupation with the "death instinct" can be read as partly an echo of the second law of thermodynamics, the entropy principle). On the other hand, particularly in his clinical papers, Freud developed a psychology of wishes, meanings, conflict, and symbolic transformation that remains undated as a fundamental contribution to a humanistic psychology. In addition to Holt, Loevinger (1966), Yankelovich and Barrett (1970), and Chein (1972) are among those who are engaged in reconstructing psychoanalytic theory to cleanse it of intrusions from physicalistic metaphors. In the terms of the metaphor of our own day, the computer, these theorists realize that the tasks of psychoanalysis (and psychology) concern the programs and processes by which information is stored and transformed, not the energy economy of the hardware (which is described literally as the conversion of electrical—or chemical—energy into heat, not as thought, feeling, or behavior). Psychoanalytic theory in this vein is congruent with conceptions of selfhood. A thoroughgoing attempt to introduce the necessary conceptual distinctions may be found in the latter part of Chein's (1972) book, my indebtedness to which is repeatedly recognized elsewhere in this volume.

I draw the image of *self as onion* from Ibsen's *Peer Gynt*, who was fated to be recast by the Button Molder if there was no core of true self left when the onion layers of his role-identities were peeled away. It is a caricature, but one that some versions of role theory approach (Thomas and Biddle, 1966). This particular role-theoretic tradition stems not so much from Mead (1934)—who emphasized interpersonal role-taking process—as from Linton (1936), who proposed a structural theory of roles and statuses to which persons accommodate. The tradition can be characterized as the theory that would naturally be conceived by Riesman's (1950) other-directed man in the same manner that Freud's super-ego doctrine casts Riesman's inner-directed man—the man with a gyroscope, not a radar—in universalized terms.

Versions of the onion model are shared by other theorists who emphasize role-playing and the situational determination of behavior. The theories are mutually congenial because they dissolve selfhood into a congeries of masks and appearances—thus Goffman's (1959, 1971) dramaturgical theory, which portrays a virtually paranoid world of schemers, connivers, and tacit accomplices who are concerned with the smooth stage management of their relationships rather than with the conduct of substantial human enterprises. Thus also Mischel's (1968) social learning theory of personality, which embraces a radical situationism that questions the utility of positing inferred dispositions of personality. "Attribution theory," popular in experimental social psychology, also focuses, in a very sophisticated way, on the *appearances* of self and personality: on what we make of the other, not on what we are in ourselves.

When it is brought to bear on *self-attribution* (as by Duval and Wicklund, 1972), it approaches the topic of my concern.

Surely these theories have a grasp on important partial truths. Their prevalence may also indicate the bad morale of our times. I am reassured by analyses presented by Alker (1972) and by Stagner (1973), however, that the empirical case for the onion view is far from established. We are not compelled to believe that by our very nature we are nothing but stuff for the Button Molder.

I cannot think of a suitable image to symbolize what I call the *self as chooser*. Writers in the existential tradition who emphasize this version of selfhood, with its attendant ethical prescriptions of good faith and authenticity, emphatically reject the onion self as a failure of human potentiality, as indeed did Ibsen in originating the metaphor. I also place the psychologists of identity in this camp: Wheelis (1958), Lynd (1958), and Erikson (1959)—though Erikson's complex vision can hardly be pigeonholed. Identity becomes problematic only in the context of choice. The cacaphony of modern culture, the erosion of traditionally accepted values and frames of meaning, has made choice especially salient—and difficult —for contemporary Western man. Participating in this ambiance myself, I would classify under this heading (and also under that of mirror) my own attempts to formulate self-determination as a theoretical and empirical problem (Chapter Eight). The chooser model too is only a partial perspective on selfhood; in comparison with the onion version, it seeks to promote our self-understanding as actors capable of assuming human responsibilities rather than merely reflecting what may be a special pathology of an alienated mass society.

For American psychology in mid-century, motivation replaced the traditional nineteenth century chapter on the will. It remains a tangled, unsatisfactory chapter, with progress apparent mainly in our knowledge of some of its neurophysiological underpinnings. Certainly, we should not seek to resurrect the will as a faculty or organ of the mind. But we need to complement the conception of separate motives operating in conflict or in fusion—as bequeathed us by both the psychoanalytic and the behavioristic lines of thought and retained in current cognitive value-expectancy models—with a conception in which the path of *some* motivational processes leads to action via choice and commitment, that is, involves selfhood.

The *self as knower* is best represented in personality theory by the work of George Kelly (1955; also Maher, ed., 1969), a humanistic psychologist and clinician who construed ordinary people on the model of scientists like himself. The flavor of his humanism is conveyed by the following passage, which applies equally to the theories of the scientist and the constructs of the layman: "Theories are the thinking of men who seek freedom amid swirling events. The theories comprise prior assumptions about certain realms of these events. To the extent that the events may, from these prior assumptions, be construed, predicted, and their relative courses charted, men may exercise control, and gain freedom for themselves in the process" (Kelly, 1955, p. 22). This too is a partial perspective that highlights one human function. It meshes readily with the versions of self as mirror and as chooser—all cognitive in their emphasis.

Finally, the *vacuum self* is my pejorative way of labeling Skinner's (1971) stalwart refusal to deal with experiential or inferred processes in the "black box" behind the person's observable behaviors. Of course the vacuum self is a denial in principle of the need for a theory of self and of the propriety of any such theorizing. All the same, Bem (1967) has found it possible to say some interesting things from the vacuum perspective that bear upon self-attribution.

Simply displaying these disparate perspectives on selfhood seems to carry several implications, which I now try to make explicit. Two of them have already been touched upon.

First, how we interpret the ideal of self-actualization depends crucially on how we conceive of the self—on our assumptions about the essentials of personhood. Maslow (1954) to the contrary, the idea that we can leap the chasm between facts and values by identifying a single syndrome that empirically characterizes self-actualizing people seems to me a will-o'-the-wisp. Of course, what we regard as self-actualizing is a matter of the values that we are committed to. And as C. W. Morris (1942, 1956) has documented, mankind has created and elaborated upon a wide array of "varieties of human value," that require contrasting "paths of life" for their realization. Man would be diminished were there not a plenitude of modes of self-actualization.

Second, our competing theories of selfhood may be more limited to particular historical and cultural contexts than their proponents recognized—and may perhaps be more valid within those contexts than their critics admit. In at least some of its features, role theory—the onion self—may be a particularly good fit to selfhood in a bureaucratic mass society; Freudian psychoanalysis a good fit to selfhood in the middle class of Central Europe during the late Victorian—or Franz Josephan—era; and existentialism a good fit to the position of intellectuals and educated youth in the cultural flux and crisis of today. There is no reason for surprise or dismay if our versions of selfhood prove historically and culturally bounded. Man as a cultural-historical actor makes himself as he creates culture and history—he is also the product of culture and history. The very terms for conceptualizing the selfhood of an existentialist intellectual will surely differ from those that fit a traditional peasant villager, a medieval monk, a nomadic herdsman, a captain of industry, a small shopkeeper, a scientist, or a factory worker. If we want our theorizing about the self to have as much generality as possible, we will do well to take our own personal and historical perspectives into account as explicitly as we can.

Even if we discount these important matters of perspective, I think we will still find panhuman features of selfhood. Good candidates for some of them have been selectively emphasized in the several conceptions of selfhood just examined. One does not have to be a true believer in any particular psychoanalytic school to accept the evidence of dreams, myth, and ritual the world over, and of madness and creativity, as pointing to iceberg-like psychic realities that have usually been ignored in sociopsychological versions of self theory, to their impoverishment. One does not have to reject depth psychology to insist that its account of selfhood would be enriched by attention, following the lead of Mead and Piaget, to the emergence of mirror-like phenomena in the developing person's transactions with the social and physical world. We do invest ourselves in and define ourselves by segmental role identities that fit the onion model; our sense of integral identity, if we have it, is at least partly illusory, a matter of unsubstantiated attribution; some-times, no doubt, entirely so. We are knowers and choosers as we hold the mirror to self and world.

The comprehensive account of selfhood, toward which a humanistic psychology should strive, will therefore have to be syn-thetic (not eclectic), articulating insights and formulations that are stressed onesidedly in the competing perspectives that we have so hastily passed in review: mirror, iceberg, onion, chooser, and knower. As often the case with competing preemptive theories, the parable of the blind men and the elephant applies, but it is a more difficult problem to put together an adequate model of the creature that is Man.

PART III

•••••••••••••••••••••
•••••••••••••••••••••
•••••••••••••••••••••••

TOWARD PRIORITIES: PSYCHOLOGICAL AND PERSONAL

••••••••••••••••••••••
••••••••••••••••••••••
•••••••••••••••••••••

A theme shared by the first two chapters in this part, Chapters Eleven and Twelve, is that we live in unprecedented times that are fraught with peril for mankind but also ripe with opportunity if we can but learn to seize it. The medical metaphor of crisis fits aptly: These are times in which what we do can make or break our future. In such times, psychology can ill afford to remain smugly academic. But reflection is in order on how we can best contribute. The nature of our resources as psychologists must be taken into account as well as the seriousness of the problems that we face.

Chapter Eleven takes brief stock of these resources and examines some of the relatively commonplace ways in which psychologists are contributing and are expected to continue contributing to the solution of the interlocking set of critical human problems. The chapter's main emphasis, however, follows George Miller in stressing the importance of psychology that we "give away" to the general public, and takes issue with the assumptive images of man that psychologists have been purveying freely—the metapsychologies em-

191

bodied in humanistic psychology and in Skinnerian positivism. The chapter argues that a psychology that is both scientific and humanistic can best contribute to helping man to gain control of his destiny.

Chapter Twelve considers a range of ethical problems with which psychology is involved. A selective review of ethical considerations that bear upon psychologists' major roles, in research, service, teaching, and public policy, begins with brief attention to the ethical code adopted by the American Psychological Association governing the conduct of research with human participants. My main emphasis, however, is on a selected set of difficult political-ethical problems that lie before us, to which an ethically responsible social psychology might be expected to contribute. Attention is focused on the "contingent future" that depends upon our present policies and actions, in keeping with the view of human agency implicit throughout the volume.

Part Three ends with an autobiographical chapter (Chapter Thirteen) originally prepared for a collection intended to introduce undergraduates to the activities of psychologists. In spite of natural doubts occasioned by ambivalent reactions of vanity-modesty-privacy, I think the chapter belongs in this volume. The attempt to combine science and humanism in psychology is a personal adventure as well as a public venture. Because deep human hopes and concerns are intrinsically involved in the subject matter, the life of the psychologist is more complexly entangled with his work in this domain than it may be in segmental, objectified areas of inquiry. In retrospect, the route by which I arrived at my present pattern of commitments continually surprises me. In the present context, this partial autobiography (I have held back some areas of cherished privacy, some of embarrassed privacy) can be viewed either as data, as context for the understanding of ideas, or as a kind of indirect argumentum ad hominem. Caveat lector!

Chapter Eleven

••••••••••••••••••••••
••••••••••••••••••••••
••••••••••••••••••••••

PSYCHOLOGY AND NEW PRIORITIES

••••••••••••••••••••••
••••••••••••••••••••••
••••••••••••••••••••••

"*R*elevance" and "new priorities" have become clichés while we are still baffled by the novel human situation that has led to their being overworked. The need for new priorities is clear to most of us, and each of us has his own favorite diagnosis—and diagnostician. The land is full of prophets who write the best-sellers that our students read in paperback and with which we teachers have to catch up: Toffler's *Future Shock* (1970), Slater's *Pursuit of Loneliness* (1970), Reich's *Greening of America* (1970), Roszak's *Making of a Counter-Culture* (1969), and now the Club of Rome's *Limits to Growth* (Meadows, Meadows, Randers, and Behrens, 1972), among the more prominent. I begin by sketching my own diagnosis, not because it is at all original but as an explicit basis for considering the relevance of psychology.

We are just becoming aware of the crazy implications of the headlong trends of change in which we seem to be involved willy-nilly. My list of these trends includes sharply rising growth curves in speed of travel and communication, production of scientific and technical information, national armament and destructive capacity,

193

energy and resource consumption, environmental pollution, population (the "explosion"), and urbanization (the "population implosion"). Any long-run extrapolation of this package of trends points
to absurdity or disaster: this is the underlying point of the book
Limits to Growth which seems to me incontrovertible, whatever the
faults of the particular simulation model. Our historical situation is
entirely novel. That an increasing number of the educated population, especially the young, share this appraisal of the human situation is also novel and belies the claim that the recent tide of alienation and/or protest is simply another recurrent specimen of youth
protest movements (Feuer, 1969).

Another way of phrasing the novelty of our situation is that
we are at the threshold of the closing of the ultimate global frontiers,
as symbolized by our moon-walking astronauts. In American history,
the frontier was the great seducer that led us to take for granted a
wasteful and reckless relationship with our environment. It was also
the great safety valve for the discontents of civilization, an equalizer
and reservoir of opportunity. The frontier closes at a time when
there are enormous inequalities that entail tensions and pressures for
which the missing safety valve is badly needed.

The economic gap between the rich countries, particularly
the United States, and the poor ones grows ominous, leading even
such a concerned ecologist as Hardin (1971) to project, without
wincing, a picture of Fortress America. Within the United States,
the politically abortive War on Poverty left the gap between the
ethnic poor—black, Chicano, and native American—and the established middle class (and affluent working class) undiminished. As
the population implosion concentrates these problems of inequality
and injustice in the cities, we face another novel problem: We have
not had time to shape a viable urban culture by the usual slow
processes of trial and error. Rich or poor, most of us are newly urban. We are no more culturally adapted to metropolitan life than
we are to the closed frontier of Spaceship Earth (in Buckminster
Fuller's phrase) or to the accelerating pace of change catalyzed by
a seemingly autonomous technology.

*In this novel and challenging but also disorienting and fright-
ening world, we are showing signs of adaptive failure.* Toffler's sum-

mary term *future shock* is a good label for our predicament. The symptoms, not only in the United States but throughout the industrialized West, are matters of salient public concern: the spread of vandalism and violence; the epidemic of drugs; meaninglessness, hopelessness, and alienation, especially but not exclusively among youth; and new searchings for the lost religion—mysticism, occultism, a new irrationalism. In the United States, all the problems that we share with the rest of the modern world have been greatly complicated by the unspeakable tragedy and shame of the Vietnam war. We are not yet in any position to reckon the final toll in demoralization and in decline in the quality of public life. It is easy, thus, for most of us to agree that new priorities are in order. In this setting— one that seems to many of us to rule out business as usual—what can psychology contribute? Is psychology relevant?

The first answer that comes naturally to a psychologist would be, Of course it is. A science-profession concerned with human experience and behavior is bound to be relevant to problems of human maladaptiveness and failure and to the reestablishment of adaptive patterns. In some sense, we surely are relevant—*if* we are doing our jobs as psychologists. If we really believe, however, that business as usual is not good enough, even for psychologists, doubts arise.

In the areas of psychology that touch closely on human social problems, we find ourselves in disarray. In social psychology, I agree with Berkowitz (quoted in Smith, 1972) that our best scientists are floundering in the search for a viable paradigm. It is hard to tell the blind alleys from the salients of advance. Where, today, are the exciting frontiers of dissonance theory in which so much experimental ingenuity was invested? In clinical and community psychology, the Boulder consensus about training and practice and their relation to psychological science—the so-called scientist-professional model—has been shattered, but all that is clear is that we have not found our new directions. Social and political activists have been active—but it is not yet obvious that we have the goods to deliver, or effective ways of delivering them. The tendency toward fragmentation, as between scientists, humanists, professionals, and activists in our societies and departments, suggests that the foundations of our alliance as psychologists in a common discipline and profession are shaky. We have problems ourselves, as we aspire to face the problems of our country and world. We are part of the problem, when we would like to be part of the solution.

I have combined a rather dismal view of psychology with a foreboding picture of the world that we face. Yet if this were the entire story, I would not have the heart to tell it. There is no denying that the risks are great, the obstacles difficult, and our resources modest, but a rich array of sensible agendas that are worthy of our committed efforts is nevertheless available to psychologists.

In what follows, I comment selectively on roles for psychology in establishing and in implementing new priorities, taking note of familiar ways in which bread-and-butter psychology can be relevant. My major stress, however, follows the lead of George Miller (1969) who maintained in his presidential address to the American Psychological Association (APA) that our main contribution to human welfare may lie in the psychology that we "give away" to the general public. I argue that we have been giving away large consignments of metapsychology—of extrascientific preconceptions about man—and that the versions that we have displayed most prominently have been a dubious gift. If we can gain clarity and perhaps find new common ground about our metapsychological assumptions, our chance of relevance will be increased substantially.

Establishing New Priorities

In establishing new priorities, primarily a political task, psychologists contribute as both psychologists *and* citizens. Especially in democratic societies, but not only in democracies, new priorities, if they emerge, result from an interactive process. No scientific elite has the answers; psychology can at best aspire to contribute to them.

As citizens, psychologists are participants in the democratic process, and there will be times when *as* citizens they will feel obliged to take a public stand. So far as organized psychology, the APA, is concerned, we should be cautious and sparing in our direct intrusion in politics. That is not where our potential strength or our competence lies. Unless the kind of consensus exists that unhappily seems to emerge only during declared wars, to politicize our organization is also to divide it and to decrease its potentiality for effectiveness. But if one believes, as I do, that the political stakes are very high when they involve the survival and future of man, the traditional political neutrality of the academic sanctuary can no longer be taken for granted. Sometimes it will have to be strenuously defended; at other times risks must be taken that admittedly jeopardize the accustomed academic values.

Psychologists and other social scientists will have a distinctive technical contribution to the dialectic by which new priorities become established, in the development of the "social indicators" (Campbell and Converse, 1971) that are needed to appraise and highlight aspects of the quality of life.

Implementing New Priorities

Psychology (and that means psychologists) can contribute to achieving new social goals that emerge from politics in a number of ways: through well-grounded *theory,* through distinctive research *methods,* through the empiricism of *applied or problem-focused research,* and through *professional skills* of consultation and human service.

Kurt Lewin's old slogan "There is nothing so practical as a good theory" still applies. The trouble is that our theories of macroscopic social behavior are not good enough: we are still chasing a paradigm. Under these circumstances, as I have urged in another context (Smith, 1972), any research psychologist whose inner light convinces him that he is on the track of basic theoretical advance should act on that conviction free of guilt about ignoring urgent social problems, though I deplore the sterility of ritualistic research that is guided by fetishism for the trappings of science more than by any inner light. It would be a shame if the present drastic shift in priorities for the support of research starves the basic research from which new theories may emerge that are practical because they are good.

In developing methods for the evaluation of social programs —methods that can be applied more powerfully when our theory is good but do not essentially depend on theoretical insight—psychologists are among those at the forefront. Campbell (1969, 1971), in particular, has advertised the advantages of treating reforms as experiments in an "experimenting society" and has contributed notably toward developing the needed methods and strategies. But there is a wide spectrum of approaches to evaluation research, ranging from the modest and informal study to the ambitious field experiment, that may be appropriate to different circumstances.

A little evaluation can be a dangerous thing, politically as well as socially, as cases like the Westinghouse (1969) evaluation of Project Head Start illustrate all too clearly. Evaluation needs to be designed in the light of the political and social context in which the findings are to be used. Whether the approach be relatively informal or a full-dress field experiment, a high level of competence and integrity is required if evaluation is to be worth doing.

Graduate training, heavily focused on the methodology of laboratory experimentation and its accompanying statistics, is seriously out of date in equipping the coming generation of psychologists for roles in evaluation and policy research. The opportunity is here to take up the slack in the Ph.D. market, if we gird ourselves for the emerging roles.

In the ensuing years, more psychologists will surely be involved in applied, problem-focused research on such topics as population growth, environmental problems, aggression and hostility, and the emergence of ethnic pluralism. As we commit our hopes to these efforts, it behooves us to be modest in our expectations and claims. The limited success of psychological research on the large problems of war and peace should be cautionary. Our main contributions to date have been in the realm of ideas rather than of firm research findings: thus, Deutsch's (1969) suggestive experimental analysis of threat, trust, and bargaining; Osgood's (1962) GRIT concept for the gradual relaxation of international tensions; and R. K. White's (1968) stress on complementary processes of attribution as a psychological ingredient in international conflict.

Our programmatic efforts to create an environmental psychology still involve more promise than delivery: bright ideas are in short supply. As for population problems, Fawcett's (1973) roundup of psychological research on fertility at least demonstrates that many psychologists are finally at work in this important area—a state of affairs to which Henry David's APA Task Force has notably contributed (APA, 1972). But the demographers and sociologists are waiting in the wings for us to fall on our faces. Modesty is in order as we try, where others have failed, to understand the motivational determinants of fertility and to identify strategies for using this knowledge to limit population growth.

When problems become politically hot—and our emerging social priorities generate heat—the heat itself becomes a barrier to relevant research. I recall the hopes that I shared with Herbert Kelman that the Ibadan Conference on Social Psychology in Developing Countries (Smith, 1968d) might address itself to researchable issues concerning national and tribal identity. In Nigeria, just before the civil war, that was too hot a problem. Only Americans and expatriate Europeans appeared at the scheduled discussions; the Africans stayed away. The indignities to which Arthur Jensen has recently been subjected suggest that important aspects of our racial difficulties may be getting out of bounds for evidential inquiry. Ethical psychologists respect the sensitivities of the people touched by their research, but they also wish to keep the realm of rational discourse and evidential inquiry as broad as possible. When people become embattled, research as well as rationality goes by the board.

In sum, there is no more magic to problem-focused research than to basic research. Ideas and creativity are essential, a favorable environment helps, and outcomes are uncertain. Few if any of our social dilemmas lend themselves to massive research attacks on the scale of the Manhattan Project.

Psychologists are just beginning to give priority to acquiring new professional competences that are required by the new social priorities. In one major development, the community psychology movement has sought to extend psychological services beyond the traditional one-to-one relationship in consultation to agencies and institutions and in the training and supervision of new careerists and other front-line workers in the human services. But practice and training for practice lag behind the programmatic statements.

Another area where new priorities require new skills is that of interdisciplinary and interprofessional collaboration. Our past experience with interdisciplinary relationships has not been very good, but new patterns with which we have had little experience are in the offing. We are used to a situation in which clinical psychology competed with the other mental-health professions, especially psychiatry, for a common ecological niche, and, on the scientific side, in which psychology shared the overlapping territory of social behavior with the other social sciences, with differences between disciplines often a matter of distinctive and thus competitive vocabularies and traditions more than of clearly distinguishable subject matter or functionally specialized approaches. In contrast, the emerging focus on social problems may thrust psychologists into working relationships with physicians other than psychiatrists (Schofield, 1969), with engineers, biologists, architects and urban planners, experts in natural resources, and demographers—specialists in domains that have little overlap with psychology but include factors that are strategic for the formulation and solution of contemporary problems that also have psychological ingredients. If psychology is to make its potential contribution to coping with these problems, psychologists will have to learn to work with specialists in these widely different domains, and even to take the initiative in establishing such interdisciplinary relationships.

Competence in interdisciplinary collaboration in this new mode is needed if psychology is to play its potential role either in problem-focused research, in policy formation, or in ad hoc problem-solving. At present, the engineers seem to be trading heavily on their transferable systems approach to assume the role of conductor of the interdisciplinary orchestra. Psychology should not leave the tough and interesting problems to the engineers by default. Here, too, there are implications for our patterns of disciplinary graduate training.

There is much to do in research and in public practice, and in training for both, if psychology is to bring its resources to bear effectively on urgent priorities. Many of these efforts will be stillborn or fruitless, but some should pay off. These efforts will not pay off directly in solutions to social problems: the solutions must necessarily be forged in the political arena. But psychologists *are* capable of contributing much more than at present to the processes of social decision and to the climate of opinion in which decisions are made.

The Psychology We Give Away

A substantial influence on the climate of opinion is the kind of psychology that we "give away" to the general public. G. Miller (1969) proposed that this is likely to be a more important contribution to human welfare than directly focused activities such as those just reviewed. The ideas that we give away in our teaching, our popular writing, and our public participation enter the common culture and change the way in which human problems are defined and dealt with. In the past, we gave the public the IQ and the testing movement (as it seems to be turning out, an ambiguous gift: the "Naders" of ethnic protest are asking that it be recalled to remove hazardous defects). In collaboration with psychoanalysis and other social sciences, we have given away a causal, as distinguished from a punitive, approach to deviancy and problem behavior—surely a gift of enduring importance. We have played obligato while the Freudians bestowed the gift of attention to human irrationality. In collaboration with other social sciences, we have given away a primarily environmentalist interpretation of ethnic differences in achievement and ability, which certainly played a part in undermining the racist beliefs that traditionally supported racist practices. Not all these gifts have worked out as giver and recipient might have liked, but taken together, they have not been trivial.

The gifts that are most salient, however, are the positivistic behaviorism of B. F. Skinner (1971) and the humanistic psychology of the sensitivity training, growth, and encounter movement. More than any other recent developments in psychology, they have caught the public eye. These gifts are as potentially important as they are newsworthy, for they concern our basic assumptions about the nature of human nature. As such, they have fundamental implications for how everyone who shares them sets his priorities, defines his problems, and conducts his life. Their implications go beyond the agenda they set for psychological science and human service.

It is essential to understand that the gifts that I am talking about proffer metapsychologies—assumptive images of man (Chein, 1972) rather than established bodies of empirically established fact. Apart from their legitimate public interest, the metapsychologies comprised in Skinnerianism and in the humanistic psychologies identify the polar extremes of orientation that divide us internally as psychologists. As long as we psychologists define our problems from these antithetical standpoints, we are not likely to hear each other very clearly. In the form that these metapsychologies are being promulgated, they do not provide an adequate stance for psychology as we face society's new priorities—or for mankind at large insofar as its self-conception is influenced by psychology. Both are dangerous gifts.

Skinner's Gift. I have only respect for Skinnerian research and for much of Skinnerian technology. Any scientific psychology will have to find a place for Skinnerian findings about the properties of reinforcement schedules, and the public generally must be indebted to Skinner and his followers for their strategies of programmed learning and techniques of behavior modification. My complaint, rather, is with the metapsychology that Skinner persists in giving away. Skinner's book *Beyond Freedom and Dignity* (Skinner, 1971) is virtually pure metapsychology, 190 proof, and it appalls me.

Skinner's frontal assault on human freedom and dignity hinges on a *residual* notion of human autonomy as causing but uncaused. Of course, such a straw-man conception of freedom loses ground with each advance of deterministic (or even probabilistic) science. But it is not the view of freedom that is implicit in accounts of responsible human action, nor, as Chein (1972) has argued in sophisticated detail, is it required by a scientific psychology. It is as a rule giver, not as a working scientist, that Skinner makes his case against human freedom and dignity. A close reading of his book shows that whenever Skinner excludes feelings and intentions, beliefs, cognitive processes, or inferred dispositions of whatever kind from a causal account of man, he is voicing a dogmatic commitment, not reasoning from evidence. This smacks of bad philosophy rather than good science.

In Skinner's best-seller, the consequences of his dogmatic positivism are concealed from the reader since, via the common language, he opens the back door to most of commonsense psychology and much theoretical sophistication that has no legitimate place in his system, under the excuse of popularization. If we take his metapsychology seriously, it should exclude our taking his book seriously, since it is couched in the language of rational persuasive argument, not of proffered reinforcements. We avoid no shocks, are dealt out no M and Ms while reading it, but are treated with the dignity of rational human beings. Neither Skinner, the creative scientist and persuasive author, nor the intelligent (if gullible) reader finds a place in Skinner's system.

Skinner's strategies and tactics have an important place in the solution of human problems since reinforcement principles cover an important segment of the causal spectrum of human action. To control the behavior of corporations, those pseudopersons in the eyes of the law, Skinnerian principles may be especially appropriate. Corporations seem typically to be pigeon brained. Suitable legislation could alter the reinforcement contingencies of costs and profits to shape the behavior of modern industry toward acceptable environmental practices. As one moves along the scale from pigeons, to autistic or retarded children, to psychotics, to fully functioning human beings, however, reinforcement principles embrace a progressively smaller portion of what a psychologist needs to reckon with.

The gift of Skinnerian man (and of Skinner's *Walden Two* [1948] Utopia) is a bad one, I think, because according to the alternative model that seems to me more defensible, what people believe about themselves and others tends to be self-confirming. To the extent that we accept it, a metapsychological model with no place for human freedom and dignity adds warrant for manipulativeness and contributes to the tide of depersonalization. Human freedom is in fact decreased and human dignity suffers if we regard ourselves and others as programmed reactors, not as human actors. If we want to *be* human actors, we get bad priorities and directives from this metapsychology.

Gift of Humanistic Psychology. My objections to the Skinnerian metapsychology should place me squarely in the humanistic camp. Certainly I agree with the self-styled humanistic psychologists in regarding man as an actor, not a mechanism. But as I move in their direction, I find myself uncomfortable with my prospective bedfellows.

As I see it, the humanistic psychology of Rogers, Maslow, and May, of Esalen and encounter groups, has made a valid contribution to the reordering of human priorities. The ready reception that the movement has met (see Back, 1972, for a historical and critical account) surely indexes a kind of vitamin lack that the affluent strata and the young experience in American life, a slighting of

important human values in a technologically driven and bureau-
cratically organized society. The new search for existential meaning,
for interpersonal communion, and for sensory awareness and love, in
its various meanings, has valid human grounds. Enough is dehumanizing in modern life for us to welcome a movement that nudges
the pendulum in the opposite direction.

Yet as a movement that touches and overlaps the counterculture of hippies, drug freaks, occultists, and new mystics, the humanistic psychologies purvey a metapsychology that strains the coherence of psychology as a discipline and has its drawbacks as a gift to
the public, except as a compensatory corrective. From the standpoint of humanistic psychology's bearing on the priorities called for
by the present human situation, I have two serious objections. One
has to do with its misunderstanding of or disrespect for science, the
other with its romantic and, I think, misleading, one-sided conception of human nature.

The humanists' stress on immediate experience leads them
to neglect the canons of evidence and of coherent conceptualization.
Humanistic psychology is advanced as an alternative to scientific
psychology by some of its proponents and by many of its students.
To be sure, Maslow (1966) had a peculiar notion of Taoistic
science tailored to include it, but in his preoccupation with the creative impulse that scientists share with artists (legitimate as compen-
sation for the prevailing emphasis on uptight methodology), he
neglected the essential character of science as a generalizing, self-
critical, self-corrective, and, therefore, on the whole, cumulative
social enterprise (Smith, 1966b). The tough problems that man
faces, most of them arising in the interplay of human behavior and
science-based technology, will surely elude solution if we discard
what we have learned about the strategies of disciplined inquiry. We
can no more afford a psychology that is humanistic at the expense
of being scientific than we can afford one that is "scientific" at the
expense of being humanly irrelevant.

The humanistic psychologists hold, and I agree, that if
psychology claims relevance to the human situation and human experience, it must take account of man as a responsible actor in a
historical world substantially of his own creating. But a strong sub-
theme shared by Maslow (1968) and Rogers (1961) that is pre-

dominant in the growth center and encounter movement sees man's essence in a largely subliminal self that is actualized as people act and experience spontaneously, in tune with their guiding impulses. In Chapter Nine, I have tried to extract ideas from Maslow's doctrines of self-actualization that can be incorporated in a potentially scientific psychology of selfhood. The notion that "salvation" lies entirely in following the dictates of what immediately feels right and joyful is not one of them. This romantic view of salvation has value as a corrective for alienation or super ego-driven puritanism. From the standpoint of an older humanism, however, it ignores the cultural creations of ethics and politics as necessities for human fulfillment in a world of interdependence but also of irreducible conflict. It fans the flames of irrationalism and encourages the tide of privatism that engulfs many of the young as they give up hope about coping with society's problems in the political arenas of the real world.

The plain fact of the matter is that progress toward reordered priorities will require head as well as heart, planfulness and effortful problem-solving as well as spontaneity, sincerity, and openness. The here-and-now orientation of the heirs of Fritz Perls does release spontaneity and cut through hang-ups, but as Zimbardo's (1969) work suggests, a truncated time perspective in the here and now releases impulsivity for either good or evil. As a teacher of undergraduates, I find the here and now a barrier to educability.

Toward a Humanized Scientific Psychology

Of course, I am suggesting the urgency of creating a humanized scientific psychology with room for emergent human freedom and dignity—and of "giving it away" as fast as we create it. I am optimistic that such a metapsychology is within reach as a frame for our scientific efforts and as a set of warranted assumptions to guide us as we bring psychology to bear on social priorities. The pediatric psychiatrist Eisenberg (1972) struck the note that I am seeking in an address entitled "The *Human* Nature of Human Nature." After a preamble in which he stated that "understanding the nature of man and his works has become a precondition for the survival of our species, as well as for the enhancement of the flowering of human individuality (p. 123)," and after discussion mainly aimed against the superficial biologism of popular ethology (another questionable gift), Eisenberg went on to say: "Man is his own chief product. The infant who discovers that he can control the movements of his own fingers transforms himself from observer into actor. The child who masters reading unlocks the treasury of the world's heritage. The adolescent who insists upon a critical reexamination of conventional wisdom is making himself into an adult. And the adult whose concerns extend beyond family and beyond nation to mankind has become fully human (p. 127)."

Such a view of man as a self-transcending actor contrasts with Skinner's giveaway psychology as much as it does with the neo-instinct theories of the popular ethologists. I think that Eisenberg's view of man fits the facts much better than Skinner's Procrustean model. Theoretical and empirical contributions, including De Charms (1968) on self-conceptions as origin versus pawn, Rotter (1966) on internal versus external locus of control, and Steiner (1971) on perceived freedom, suggest that people's capacities for self-determination—for freedom and dignity, if you will—are accessible to causal analysis. The Piagetian tradition in developmental psychology and the Meadian tradition in interactionist social psychology provide rich intellectual resources for the humanized view of man.

The image of man that we purvey, the metapsychology that we give away, does make a difference. I return to Skinner for two examples. One concerns schooling. Skinner (1968) has highlighted the inefficiencies of prevailing teaching methods and has provided models for specifying desired behavioral outcomes and shaping the behavior of the trainee to achieve them. But note that I write *trainee*. Those aspects of schooling that can properly be called training stand much to gain from a Skinnerian analysis (even though reinforcement theory plays little role). What, however, of the traditional objectives of education, which remain valid though Skinner cannot talk articulately about them? If our hope is to educate responsible, wise citizens and leaders who are capable of choice, of enjoyment of a wide range of human experience, and of the *creation* of values, then our objectives are not specific trainable behaviors but emergent attributes of the person. As long as we are capable of conceiving such distinctively human goals, it is poor policy to rule them out by adopting an impoverished model of man.

Skinner's technocratic view of the design of cultures, which follows from his model, provides a second example. At the center of the web in Skinner's book *Walden Two* is the scientist-planner who arranges the contingencies. The rest of the life of the community is programmed; if wisely so, the hive will persist in contentment indefinitely. As in Huxley's book *Brave New World*, however, we unreconstructed "savages" may well reject this conception of human felicity. In contrast, a view of man that is respectful of human agency would consider the collaborative initiatives of the participant citizen as valuable in their own right. The ideal—so imperfectly realized—of government of the people, by the people, and for the people has not yet perished from the earth.

Skinner's Utopia, like all Utopias, avoids the question of how we get from here to there. The humanized version of man in society that I have been advocating at least casts in sharp focus our central political dilemma: how can we deal adequately with the difficult, interconnected, long-run problems that we noted (which requires planning, coordination, and seemingly centralization of authority, even on a global scale)` and at the same time enhance individual freedom and flexible interdependence? How can we move toward these difficult goals, starting from where we are in a world of autonomous nation-states with vastly unequal resources, and, in the United States, with an increasingly divided citizenry whose attachment to the national community has faltered? This dilemma is too big to be left to the politicians—or to the political scientists.

I should add that the metapsychological model of man that we espouse, whether we export it or not, also determines our beliefs about what is ethical in our relations as psychologists with the human "subjects" of our research—a matter about which psychologists are in strong and principled disagreement. The human use of human subjects that Kelman (1968) has called for takes higher priority if, as psychologists, we think of the human participants in our research as people, not as objects to be manipulated, in a relationship that may be collaborative, reciprocal, or exploitative.

Since the decline of traditional religion as a potent social force, modern man's collective self-concept has been in trouble, to which psychology has contributed in a small way. The frightening trends that throw us into future shock compound the difficulty. We are in danger of losing faith in man, as we are losing faith in our society. At the least, we psychologists should not be giving away dehumanized conceptions of man that aggravate the problem when these conceptions are in no way compelled by scientific data. More ambitiously, we should bend our efforts to develop a humanized science that is compatible with human freedom and dignity.

The traditional, hackneyed goals of scientific psychology—"the prediction and control of behavior"—appear in an interesting new light as we consider alternative models of man in the context of future shock. The stock in trade of the futurologist is the projection of trends—prediction. We are told that we must adapt to these trends, to learn to love them. But human survival, we are coming to realize, requires us to learn to shape and control the alternatives—unprecedented but humanly possible. If we fail to gain control of them, it looks as if we may be lost. If we succeed by means of centralized technocracy, as Skinner's model suggests, we may also be lost—lost as we have known ourselves in the great humanistic tradition of history, the arts, and literature, and in the little traditions of ordinary human life. If we manage to educate ourselves toward the collaborative political solution of these problems, guided by all the scientific resources that we can muster focused on enhancing people's capacity for intelligent choice, the result could indeed be a cultural mutation, the step to man that the polymath John Platt (1966) has heralded in much the same context of concerns.

Chapter Twelve

••••••••••••••••••••••
••••••••••••••••••••••
••••••••••••••••••••••

PSYCHOLOGY AND ETHICS

••••••••••••••••••••••
••••••••••••••••••••••
••••••••••••••••••••••

*F*or a psychologist who is not vested with the theological or the pastoral or the philosophical mantle to venture to talk to others about matters of ethics—rather than tending to the ethical problems in his own sphere of action— would seem to require some mixture of hubris and *chutzpah*. Since my claims as an ethical commentator are modest, I must set the context for my remarks so that my qualifications as a citizen-psychologist stand in for my obvious lack of special competence as a student of ethics.

Perhaps I can best serve this purpose and at the same time expose my stance on ethical issues if I begin with some brief comments on Diana Baumrind's excellent paper in the symposium for which this chapter was written.[1] Since I put in several years of hard

---

[1] The symposium focused especially on the code of "Ethical Principles in the Conduct of Research with Human Participants" adopted by the American Psychological Association (reproduced later in this chapter). In the symposium Diana Baumrind gave a searching critique of the code and its approach to ethical problems, objecting to the pragmatic compromises embodied in it. The initial part of this chapter is addressed to her criticism, but is intelligible without the context of her remarks.

209

intermittent work as a member of Stuart Cook's Committee on
Ethical Standards in Psychological Research that produced, after
numerous revisions, the American Psychological Association document that Ms. Baumrind has subjected to such searching criticism,
it is only fair to say that, *unless* I were allowed to say a few words
about her paper, I should find it hard to get on with the chapter.
Throughout the work of our committee, Ms. Baumrind was our
most articulate critic. Her paper for this symposium develops her
critical perspective in full explicitness, and I regard it as a substantial contribution to our shared objectives of raising the level of ethical sensitivity among psychologists and of improving the ethical level
of common practice in psychological and other social behavioral research with human participants.

Quite properly, Ms. Baumrind set herself a task different
from that of the committee. As a concerned, ethical individual, she
has worked out her own coherent ethical perspective, developed in
her paper in explicit relationship to the well-explored alternatives of
ethical philosophy. She has applied that perspective to current practice in psychological research and to the Cook Committee document,
letting the chips fall where they may. For an individual critic, this is
the strategy of choice—the way most likely to affect our actual ethical standards and behavior. Since I find both Ms. Baumrind's premises and conclusions attractive (though she is surer of her ground
than I can be of mine) I wish her well; I hope that as a result of
her educational efforts, the next version of the APA code and commentary moves in the direction of her recommendations.

The committee's appropriate task could not be the one that
Ms. Baumrind assigned herself. In the human world we live in,
ethical issues are indissolubly commingled with political and educational ones, at least whenever the stakes are socially important.
Divergent interests and value perspectives compete with one another
politically; and efforts to raise one another's sensitivity to ethical
considerations, to promote ethical awareness and ethical action as
we ourselves best understand it, are inherently educational. A
heterogeneous committee responsible to the membership of the
American Psychological Association necessarily encountered ethical
issues in a political and educational context unlike that of a single
concerned individual. Even if we on the committee had been able to

agree among one another on ethical first premises (although we educated one another and moved a considerable distance toward a consensual perspective, we could not claim *that*), we could not have imposed any singleminded view on the congeries of experimentalists and humanists and others that constitute American psychology—Festingerians; Skinnerians; Rogerians; students of test scores and stress, creativity, conformity, cognitive coding and conservation—virtually all of them persons of goodwill who regard their differing versions of the psychological enterprise as ethically legitimate.

The initial tack we took was empirical. We assembled, studied, and classified an enormous number of actual concrete instances of ethical issues, conflicts, and decisions in psychological research with human beings, collected in successive waves from questionnaires sent to fully two-thirds of the APA membership list. We also interviewed a large number of psychologists who occupied special positions that were likely to entail an informed and considered perspective on ethical issues in psychological research: for instance, department chairmen, journal editors, members of review panels, and writers on research ethics—including Ms. Baumrind. We eventually broadened our sights to include nonpsychologists whose perspectives we expected to be relevant to our task—especially in sociology and philosophy. All of this was in the attempt to assure that we addressed ourselves to real issues and that the perspectives that we brought to bear on the issues engaged and reflected the ethical thinking of the discipline, not just our personal principles or consciences.

From this foundation, we attempted to codify the principles that were involved in ethical decisions in the array of incidents before us. This was not an armchair job; it involved long and heated debates and reconsideration. Eventually we came forth with a draft version of principles and illustrative incidents that we published for reaction by the entire APA membership and sent to a large number of individuals, organizations, and local groups with a special invitation for comment. The reaction was explosive: it almost convinced us that our task was impossible. We were attacked from both flanks. (The comments were often accompanied by a few polite words recognizing our good intentions and hard work, and commiserating with our obvious failure.) On the one hand were those like Ms. Baumrind who saw our product as a charter for Machiavellianism, an excuse for unethical practice. On the other were as many who were sure that our proposed code would put scientific psychology out of business and who regarded the very publication of the draft document with its included incidents as an unmitigated disaster, perhaps even an unethical act. Still there were others who found our long document with its detailed, I was about to say Jesuitical, analysis simply unreadable.

Chastened, we went back to the drawing board for a thoroughgoing revision—this time better informed about the political and educational problems that were enmeshed with the ethical ones, and impressed by the *lack* of ethical consensus among honorable persons in our discipline. We became more explicit in our realization that we could not be lawgivers, only sensitizers. We succeeded in compressing the many subprinciples of our first draft into a decalogue of ten principles that phrased important ethical ideals. But, perforce, we eschewed the role of Moses. With important exceptions, we avoided the categorical "Thou shalt not . . . ", substituting, in effect, the more cautious "Thou shalt worry deeply, consult with others sincerely, and be prepared to justify thy decision to thy peers and the public if . . . "—if considerations of scientific gain seem to justify a limited compromise of ethical ideals. The Talmud or commentary that accompanied our decalogue discussed in detail the same ethical issues that had been dealt with in our previous, unacceptable document, taking into account the reactions that our earlier version received. Perhaps because the earlier version had aroused such anxiety and animosity, our revision proved widely acceptable when distributed for reaction to the entire membership. With only minor changes, it was adopted in December 1972 as an official document of the American Psychological Association (Ad Hoc Committee, 1973). (The full title is "Ethical Principles in the Conduct of Research with Human Participants.")

> The decision to undertake research should rest upon a considered judgment by the individual psychologist about how best to contribute to psychological science and to human welfare. The responsible psychologist weighs alternative directions in which personal energies and resources might be invested. Having made the decision to conduct research, psychologists

must carry out their investigations with respect for the people who participate and with concern for their dignity and welfare. The Principles that follow make explicit the investigator's ethical responsibilities toward participants over the course of research, from the initial decision to pursue a study to the steps necessary to protect the confidentiality of research data. These Principles should be interpreted in terms of the context provided in the complete document offered as a supplement to these Principles.

1. In planning a study the investigator has the personal responsibility to make a careful evaluation of its ethical acceptability, taking into account these Principles for research with human beings. To the extent that this appraisal, weighing scientific and humane values, suggests a deviation from any Principle, the investigator incurs an increasingly serious obligation to seek ethical advice and to observe more stringent safeguards to protect the rights of the human research participant.

2. Responsibility for the establishment and maintenance of acceptable ethical practice in research always remains with the individual investigator. The investigator is also responsible for the ethical treatment of research participants by collaborators, assistants, students, and employees, all of whom, however, incur parallel obligations.

3. Ethical practice requires the investigator to inform the participant of all features of the research that reasonably might be expected to influence willingness to participate and to explain all other aspects of the research about which the participant inquires. Failure to make full disclosure gives added emphasis to the investigator's responsibility to protect the welfare and dignity of the research participant.

4. Openness and honesty are essential characteristics of the relationship between investigator and research participant. When the methodological requirements of a study necessitate concealment or deception, the investigator is required to ensure the participant's understanding of the reasons for this action and to restore the quality of the relationship with the investigator.

5. Ethical research practice requires the investigator to respect the individual's freedom to decline to participate in research or to discontinue participation at any time. The obligation to protect this freedom requires special vigilance when the

investigator is in a position of power over the participant. The decision to limit this freedom increases the investigator's responsibility to protect the participant's dignity and welfare.

6. Ethically acceptable research begins with the establishment of a clear and fair agreement between the investigator and the research participant that clarifies the responsibilities of each. The investigator has the obligation to honor all promises and commitments included in that agreement.

7. The ethical investigator protects participants from physical and mental discomfort, harm, and danger. If the risk of such consequences exists, the investigator is required to inform the participant of that fact, secure consent before proceeding, and take all possible measures to minimize distress. A research procedure may not be used if it is likely to cause serious and lasting harm to participants.

8. After the data are collected, ethical practice requires the investigator to provide the participant with a full clarification of the nature of the study and to remove any misconceptions that may have arisen. Where scientific or humane values justify delaying or withholding information, the investigator acquires a special responsibility to assure that there are no damaging consequences for the participant.

9. Where research procedures may result in undesirable consequences for the participant, the investigator has the responsibility to detect and remove or correct these consequences, including, where relevant, long-term aftereffects.

10. Information obtained about the research participants during the course of an investigation is confidential. When the possibility exists that others may obtain access to such information, ethical research practice requires that this possibility, together with the plans for protecting confidentiality, be explained to the participants as a part of the procedure for obtaining informed consent.

If a camel is a horse designed by a committee, one can hardly expect such a document to be purely equine, given the process by which it was conceived, gestated, and brought to delivery. It a piece and a product of political and educational process in the realm of practical ethics, not an instantiation of abstract ethical philosophy. I believe that the wide participation of psychologists in its production has been an important venture in ethical education and that the document itself will prove helpful. But its principles and commentary do not solve the ethical problems of psychological research with human subjects; rather, they *display* these problems and put the responsibility for complex ethical decisions where it belongs, on the individual psychologist (who is obliged, of course, to take steps to counterbalance inevitable personal bias).

As in the venture of the Cook Committee, I am concerned in the remainder of this chapter with practical ethics for psychology and psychologists—ethics that are inextricably entangled with politics and education. I do not write from a technical philosophical position. The fact that in one of my roles I am an administrator as well as a psychologist leads me perforce to give substantial weight to the reality of conflict and to the necessity of compromise and accommodation if desirable human ends are to be realized. I readily grant Ms. Baumrind's point that an ethics of consensus can hardly be adequate philosophically, but I would stress, all the same, that the ethical consensus that *does* exist within a discipline or its components makes a big difference in how members of the discipline behave. Therefore I think it important to push consensus in the direction of humane values.

I share with Ms. Baumrind (but not with B. F. Skinner [1971]) a view of man as an actor, who at his best and in favorable situations is capable to an important degree—a crucial degree —of making responsible decisions. Such a view seems to me required if talk about ethics is to make any sense at all. I have stated this basic assumption carefully, recognizing that responsible decision is a difficult attainment, not a gift to be taken for granted. I also recognize that many positivistically inclined psychologists who do not conceive of man as a moral actor are nevertheless ethical in their own actions and favor good ethical practice. I only assert that the preconceptions of these positivists ill accord with the terms of ethical discourse.

I also share with Ms. Baumrind (but in this case not with Maslow [1971] and similarly inclined humanistic psychologists) a sense of the reality of evil, which in my nontheological sense means that human beings cannot be assumed *naturally* disposed to always know their own good and to act in terms of it, and that in following their own natural impulses they can quite readily do harm to one another. We do not live in the Garden of Eden that some humanistic psychologists, and many of the romantic young, would like to wish into reality. (Here I find common ground with another humanistic psychologist, May [1972].) Our biological programming by no means guarantees that if the plant of human potential is properly watered, good will come of it. So serious ethical and political issues inhere in human action. If we are to be true to our never fully realized potential for ethical responsibility—or if we are to survive as a unique species—we must draw on the funded experience of man's history as a conscious, self-critical being. We must also look ahead, as best we can, in our utterly novel situation in which we face ultimate limits to growth (Meadows and others, 1972), with the closing of the global frontier and our dawning realization that, willy-nilly, mankind shares a common fate.

In discussing future prospects and challenges with respect to psychology and ethics, I will approach the future, which is most uncertain, by way of the present, which we think we know. As for the present, I will review some ethical issues that arise in each of the four roles encompassing the activities of psychologists: research, human services, public policy, and teaching. The issues that I highlight are ones that I expect to be with us for at least the short-term future. I will then speculate about some issues for which I think we should be readying ourselves.

My comments on ethical issues connected with the psychologist's research role are brief, since the extensive report of the Cook Committee is readily available. I focus rather on what might be seen as an emerging new commandment, formulated by Ragner Rommetweit (1972) in a discussion of European philosophy of the social sciences: Thou shalt not seek knowledge about thine Brother that cannot be converted into self-insight in Him. This commandment sets supreme value upon the integrity of human beings as conscious actors and forbids the acquisition of knowledge that can be used manipulatively. While the statement is extreme and Rommetweit regards it as unworkable, it brings into focus an ethical concern that is widely shared. People can be treated as objects of research, in this view, only insofar as what is learned adds *directly* to their resources as subjects. (It is odd, isn't it, how the term *subject*

or *S* has reversed its connotation in the current psychological literature—so markedly that the Cook Committee replaced it with the
term *participant*. From a researcher's standpoint, the human subject *is* an object.)

One can agree wholeheartedly that it is desirable for psychological science to add to people's resources for self-understanding—and even argue that one of the basic justifications of the psychological enterprise is that collectively, in the long run, it tends
towards this end—while still regarding it as undesirable to forbid any
inquiry that cannot have this result. As Rommetweit points out, any
application of the principle to actual decisions about whether or not
to undertake particular research with particular people must pre-
suppose foreknowledge of what can be communicated to the subject
and understood by him. Such knowledge is often unavailable, and
one readily thinks of instances (for example, research with infants
or young children, or with the mentally retarded, or with the
severely disturbed) where what is learned from research cannot be
converted to self-insight yet is surely of value to those charged with
the subject's nurture or care, to the subject's benefit. The commandment as stated converts a positive ideal—the enchancement of the
other's humanity—to a negative proscription: research that does not
contribute directly toward achieving the ideal must not be undertaken. The former is acceptable, not the latter. A humane scientific
psychology needs more complex, less restrictive ethical guidance.

That, in Francis Bacon's phrase, "Knowledge is power"
gives rise to ethical dilemmas even in the human sciences where
knowledge is faulty and fragmentary. A generation disenchanted
with power for whom science and its rationalism have lost their
mystique finds it easy to think of placing whole areas of inquiry off
limits. Given Man's intrinsic dependence on knowledge, that would
be a sad mistake. We should rather focus our ethical concerns on
the humane and respectful treatment of the research participant and
on the uses to which our psychological knowledge is put—a matter
we next consider.

It is in regard to the applications of psychology to human
service—in regard to psychology as a profession— that ethical issues
were first considered explicitly in the discipline. The traditional ways
of maintaining ethical practice in American clinical psychology face

some perplexing challenges in a day of encounter groups and nude marathons, of wildly democratized psychotherapeutic fads in which a randomly drawn undergraduate may well turn out to fancy himself a Gestalt therapist. These problems may be practically troublesome, but they do not raise fundamental new ethical issues. They speak to what is evidently a deeply felt "vitamin lack," in some strata of contemporary society, that must somehow be assuaged whether under responsible professional auspices or not. Underlying the confusions that this cultural malaise entails are some serious ethical perplexities.

One perplexing situation arises from the crisis of confidence that clinical (and community) psychology shares with the other helping professions; the effectiveness of its kit-bag of helping techniques is questionable. Outcome research on psychotherapy is out of style because of its dismally unimpressive findings. To a greater extent than we like to admit, psychotherapy is not an applied science; with the important partial exception of the behavior therapies, it is an art little connected with established scientific principles and only weakly supported by evidence. So is its practice ethical? In an era sensitized to the perspective of cost/effectiveness, one has qualms.

Without wishing to provide a reassuring answer too quickly, I do not wish to leave the matter defined wholly in terms of cost/effectiveness. Human suffering, anxiety, self-doubt, estrangement, and guilt have always been with us. People need somewhere to turn for comfort, reassurance, and attentive communication; when their traditional recourses are unavailable or unsatisfying for whatever reason, new professions arise to fill the void. If the new professions "cure," so much the better; perhaps it may be enough that they *care*. The ethical problems of responsible and professionalized caring are well known to the priesthood. This function has been adopted from the priesthood by the mental-health professions.

But the priestly role is a risky model for a profession that also regards itself as an applied science. Another aspect of the role—the prescriptive one—seems to put the mental-health practitioner in a dubious ethical position. What is the good life, and how ought Man to live? Once the traditional and theological answers are no longer taken for granted and people are left on their own to make the choice, they may turn for guidance to the mental-health professional as a scientific guru. But science knows little more than "scientology" about these matters. Psychological science can develop contingent knowledge about the consequences and side effects of particular value choices or about the conditions under which particular values can best be realized. In uncovering covert processes such as rationalization or displacement, psychology can suggest more stringent criteria of authenticity than were previously common. In tracing the interconnections that tie together the various facets of a syndrome like authoritarianism, it can enrich or complicate the context of choice for child-rearing and living. But psychology can only describe and elaborate upon human ends, not prescribe them. Psychologists risk becoming inauthentic themselves if they accept in the name of science the guru image that is so readily projected upon them.

To view the helper's role in this way is to regard a *collaborative* relationship as ethically preferable to either a prescriptive or a manipulative one. The ideal is a coequal relationship between mutually respecting and caring persons. But it is intrinsic to helping relationships, be they parental or educational or therapeutic, that they are asymmetrical, not fully mutual. The helper is in at least some respects wiser or more experienced or more competent or less upset than the helped; that is why his help is sought. The practical ethics of helping requires the helper to plan and guide his part in the relationship in order to increase its mutuality, in order to enhance the competence of the helped to participate as an equal and make the choices that are right for him. Entrenched dependency is the pitfall. Skill in so conducting a relationship is not spontaneous; it is a discipline that must be learned. That does not mean that we need to condemn it as manipulative. Outright manipulation, as in the behavior therapies, seems warranted, under careful safeguards, to the extent that the helped are beyond the reach of collaboration (as in the case of autistic or mentally retarded children) or to the extent that the client can in effect be made a collaborator in the manipulative process (as in symptom-oriented behavior modification).

The service contexts that I have touched on center upon individual helping relationships, whereas the psychological professional who serves an institution—a school system, a hospital, an army, a business, or a prison—faces other problems to which we have become sensitive. Institutions have their own purposes, which may not coincide with the interests of each of their members or with those of other citizens. And institutions differ in their resources, their power to command the services of professional psychologists. When psychologists are available to industry and government but not to the poor, the situation is ethically troubling.

Applied psychologists who work in such institutional contexts must often steer their way through complex ethical shoals. We are aware of the opprobrium suffered by military psychology in the eyes of many during the Vietnam war. As individual psychologists, we naturally have different answers concerning the conditions under which it is ethical for us to participate. I see no general solution to the problem, but perhaps it may help to view it in a broader context. The ethical difficulties that confront applied psychology hinge on its embeddedness in inequity and injustice in the environing society. To the extent that psychologists as citizens can join effectively with their fellows in reducing inequities and correcting injustice, the ethical dilemmas entailed in their participation in established social institutions are mitigated. Here ethics and politics merge, and we come to the ethical problems associated with psychology's participation in public policy.

Currently, in the sphere of public policy, psychologists who are concerned with human welfare cannot help being so preoccupied with political frustration that ethical issues hardly come to the fore. As this is written in the second Nixon term, it is not a time when government listens to our voice as psychologists, and as citizens we are too few to be taken seriously as a political force. As we register to our dismay the drastic retrenchment in the national commitment to human welfare, our mood tends toward impotent rage—understandable, to be sure, but not impressive either ethically or politically.

In what we can hope is a political off-season, it is through our previous works, particularly the testing movement, that our influence is most felt. Here psychologists are involved in dilemmas that are at once ethical, political, and technical-scientific. A technology that we developed in the service of equal opportunity on the basis of individual merit is widely seen as a bulwark of the existing social hierarchy, a bastion of "institutional racism" that pins self-confirming labels on people, especially children and youth, in order to perpetuate the cleavage between haves and have-nots. (See Smith, 1969b.)

This is not the occasion to examine the tangled issues concerning the substantial element of truth in this charge, and the dubious alternatives that are available to the use of tests. I would like to suggest, however, that the testing movement in psychology has unwittingly contributed to the prevalence of a unidimensional scale of merit that is applied to both individuals and institutions. Johnny, I.Q. 140, is better than Mary, IQ 115, who is better than Juan, IQ 95. In the same vein, Harvard is better than Ohio State, which is better than Podunk State, which in turn is superior to Centerville Community College (see Jencks and Riesman, 1968). In this case, selectivity is the criterion. Widespread commitment to such a preemptive evaluative dimension is humanly damaging. Perversely, the more reliable and valid our assessment of people and of educational institutions, the more damaging is our assessment to the self-respect of those who fall short on a single scale and to respectful relations among people and institutions that know one another's placement on it. We are preserved—to the extent that we are—by the technical deficiencies of our evaluative procedures.

Psychologists would do well to be less defensive about the IQ, which is a practical index of real but limited value, and more concerned about contributing, if they can, to an evaluative perspective that balances a wider variety of loosely linked dimensions. Who, except narrow academics, would seriously argue that the IQ exhausts the range of valued human qualities, talents, and virtues, or, for that matter, that it predicts much besides *academic* performance —except crudely? Our rapid progress toward nearly universal higher education that is probably loosening the previous tight linkage between educational attainment and subsequent occupational prestige (with some attendant confusion and personal disappointment) gives us a first chance to loosen the stranglehold that the unidimensional evaluative schema has had upon us.

As I focus on psychology's teaching role, I am concerned not with the student-teacher relationship, which indeed has its ethical problems, but with psychological education in the broadest sense— with the psychology we give away to our students and to the public at large, which, G. A. Miller (1969) thinks, is our most substantial contribution to human welfare (see also Chapter Eleven). From an ethical perspective, the most important aspect of the psychology we give away is the image of man that we convey explicitly or implicitly, the assumptions about man's potentialities and limitations, and about his relations to the meaningful world of responsible human action and to the natural-science world of energy transformations and blind causation. The image of man that we purvey is important because man is a uniquely reflective creature. He has beliefs about himself as an individual and as a species; individually and collectively, he has knowledge about his past and expectations about his future. All these beliefs and expectations enter as determinants of human choice and human action. So it matters what Man believes about himself. Psychology as a vastly popular academic subject has much to say that bears upon man's self-perception. For a teaching psychologist (and in one way or another we are all teachers), a first step toward responsibility is to realize that most of what we have to say concerning our image of man is metapsychology—a matter of prior assumptions or stipulations that constitute the very terms of psychological fact—not of empirical, evidential, scientific conclusions. We need to examine the psychology that we are giving away from this perspective.

B. F. Skinner's (1971) best-seller *Beyond Freedom and Dignity* provides a convenient target for my ethical concerns since it caricatures the positivist tradition that has been the mainstream of American behavioristic psychology. As I noted in Chapter Eleven, the book is virtually pure metapsychology, 190 proof, and it appalls me in spite of my respect for Skinner's great scientific and technological contributions. As I argue in Chapter Eleven, Skinner's metapsychology that denies human freedom and dignity is stipulated a priori, not established empirically. And it has ethical consequences. As Arthur Koestler put it humorously over BBC (*The Listener*, February 22, 1973), "If you tell an American college undergraduate that he is nothing but an overgrown rat, obeying the same laws as the rat obeys in the Skinner box, he will grow into an overgrown rat and grow whiskers and bite your finger." Or, more seriously, he may be likely to assume a manipulative rather than mutual relationship to his fellows, and he may be less likely to attempt responsible ethical choice as he faces his own future and that of mankind. Cumulated across many undergraduates and the reading public, the likely effects can make an important difference. I am trying to counteract them!

Of course an alternative metapsychology is possible, more in accord with human experience than Skinner's and equally compatible with a scientific psychology—indeed more so, since it makes fewer dogmatic exclusions. I have tried to sketch its outlines in Chapters Nine through Eleven; Chein (1972) contributes substantially to its basis.

Having sampled some of the ethical problems that are raised by psychology's present roles, we can look toward the future. For the immediate future, the old weatherman's best prediction probably holds: tomorrow's weather will be like today's. As we look ahead, the grim question of whether there is to be any future at all arises. Between the Cassandra prophets of doom and our own natural tendency to bury our heads in the sand when faced with ominous uncertainty, it is particularly hard for us to think constructively about the distant future (see Smith, 1973b).

John Platt (1971), the polymath biophysicist-futurologist, has helped me to get my own head straight in thinking about the future by breaking it down into three segments: the *ballistic* future where a modified "weatherman's prediction" of projected trends holds because causal processes that are presently underway cannot feasibly be deflected; the conditional, *if-then* future in which predictions hinge intelligibly on human decisions and actions that are presently open to us; and the *guesswork* future of prophecy and of positive or negative Utopias, in which the chain of if-then contingencies becomes so complex that no deterministic or even probabilistic prediction can sensibly be made on an evidential basis. Obviously, these three futures are not fixed segments of the calendar: the cuts in time are placed differently for different aspects of different issues. In the small world of our personal lives, the three segments march in rapid sequence. In the larger world of public policy, the time scale is necessarily broader. Projections of future population growth, for example, are ballistically fixed within definable limits well into the twenty-first century by the present age-structure of the population and weatherman predictions about death rates.

(The relativity of Platt's distinction—its heuristic rather than substantive status—is illustrated by the fact that a genocidal nuclear world war could upset the ballistic prediction. If we entertain *this* contingency, the whole future slips into the if-then category.)

This tripartite schematization of the future helps us to organize our practical thinking in ways that are relevant to ethical issues. In the ballistic future, all we can do is adapt or adjust. Our coping, of course, can be more or less intelligent and effective, more or less attentive to the long-term context in which our options are open. The prophetic future is the terrain in which we can exercise our imaginations with Utopian thinking, which can be useful to us so long as it does not lull us into carelessness or scare us into desperation and apathy. Psychologists could contribute much more than they do to the formulation of human goals were they to project more Utopias that incorporate their psychological assumptions and knowledge. That Skinner (1948) set an example for us in his book *Walden Two* is to his great credit, whatever one thinks of his model of a desirable future (I don't like it).

It is the intermediate future of if-then contingency that deserves our closest attention, as the segment in which present human decision and action can settle our fates one way or another. It is here that contingent knowledge, the stock-in-trade of science, can be brought effectively to bear.

My complaint about much futurological speculation is that the projected trend lines that it is so fond of neglect the tripartite distinction. I am thinking of those familiar exponential curves that tend to end in absurdities—for instance, the entire American population belonging to the American Psychological Association by the turn of the century (that was E. G. Boring's straight-faced extrapolation) or the death of the human enterprise in a chaos of overpopulation, pollution, and the depletion of energy resources. These are prophecies rather than scientific if-then predictions. If we understand them in the ballistic mode, we are as likely to be paralyzed by them as mobilized to disconfirm them—clearly the intent of the more apocalyptic predictors (cf. Meadows and others, 1972) who see themselves as voicing a self-disconfirming prophecy on the model of predictions of traffic fatalities by the National Safety Council before each major holiday weekend.

One of my main complaints about the prevalent popular metapsychologies, positivistic *and* humanistic, that psychologists are most conspicuously giving away to the attentive public is that their models of man provide little place or support for man as a planner for this middle-range future in which our fates are decided by our present actions or inactions. I agree with Skinner (speaking at the University of Michigan, April 20, 1973) that man's fate is currently in the balance and that deliberate planning, using all the resources of science including scientific psychology, is needed if we are to avert catastrophe. But Skinner's positivistic metapsychology of environmental determinism—his input-output analysis with an empty organism (the black box)—leaves no place for the citizen-planner. Frazier, the benign technocrat of *Walden Two*, enters as a deus ex machina. So, for that matter, does Skinner himself; as I have noted, there is no place for the creative scientist in Skinner's system. Skinner's official model of man, if we believe in it, deprives us of the freedom and dignity and ethical responsibility that we need if we are to shape our conditional future toward human ends.

As for the popular versions of the humanistic psychology linked to the sensitivity-training and encounter-group movement (Back, 1972), they have been so preoccupied with reaction against the dehumanized rationality of positivistic science and technology that in the spirit of romantic escapism, they encourage people to neglect the real contingencies on which our future depends. Turning on to the here and now may be a therapeutic corrective that is useful to self-alienated victims of an unsuccessful search for meaning in modern life; in man's present predicament, however, it could spell disaster as an enduring posture. As an *alternative* culture, the so-called counterculture with which humanistic psychology resonates enriches the dimensions of modern life. As a *successor* culture, it could be suicidal.

A variety of challenges crowd into view, with ethical issues attached to each, if we focus on the intermediate future, which can be either menacing or promising depending upon what we decide to do about it. Thanks to the scientific fruit of the tree of knowledge, we can no longer blame our present and prospective misfortunes on acts of God. In most emerging problems, human behavior is the stumbling block. Such familiar problems, each potentially solvable in the contingent future but each an interlinked source of potential disaster, are the control of nuclear armaments, the world population crisis (especially acute in the impoverished "developing" countries), environmental pollution and the disruption of life-sustaining eco-systems, and—now coming into view—the energy crisis that results from the American habit, formed on the reckless frontier, of squandering resources. Because these problems have been the subject of much sophisticated discussion in the public domain, I bypass them in favor of three others where public attention and concern is needed. None of these problems can be considered the private property of psychology, yet each has its psychological ingredients. Difficult ethical issues lurk near the core of all three.

The first problem, one special to the United States and the industrialized countries, concerns the enormous disparities that exist between our sector of the world and the rest of it. From a ballistic perspective based on intransigent facts that can hardly be altered sufficiently to reverse current trends in the near future, these disparities are almost bound to increase. Do what we can, we of the haves are likely to face before long an overpopulated, underfed world of have-nots in which periodic famines rage and life deteriorates Calcutta-style. We cannot conceive of raising this impoverished world to anything like our present (and ever-expanding) rate of energy expenditure: even if an inexhaustable source of nuclear energy should become available, I am told that to do so might raise world temperatures to a level that would disrupt the supports of life as we know it. How are we to orient ourselves to such a world of poverty and extreme distress? The concept of Christian charity suggests an ethical solution—voluntarily beginning to reduce our expenditure of energy and resources, while assisting the poorer countries toward a level of material life equal to our own. Such a prospect in keeping with Christian ethics will probably seem to you (as it does to me) less likely than the prospect of our harden-ing our hearts, building a figurative Chinese Wall around our affluence, and attempting to brazen it out, perhaps with imperialist military ventures and the support of client nations. The prospect frightens me, as a civilization that is "saved" in such a way is surely lost. Our democratic freedoms would receive short shrift. Perhaps in the trauma of Vietnam and its sequelae we are experiencing a foretaste of what may befall us if we do not prevent such an outcome and choose a better fate for ourselves and others.

The basic ethical problem is one for all, not especially for psychology. The problem is acute for the official Catholic Church, given its stand on matters affecting the population issue. (See also Chapter Six.) For psychology, the present ethical relevance is a matter of priorities. Some of us can already see this potentially grim future looming on the horizon. The challenge, in our research, our teaching, and our representations with respect to public policy is to mobilize our commitment and our competence toward the pro-human alternative while there still is time. Optimists like myself by temperament can find some cause for taking heart in the small but increasing stream of psychological research on altruism (for example, Macaulay and Berkowitz, 1970), which has begun to compete with our long research preoccupation with hostility and aggression. Perhaps more important is the emergence of a new quasi-religious concern for Man's unity with Nature, in which the old American shibboleth "The bigger the better" is coming to be seen as the cultural aberration that it clearly is. Psychologists are only beginning to interest themselves in this potentially crucial change in our value system.

A related problem and challenge, which will be exacerbated by the pressures to be expected in connection with my first problem, concerns what we are to do, nationally and internationally, about the cultural identity and interdependence of peoples in a shrinking world. A generation ago when the old colonialism was collapsing, we could be more optimistic than seems possible today. As we presently look about us, we see a world of new and mutually hostile nationalisms, and a society of our own in which submerged groups (for example, the Indians, of whom very few white Americans had previously been aware as *people*) are clamoring, sometimes violently, for recognition and for equity that seems entirely beyond their grasp. The ethical, the political, and I should think also the aesthetic desirability of some kind of cultural pluralism seems increasingly obvious to many of us. Psychologists, fortunately no longer entirely white ones, are inevitably drawn into the fray. The issues become entangled with the problems of IQ and test technology, touched upon earlier, where some psychologists act as though they have a vested interest in the unidimensional evaluative schema that I earlier deplored.

For psychologists of whatever ethnic identity, the special ethical problem in this area seems to be how to maintain scientific and intellectual integrity and at the same time compassionate respect for people from other groups, in dealing with issues close to people's sense of identity and selfhood. There has been a good deal of understandable but regrettable foolishness perpetrated on all sides.

A third problem that strikes me as more serious than liberal psychologists realize, concerns authority, or law and order in the current debased phrasing. Hobbesian social philosophy becomes reinvented as Hobbesian features of disorder and violence rise to prominence in the contemporary social world. Psychologists on their part assume that they have laid the topic of authoritarianism to rest, when they merely have abandoned it. Little has been done with Erich Fromm's (1941) valuable early concept of rational authority. Much more than sociologists, psychologists seem intellectually and morally uncomfortable in this area of concern. Meanwhile, the steady long-term attrition of arbitrary traditional authority, be it in Church, State, school, or family, seems beyond question, as is the fact that the relative vacuum of legitimate authority that has ensued, together with the rapid rate of change in these matters, has left severe social problems in its wake. My fear is that unless we cope adequately with the basis of social order, drastic antidemocratic, antihuman solutions may be sought successfully by some and imposed upon the rest of us. While I far from bemoan the passing of traditional authority, I think it urgent to explore viable alternative patterns. The challenge to psychology is to contribute ideas and evidence to this venture. Again, the issues are difficult in part because they are value-laden and readily become ideological.

Perhaps you wonder why I did not put at the head of my list one popular topic that I have not mentioned: the control of the mind. The reason is that this topic does not strike me as a priority matter. I think a lot of poppycock has been said about it, from the false alarm about subliminal perception in the service of "hidden persuaders" (would that *all* advertising were subliminal!) to the furor about brainwashing (a drastic process that is real enough, but no Pavlovian mystery) to the proposal of drugs for pacifying aggressive Presidents and the dramatic report of electrically wired bulls programmed to stop a charge in their tracks. Humanists have taken inflated newspaper speculations at face value, and are running scared—when they leave off pooh-poohing scientific psychology.

As a citizen, I am concerned with the monopolistic control of the media by crass materialistic commercialism, and I am alarmed when the President appears to take lightly the traditional liberties of the press. I think the public is often manipulated, but the manipulation that I fear takes quite traditional forms, applied with more potent technical resources and perhaps with greater ruthlessness. In spite of the mystique encouraged by psychologists in the advertising industry, I do not think that psychology possesses much special knowledge that is readily converted into this kind of power. No psychologists were called upon to assist in Watergate.

We know enough about the incredible complexity of the electrochemical processes and related neural structures that somehow underlie human experience and action to make the wise guess that in the foreseeable future our advances in understanding this complexity will be gains in understanding in *principle* rather than in full actuality. I am not afraid, short of the remote future of positive or negative Utopias, that memories or compulsions will be implanted in us by wiring us up or feeding us RNA. Neither am I afraid that Skinner's strategies and tactics of behavior modification will be used to shape our actions according to somebody else's pleasure. In the limited but important spheres in which Skinner's strategies have been effective, I attribute their success as much to the general commonsense and psychological acumen of the applied Skinnerians as to the power of Skinnerian theory. My concern with Skinner is with the bemusing effect that his speculative metapsychology may have on us, not with the insidious power of his scientific theory and techniques.

Psychology that takes ethics seriously has a fundamental challenge to contribute in understanding and in professional practice to the development of people who, in interdependence, are capable of taking charge of their lives and shaping their future in accordance with emerging requirements of human nature. In this continuing interactive and dialectical process, human nature itself will be modified, as will the human situation. Short of disaster, there is no visible end to this process—no equivalent to the Marxist's classless society or to the traditional Catholic eschatology as a static goal. But I would not wish an end to history. I prefer the continually advancing contingent future that can be shaped by human action to Utopia or the Heavenly City.

I conclude this chapter on what should be the concern of the ethical psychologist by referring again to John Platt. After reviewing what he regarded as the extraordinary unprecedented threats that mankind faces, which also represent opportunities if man can overcome them, Platt (1966) suggests, in a grand image, that if we *somehow* surmount the crises that lie before us, our human nature will be qualitatively transformed, just as our primate forebears became protopeople through tool-using and speech and our savage ancestors were transformed to peasants and city dwellers by the invention of agriculture. Platt spoke of this hoped-for transformation as the step to man, the title of his book. Platt is not a psychologist, and he left the nature of the transformation that he heralded a mystery. For a psychology that is both humanistic *and* scientific, I can think of no greater challenge than to contribute to understanding and bringing about this step. Our future depends upon it.

Chapter Thirteen

• •
• •
• •

TOWARD HUMANIZING SOCIAL PSYCHOLOGY

• •
• •
• •

I am a social psychologist and have so regarded myself since long before I had any clear idea of what the field was really about. (My first secure sense of the shape of the field came only after I had been teaching it for a couple of years: the conventional course of lectures may be a deplorable mode of instructing the student, but it is an excellent way of educating the instructor!) But as a sample of one, I have been deviant, not at all typical of the field as it has developed over the past two decades.

In an era when laboratory experimentation was the main order of the day, I did none except as a student. My research has mainly involved interviewing and survey analysis, and even so, I cannot regard myself as primarily a research psychologist. I have taught undergraduate and graduate students for fully a quarter-century at Harvard, Vassar, N.Y.U., Berkeley, Chicago, and now the University of California at Santa Cruz, for some students a good teacher but I have never regarded myself as particularly skillful. I have been an editor of psychological journals. I have been an academic administrator as a department chairman at Vassar and Chicago, as a research institute director at Berkeley, and now at Santa Cruz as what would elsewhere be called a dean of social sciences—but throughout I seem to have retained much of the ambivalence toward administrative roles that is instilled by the research-oriented values of graduate education. I have invested a good deal of time in the affairs of the American Psychological Association and in participation in government advisory committees. I have maintained close intellectual relations with colleagues in clinical and developmental psychology and in the mental-health professions without ever being a mental-health professional, while, outside of psychology, I have also at one time or another been in good communication with political scientists, sociologists, and, to a lesser extent, anthropologists. All these activities, most of which are unrepresented in what follows, are part of my identity as a psychologist.

And, with increasing clarity, I have struggled to make sense of an emerging three-way commitment: to a psychology that seeks to come to grips with human experience (and is in that sense humanistic), to a psychology that broadly abides by the rules of the game of science as a public, self-critical, and therefore cumulative social enterprise, and to a psychology that bears helpfully on urgent social problems. These commitments have made me a generalist—at a time when specialization has been the trend. The things I have done that have pleased me most, in writing and teaching and consultation, have been efforts at conceptualizing, cutting across established boundaries, rather than the direct products of my research. To an extent greater than I sometimes like to admit, I have been an "armchair psychologist." If there is an Establishment in psychology and the social sciences, I am surely a member, but—I hope—something of a maverick. Since this disorderly and atypical career seems to have made more sense, after all, than I should have had any reason to expect, it may be useful to myself and to others to probe lightly into some of the circumstances behind the pattern of my commitments. My path was certainly not guided by much foresight and rational decision.

I came from an academic family with virtually no contacts in the business world, and when I began college at Reed in 1935, I took it for granted that I would go on to some professional or graduate school. Through my father, an English professor and dean at a then inconspicuous western state university, I knew more about Ph.D. training than about the launching of any other career. Following childhood interests in natural history—especially insects and fossils—I first saw myself as a biologist; brilliant teaching that I encountered in my freshman year lured me to history. But it was the professor, not the field that had attracted me, as I learned when as a sophomore I had to endure mediocre teaching in the subject. By then, I had begun to become seriously interested in psychology, for a tangle of reasons that I imagine is not uncommon.

There was a great teacher: William "Monty" Griffith, a huge, brilliant Rabelaisian figure of a man who, as I learned later, regarded himself as a failure because he could never bring himself to complete his doctoral dissertation but who was then very much a success in making psychology real and interesting to bright students. There was delayed adolescent confusion (I was two years young for my class), in which late bull sessions with friends, deepening involvement in student radicalism (Depression-style), and the fascination of Portland's small Bohemia for a very proper and socially timid small-town boy came to compete all too effectively with the automatic role of good student that I had previously played so successfully. (There was guilt and anxiety, too, about classes missed, work undone, and the resulting scholastic tailspin.) And there was a girl, a senior psychology major, my devotion to whom carried over to her field.

I could claim with some validity that psychology represented an ideal synthesis between the thesis of biology as my initial undergraduate interest and the antithesis of humanistic history and my family background, but I was mainly drawn to psychology because of preoccupation with my own inner problems. By then I was enrolled in premedical courses with a predictable goal of psychiatry in mind—but the academic collapse that cost me credit for half my junior year ruled out that possibility. In a mixture of shame at my failures, wry satisfaction at having salvaged something from what threatened utter disaster, and misgivings about the future, I transferred provisionally to Stanford the following summer. Yet I have always been grateful to Reed for letting me discover myself, however painfully. At that time it was not yet possible to read about Erik

Erikson's "identity crisis" that he added to the common vocabulary. Reed with its intensely intellectual nonconformity and its potent self-sustaining culture shared by students and faculty provided a high-risk, high-gain educational setting in which identity crises were provoked and new identities forged. For me, it was a kind of salvation, but of course I think so because the "I" that looks back was essentially formed there.

Stanford was a success, capturing me irrevocably for psychology, and I stayed on a second year for a master's degree, working with E. R. Hilgard on Kurt Lewin's new topic of "level of aspiration." (I also did a study of human learning with him: Hilgard and Smith, 1942. From Hilgard, then young and newly from Yale, I learned valuable lessons about digging for the *psychology* in a problem, as he liked to put it: getting behind the trappings of method and stylish topic to underlying questions that are psychologically interesting. An acute nose for psychological problems, as Hilgard has always had, is what differentiates good psychology from ritual busy-work, of which there is too much.) My interests in psychology, as I remember them, were not yet focused, but they turned toward a personality-social-clinical direction and both my gradually relaxing Marxism and my perennially hypersensitive social conscience inclined me to social psychology. For further doctoral training the excellent choice between Harvard and Yale was opened to me.

One of my Stanford mentors, C. P. Stone, with whom I had published a minor rat study (Stone and Smith, 1941), urged Harvard; another, Lewis Terman of the Stanford-Binet—the grand old man of the department—urged Yale, and my reading with Hilgard in Clark Hull's early system-building in behavior theory might well have tipped the balance that way. But I still possessed no real basis for intelligent choice, and, as I remember it, I made the decision for Harvard on the flimsiest and most nonrational of grounds —a girl who was going from Stanford to Radcliffe. Also my father's Harvard Ph.D. probably had more to do with my choice than I then liked to admit.

Only later did I realize how decisive the choice had been. The pre-war Harvard department was a collection of nonconsensual prima donnas: Gordon Allport, Henry Murray, and E. G. Boring, among those who became particularly important to me. Yale in contrast was the base for a vigorous consensual research group dominated by Clark Hull and his neobehavioristic learning theory. Had I gone to Yale, I would surely have been assimilated to the "Yale school" and launched upon a clear trajectory of research agenda. At Harvard, graduate students were exposed rather to a remarkably stimulating cafeteria of choice. Like Reed, my experience was high-risk, high-gain, as I look back on it. For many, the experience was disorienting. Fortunately, I came out more my own man.

Two major things happened on my route to psychology during my year and a quarter at Harvard, before I was drafted into the Army right after Pearl Harbor. The main focus of the first year was a horrendously demanding intensive-extensive "proseminar" chaired by Boring, the great historian of psychology, and involving several other faculty in their specialties. When this seminar had been capped off by the fearsome preliminary examinations for doctoral candidacy, I surely knew more book-and-journal psychology than I have ever since. My psychology was crammed in every which way, and I had to rely upon a cooperative unconscious to organize and digest the jumbled facts and theories—something that has always worked for me, though I gather it is generally not well-advised practice. Students today whose graduate training makes less heroic demands on them are missing something.

The second major happening was my first encounter with two memorably contrasting representatives of personalistic psychology, in the charismatic figures of Gordon Allport and Harry Murray. (Saul Rosenzweig (1970), whose Harvard years were somewhat earlier, has felicitously matched Murray, Allport, and Boring with the id, the ego, and the superego in Freudian psychoanalysis: the fit is uncanny.) At the Psychological Clinic, an old yellow clapboard building, where I had a cubbyhole and an intellectual-social home, Murray made the study of human fantasy seem a royal road to the understanding of hardly formulated human depths, and made us— students and junior colleagues—feel like bold explorers. Up in the chaster environment of Emerson Hall, Allport expounded on the unique individual and fended off as best he could the hostile forces of psychoanalysis (at the clinic) and of behaviorism and positivism (elsewhere in America). He taught us how to formulate and write life histories, and (in this, joining with Murray) involved us in trying to apply the slim resources of our psychology to the real-life problems of civilian morale in the tense period when a neutral America watched the ominous war in Europe. (Our seminar papers were supposedly circulated in Washington, and this impressed us.) Allport emanated an atmosphere of "high seriousness," of social and ethical concern.

In the fall of 1941 I sought to delay being drafted by joining the psychoanalyst Walter Langer in work on the psychological analysis of various countries for his brother William Langer, then head of the Office of the Coordinator of Information, the predecessor of the Office of Strategic Services (oss). I shudder to think of the callow hypotheses I promulgated about the character structure of the Finns and the Portuguese in this primitive attempt at culture and personality study from secondary sources in English. The gains were a U.S. Civil Service appointment form as junior psychoanalyst (which I still treasure as a souvenir) and remaining at Harvard in a time of high intensity, when refugees from Hitler's Europe—especially Frederick and Gertrud Wyatt who became my life-long friends —were bringing a complex and fascinating cosmopolitanism to an already heady atmosphere.

Six graduate students, including Silvan Tomkins, Robert Holt, John Harding, and myself, rented a slum house near Harvard for $5 a month apiece, where by our parties we probably hastened the breakup of the Psychology Department whose tensions we sought to dispell. But Pearl Harbor came, and I was drafted immediately after—the first in the department to leave for the war. Characteristically, I was afraid after my warm and enthusiastic send-off that I might be rejected and have to slink back.

As a reluctant draftee in a war in which virtually all of my generation believed, my first experience was unacademic but psychologically invaluable: immersal in the tough and colorful culture of young working-class Americans, mainly Texans. A good contrast from Harvard and from my whole previous life! Later on as an enlisted man and as an officer, I took a turn at several aspects of personnel psychology (which I never felt tempted to make my professional specialization); finally I joined the Chicago sociologist Samuel Stouffer's research branch of the Army's Information and Education Division, working first with the psychologist Carl Hovland on experimental studies of the impact of orientation films on soldier attitudes, and then on sample surveys of various aspects of soldier morale, attitudes, and motivation—in the United States, in the Mediterranean theater, and at the very end of the war, in the Pacific. The assignments entailed a lot of responsibility; the work was exciting and important. We were doing "relevant" research on topics such as the AWOL and desertion problem among the veteran troops on the Italian front, psychoneurotic breakdown in combat, officer-enlistee and Negro-white relations in the Army, and the venereal-disease problem among troops in Italy and in the Philippines. When after four years I got out of the Army as expeditiously as I could, I was really a psychologist, not just a student of psychology.

My fate in the Army had fortunately involved me with three major strands in the making of social psychology as it emerged vigorously in the post-war years. One major strand, survey research and analysis as heavily influenced by Stouffer's group, has been a primary source of data for public-opinion research and descriptive social psychology, especially as practiced by sociologists. And the experimental study of persuasive communication and attitude change —another major strand carried forward in the 1950s in a highly productive program at Yale led by Carl Hovland—was a direct outgrowth of the experimental Army studies in which I had served a brief apprenticeship. I add Hovland to my list of great teachers for his uncommon gifts in Socratic questioning, which brought clarity out of obscurity in the design and interpretation of research, but he did not succeed in making me an experimentalist. I returned to go to Harvard, not to Yale.

The third major strand was symbolic interactionist sociology as represented by Arnold Rose, later an eminent sociologist but then incongruously an enlisted man teamed up with me, an officer, in North Africa and Italy. From our running dyadic seminar for more than a year, with the kind of close association that a joint overseas assignment can develop, I "internalized" much of the Chicago tradition of social psychology as a specialty of sociology, not psychology. I also was reeducated in the social psychology of prejudice and race relations, vicariously benefitting from Arnold's just completed experience as junior collaborator in Myrdal's classic study of the Negro in America (1944). His prickly sensitivity to unjust status differ-

ences, which I felt uncomfortably on many occasions, very likely
saved me from overidentifying with my officer role.

When I was finally released from the Army at the end of
1945, I was filled with a sense of urgency to disclose the "real"
story that our inquiries and my privileged vantage points made me
want to tell: my old romantic radicalism was still there. I had the
idea of writing a popular muckraking book that would draw upon
our Army data, and, after getting my Ph.D. degree, of going into
applied sociopsychological research, maybe under the auspices of a
labor union. The point of decision, when I had to decide whether or
not I was selling out, occurred very shortly when Stouffer invited me
to join with several other former members of the research branch,
civilian and military, in the reanalysis and write-up of the vast data
from our studies for the Army—an undertaking that eventually led
to the publication of the books entitled *The American Soldier* (Stouffer and others, 1949). This was a realistic opportunity and challenge
that made more sense to me than embarking on journalistic crusad-
ing, for which I had no preparation or models.

My chapters in *The American Soldier* composed my first
major piece of published work. I analyzed the pertinent survey data
and wrote about the motivations that sustained troops in ground
combat, about the special situation and the attitudes of soldiers assigned to the "rear echelon," and about the predicament of green
replacement troops assigned to veteran combat units. This was good
practice in the older style of survey analysis, using the IBM counter-
sorter with decks of the already efficient punch cards of coded data.
I still like the direct contact with emerging findings and the flexibility of analytic tactics with the counter-sorter better than the distance
imposed by the efficiently programmed analyses that are required
by modern electronic computers. (I pay tribute to Stouffer's mastery
of this research style in my biography of him in the *International
Encyclopedia of the Social Sciences* (1968f).

Later on, I experienced a mixture of pride and chagrin when
Merton and Kitt (1950) reinterpreted my analysis of the replacement data in their classic paper setting forth a generalized theory of
"reference groups," groups to which one refers comparatively in appraising one's own situation. I had presented and discussed some
provocative comparisons, drawn from surveys of divisions that were

waiting in England for the invasion of Normandy: combat veteran infantrymen in veteran divisions that had seen various amounts of previous action in the Mediterranean theater versus green replacements in the same veteran divisions versus infantrymen in completely inexperienced divisions. In their willingness for combat, for example, the replacements stood squarely between the veterans and the inexperienced troops (the veterans being by far the most unwilling); in their attitudes toward their noncommissioned officers replacements were by far the most favorable; while in their confidence in their own ability as combat leaders they were the lowest. I had offered a commonsense interpretation of this mixed pattern of morale indicators. In some respects, the replacements partially took over the attitudes of the veterans around them (thus their intermediate willingness for combat). But they also reacted to the fact that their new outfit and its members had the prestige of combat experience (thus, their more favorable attitudes toward their noncoms, and also their pride in their companies). Yet in comparison, the replacements naturally felt ill equipped to take the lead in combat. Well and good, but I later envied the imagination of Merton and Kitt who were able to cast these ad hoc interpretations into the coherent, generalized framework of reference-group theory, as following from the fact that veterans were a positive reference group for the replacement soldiers in the veteran divisions. The general account is elegant and simpler.

Back, then, to Harvard, where I had only the dissertation to finish to attain the Ph.D. that I still coveted. I opted to take my degree in the new Department of Social Relations, a pioneering interdisciplinary venture joining social and clinical psychology with sociology and cultural anthropology, rather than in psychology from the now residual department. During the summer of 1946 when I was winding up my writing for *The American Soldier,* I was also working with Jerome Bruner and Robert White whom I had known as junior faculty in the pre-war department. We were planning a research project on the personal dynamics of public opinion that was being generated in the new Laboratory of Social Relations at Harvard, which Stouffer was shortly to join as director. I returned to Harvard in the fall, technically still a graduate student but also project director of our joint study at the clinic. Being the director helped a lot: at that point the petty indignities of the unadulterated graduate-student role would have been hard to take.

The study on which I embarked with Bruner and White was the investigation of personal determinants of attitudes toward Russia that, some years later, resulted in our book entitled *Opinions and Personality* (1956). (Conflicted delay in getting things written up has always been one of my problems.) Bruner at that time was still primarily identified with social psychology and public-opinion research; he was just at the point of initiating his studies of personal factors in perception that formed the bridge to his later brilliant career in cognitive research and developmental psychology. White was a careful and original psychologist of personality in the broadly psychoanalytic tradition, who combined many of Murray's interests with something of Allport's disciplined and well-controlled style. This set of commitments naturally inclined him to the reformulation of Freudian ego psychology, as in his subsequent work on competence (White, 1959), which influenced my thinking profoundly.

Our study had two major components. At the clinic, a large group of investigators studied the personalities and the opinions of Russia of ten adult men, in repeated sessions over several months that included intensive interviews, projective tests, and tests of cognitive abilities. The senior members of the investigating group met as a diagnostic council to arrive judgmentally at a formulation of each case. They followed research traditions established at the clinic by Murray in his classic book *Explorations in Personality* (1938), which I had read at Stanford, and which had added to the appeal of Harvard to me. Each member of the council was responsible for administering at least one procedure and for formulating at least one case. Among the subjects of our study, my special responsibilities were the Communist "Hilary Sullivan" (Smith, Bruner, and White, 1956, pp. 154–188) and the accountant "Clarence Clark" (pp. 203–210). Significantly in terms of my persisting later interests, I selected for my part of the data collection a two-hour semistructured recorded interview on personal values and religious sentiments. According to our plan, the intensive clinic study was to provide us with the kind of rich qualitative data about people's opinions in the full context of their personalities that would enable us to refine and elaborate our understanding of the kinds of relationships obtained between opinions and personality. (We understood that the qualitative study of ten cases could not provide solid evidence to test particular hypotheses.)

The second major component of the study, an interview survey of a representative sample of adults conducted in Springfield, Massachusetts, provided quantitative evidence for some of the relationships that we thought we discerned in the earlier phases of the clinical investigation. I analyzed these data for my doctoral dissertation (1947a, 1947b).

It was the intensive, qualitative study that most fascinated me. I discovered that an interviewer who listens intently can learn a great deal about matters that are important in people's lives—by asking them as well as reading between the lines—and that what one learns in such a direct, essentially *collaborative* relationship may be even more important, or at least more relevant to understanding what the other person thinks and does, than the beguiling results of inferences from projective techniques and fantasy characteristic of depth psychology. I also learned that the psychopathologically slanted Freudian account of defense mechanisms gives an impoverished and distorted picture of the versatile adaptive strategies that "normal" people use in coping with their life situations.

Before the book *Opinions and Personality* took final form, the three of us had many discussions in which we progressively reformulated the natural history of opinioning in order to arrive at our final data. We discerned among the ten men whom we had come to know so well three basic modes in which their opinions bore on their processes of adaptation: *object appraisal,* in which the opinion or attitude reflects a sizing up of the relevance of its object for the person's values, interests, and concerns; *social adjustment* (I would now—see Chapter Three—prefer to speak of *mediation of self-other relations*), in which holding or expressing an opinion promotes a desired relationship with other people or a desired identity; and *externalization and ego defense,* in which the person's opinions serve as a kind of projection screen for the expression or working out of one or another of his unacknowledged inner problems. The same pie could have been cut along somewhat different lines, as it has been by other theorists (for example, Katz and Stotland, 1959), but I think our clinical, qualitative study established quite definitively that theories are simplistic and inadequate if they try to reduce the psychological basis of opinions to some single process, such as projection or displacement. Our theory also provides an explicit place (in object appraisal) for the kind of rational processes that seem essential for human dignity but had been too much ignored by clinical and social psychologists—a theme to which I returned much later (see Chapter Three).

If I had become a psychologist by the time I left the Army, I was duly anointed when I gained the doctorate in the fall of 1947, after writing my thesis in six harried weeks (also the first six weeks of my marriage: my wife suffered cooperatively!) in preparation for my initial academic job on the Harvard faculty. I have written in some detail about my becoming a psychologist because these steps should have particular meaning for students of psychology. The career vicissitudes that followed are of less interest here, and I will therefore touch on only a few salient turning points as I review the development of my thinking and activities as a psychologist.

One turning point came early. As a new assistant professor in the Harvard Department of Social Relations, I thrived on the interdisciplinary atmosphere and on my new responsibilities in teaching; I was also in charge of the tutorial system and honors program. But I found myself increasingly paralyzed by sensed pressures to get on with significant independent research. I was reacting most unconstructively to the competitive atmosphere of the department. Hoping that I would find therapeutic help as well as useful training, I embarked with Dr. Helen Tartakoff in a personal psychoanalysis as a research candidate at the Boston Psychoanalytic Institute. (I was able to use the G.I. Bill.) But a year of analysis left me even closer to sheer panic. When the opportunity arose, I fled to an excellent teaching and administrative position at Vassar.

In retrospect, I have never regretted doing so. I do not believe that, had I stayed with my analysis, I could have worked through the special reasons for my hang-up at Harvard in time to deal with the very real problems it created. At that juncture, flight on relatively good terms was the best thing I could do. I often think back on this experience as I see young untenured faculty reacting in equally nonconstructive ways to the pressures of appraisal and "publish or perish." I also gained substantially from my very incomplete exposure to psychoanalysis, although I did not stay with it long enough for it to help me solve my problems. I learned experientially something of what psychoanalysis is about—which has given me a sense of perspective in my occasional reading in the psychoanalytic literature. I also learned a good deal about myself, posing issues for an informal self-analytic agenda that I have practiced from time to time ever since as they have taken new forms in my changing life situation.

I became well acquainted with the ghosts of my childhood relations with my parents, who now appeared to me loving but in essential respects very inadequate and conflicted people who held inordinately high and narrow aspirations for me. In knowing and living with myself I prefer to recognize these ghosts even if I cannot exorcise them. I saw clearly how some of my still recurring problems in my psychologist work-role—sometimes paralyzing self-doubt and guilt that have blocked me from research and writing in ways reminiscent of my debacle at Reed—also had roots in my vulnerable past as a fat, unathletic boy two years younger than my classmates—an inadequate player of the male role all the way through adolescence. Perhaps most important, I painfully discovered the great gulf between intellectualized "insight" and real personality change, the absence of any magic, black or white, in psychotherapy. (But I continue to value insight for its own sake—being who I am, I could not do otherwise.)

Another formative experience, after three years at Vassar, was four years on the staff of the Social Science Research Council in New York, ending in 1956. In staffing several research planning committees of the council that dealt with matters as diverse as cross-cultural research on socialization and the problems of foreign students, I performed an honorable but largely unsung role of midwife to other people's research ideas—and learned how to write creative minutes, a knack that has since served me in good stead. I was also cultivating the interdisciplinary perspectives sown in my associations in the Army and in the Harvard Department of Social Relations. Of course, I ran the risk of losing my standing and identity as a psychologist, as I very likely would have had I not at the same time been serving as editor of a major journal in personality and social psychology—another midwife role, but one more honored.

Because I was still young, and felt younger and short of self-confidence, I was more tolerant then than I could be now of the careful and meticulous busywork that predominated in my journal as in most others. While I favored substantial reports, I was necessarily chary about imposing my own private standards on the journal over which I held temporary stewardship. As an editor for the American Psychological Association, I was perforce partly a bureaucratic functionary. The kind of personal editorial leadership exercised by Gordon Allport in an earlier era of the same journal was no longer possible, or so it seemed to me, and that was a loss.

Meanwhile, my family was growing, and the children (three boys and a girl engendered before my wife and I became aware of the population crisis) became for me, an only child, a crucial part of my education as a psychologist—though a part that I felt strongly should be kept human rather than scientific. While I was still teaching at Harvard, I remember encountering Gordon Allport on the steps of Emerson Hall with the exultant news of the birth of our first son, and my dismayed exasperation at his benediction, "Marvelous, Brewster. Every psychologist should have a child and a dog." In fact, my wife and I bought a Siamese cat to "raise by the book," as an only half-facetious strategy for working out what we feared might be our propensity for raising our child by a book. (We developed a very neurotic cat, and found it the highest praise when friends said that the young Smiths did not act like psychologists' children.) Spock was useful, all the same, mainly for his reassurances and medical advice. Mostly we felt that our child-rearing techniques were heavily determined by who we were, what was possible for us. If we did not apply much psychology in raising our children, I could still learn from them much that books and journals can never provide, and from self-discovery in the new role of grown-up that children impose upon their parents. A whole set of assumptions about language learning was ruled out for me by our first child's first word—when at maybe eighteen months he pointed up, sharing delight, to say "Moon!"

In 1955 circumstances cast me as an officer of the Joint Commission on Mental Illness and Health, a venture established by act of Congress that, in spite of being enmired in the baroque interprofessional politics of medicine, psychiatry, and psychology, eventually produced an important report (Joint Commission, 1961) that helped shift the emphasis from the grim state hospital to community-based approaches in the treatment of severe psychological disturbance. In working with task forces and committees of the Joint Commission, I discovered that my perspectives and sense of strategy as a social psychologist were useful and sometimes influential. I also began to get the hang of the difficult and complex interrelations between scientific information, professional expertise, and the political maneuver and accommodation that are involved in any attempt by psychologists or allied scientists and professionals to influence public policy. This is a matter with which I have since become increasingly concerned as I have learned that translating knowledge into social policy is inherently a matter of politics, with the most frustrating difficulties lying more often on the political side rather than in lack of knowledge.

Involvement with the Joint Commission confirmed my interest in the theoretical, pragmatic, and value-related issues caught up in the slogan-term "mental health," which had already been stimulated by Marie Jahoda (1950), my friend and associate at New York University where I held an academic position in psychology from 1956 to 1959. She was a psychoanalytically oriented social psychologist somewhat senior to me, and her interests and social values appealed to me as much like my own. Bad mental health is readily identified in insanity or psychosis (though whether it is helpfully regarded as a disease in the conventional medical sense is quite another matter.) But what do we mean by positive mental health? I participated in Jahoda's attempt to deal with this problem for the Joint Commission by chairing a seminar of thoughtful humanists, psychoanalysts, and psychologists who discussed early drafts of her report (Jahoda, 1958).

Under this stimulation, my own thinking underwent various changes, coming to a temporary equilibrium with the view, expressed in a paper (1961) that has often been reprinted, that mental health is not a scientific concept but rather a chapter heading for whatever *evaluative* perspective on human personality we may want to develop. (See Chapter Seven.) Just what value standards we decide to employ—whether adjustment, or autonomy, or realism, or capacity for love or work or untroubled sleep—is a matter of

ethics or politics, not of science, although psychology can contribute
to the consideration of value choices by developing evidence about
the causal antecedents of particular valued qualities and about the
consequences for other values of giving priority to any particular
value. A major line of sociopsychological research, for example, has
brought to light a number of generally unwelcome features that
seem to be linked empirically to the values that characterize the law
and order mentality. Because of their knowledge, people who know
about the authoritarian personality—with its ethnocentrism, punitive moralism, and black-and-white categorical thinking—are likely
to make value choices that are different. They may raise their children differently and favor different social policies than they would
otherwise.

     This way of thinking about mental health may be con-
sidered armchair psychology, but it represents, I think, a potentially useful kind of psychological contribution. For one thing, the
approach punctures the claims of those who would use the language
of mental health to give a scientific aura to the promotion of their
own values, be they conformist or nonconformist. It helps to immu-
nize us against the pretensions of the mental-health professions as a
new priesthood. The next turning point for me was no armchair
matter, as it plunged me into field research in West Africa and
brought me, once again, into a close collaborative relationship with
the subjects of my research—the first contingent of Peace Corps
volunteers to go overseas. The results of the research, and of the research experience, changed my thinking about a number of matters,
including mental health.

     By this time I was at the University of California at Berkeley,
where I remained for nine years. In 1961, Berkeley had a summer
training program for Peace Corps volunteers who were to go to
Ghana as secondary school teachers, although only a minority of the
group of fifty who entered training had had previous teaching experience. The clinical-counseling psychologist Nicholas Hobbs, a
good friend and fellow veteran of Joint Commission battles, had
taken on the important task of directing selection for the Peace
Corps. He persuaded me to coordinate selection during training at
Berkeley, holding out the carrot that I could include experimental
test procedures and would be encouraged to negotiate with the

Peace Corps for a follow-up study in Ghana to evaluate measures used to predict effective performance overseas. I leaped at the opportunity, not only because I too had caught the excitement of the Kennedy Peace Corps in its early days but because I saw it as a chance to flesh out my thinking about positive mental health by the close study of able young people as they coped with a novel and challenging situation. I was also fascinated by the opportunity to see the new Africa firsthand.

In this first round of Peace Corps selection-in-training, primary reliance was placed on psychiatric appraisal interviews, from which it was possible to extract reasonably satisfactory ratings of mental health as evaluated by competent psychiatrists. For research purposes, I included pencil-and-paper measures of authoritarianism on the expectation that the supposed ethnocentrism and psychological rigidity of the volunteers who were high in this trait might be expected to interfere with their performance in Ghana. The third research measure, which was almost more than the traffic would bear given the volunteers' growing impatience with "shrinks," was developed by a brilliant graduate student, Raphael Ezekiel, who was working with me at the time on the topic of time perspective—people's views of their personal future as a potential determinant of what they do with their present lives. Ezekiel had the volunteers write brief mock autobiographies, first imagining what their lives would be like five years hence, and then sketching their lives at age forty. With the help of other graduate students as independent judges, Ezekiel rated each essay for the degree of differentiation with which the future was presented, the extent to which the future state of affairs was produced by the person himself, and the presumed amount of persistent effort that would be required to bring it about. These ratings also yielded a summary score. We salted these data away as the volunteers left for Africa and their new roles.

I had been developing preliminary plans for a quasi-experimental comparison of schools with and without Peace Corps teachers, but the Peace Corps administration and I had the good sense to get me to Ghana at Christmastime, 1961–1962, to scout things out before firming up my research plans. (The family suffered, but we had a special Christmas when I got back.) Not untypical of field research, I found that I had a serious job before me in gaining the confidence of the local Peace Corps representative, of suspicious government officials, and, most important, of the volunteers themselves, a number of whom I accompanied on a holiday jaunt to northern Ghana. It immediately became clear that I could expect nothing from questionnaires but would probably receive full cooperation in the authentic give-and-take of informal interviews. It also became clear that any kind of controlled comparison would be politically and practically infeasible. Should I go ahead or call the study off? I decided that a full description of the volunteers' experience would be worthwhile, and, properly analyzed, it could be related usefully to our data collected during the training period. By then I had been captivated by developing Ghana and much attracted by the volunteers whom I had begun to know as friends, so it would have taken a real disaster to make me drop the study.

The next two summers, Ezekiel and I returned to Ghana armed with an interview guide based on what I had learned on my first visit and made long tape-recorded interviews with the volunteers at their schools all over the country. We stayed with the volunteers, and we often did the interviewing late at night by flashlight or lantern to the accompaniment of rain-forest noises. The better part of another year was required to develop and apply an appropriate systematic and quantitative way of analyzing the information in the rich interview protocols as they were typed up—in this I had the help of an able group of graduate students. There had been thrills aplenty in our arduous field work, but the pay-off was delayed until the results of our analyses began to pour forth in computer printout. They were internally coherent; they made sense! And, by then, we had the uncommon advantage of knowing each "unit" in our statistics as a person. (More than a decade later, I am still in touch with most of them—a sign that I had managed to achieve a kind of collaborative relationship in psychological research that I wish could be more prevalent.)

Ezekiel (1968) and I (1966a) have written at length elsewhere about what we found, which shattered some stereotypes about the "good" Peace Corps volunteer and was useful, or ought to have been, to the Peace Corps administration. Here I wish to discuss only how our findings affected my thinking about positive mental health. As it turned out, the psychiatric ratings showed no overall relationship to any of the indices of Peace Corps performance that we developed. Neither did authoritarianism (Smith, 1965a), perhaps because none of the volunteers was extremely authoritarian and perhaps also because of the markedly authoritarian atmosphere that turned out to be characteristic of Ghanaian education. Ezekiel's measure based on the mock autobiographies was the only procedure in our battery that helped to predict performance.

The results made sense in terms of what we thought we had seen in our direct contact with the volunteers in their job setting. Freedom from anxiety or minor neurotic symptoms had seemed quite irrelevant: a good many of the most effective volunteers had their quirks; some of the least effective were shockingly "healthy." What made the critical difference among these generally able and well-intentioned young people was whether or not the volunteer engaged himself fully with the task, investing himself to the hilt with unreserved commitment. The volunteers who really invested themselves took the difficulties they encountered in stride as challenges; they might have been frustrated but could not conceive of being bored. Other, less effective volunteers were more reactive than active; they tended to devote their energies more to adjusting to their situations than to making the most of their opportunities. We found it impossible to classify the "real" difficulty of the situations faced by the different volunteers, since the same objective situation that was frustrating to one sort of volunteer was attractive and challenging to the other. Ezekiel's autobiography ratings seemed to have tapped, though crudely enough, the volunteer's predisposition to cope actively with his life situation, with full self-commitment. The aspect of psychological effectiveness on which we focused appeared to me closely akin to R. W. White's (1959) concept of competence as being based upon intrinsic motivation to have effects on one's environment.

Back to the armchair, or rather to the conference and seminar. In the mid-1960s I was a member of the Social Science Research Council Committee on Socialization and Social Structure, which had the mission of setting new directions for research on how society fits people to play its roles. Mainly, perhaps, we were educating each other, in a stimulating group that contained three sociologists and three psychologists (John Clausen, Orville Brim, Alex

Inkeles, Eleanor Maccoby, Ronald Lippitt, and I), all good friends
who had met together over a period of years. For the committee, I
took on the task of examining leads in the research literature that
would help us understand the conditions that promote the development of competence, in White's sense of motivationally based psychological effectiveness (which also seemed to me to be the sense
indicated by my Peace Corps study—a rather far cry from my earlier
relativism about values and positive mental health [Smith, 1961]).
I had the help of a specially convened research conference that
brought together specialists from a variety of fields. In the resulting
essay (1968c) that I eventually produced after much travail, I proposed that the motivational core of competence is a cluster of attitudes toward the self as potent, efficacious, and worthy of being
taken seriously by self and others. (See Chapter Seven).

Such a cluster of attitudes sets a kind of self-fulfilling prophecy in operation. In the favorable case, the individual has the confidence to seize upon opportunities as they present themselves. He
tries. He therefore acquires the knowledge and skills that make successes more probable—which in turn lend warrant to his sense of
efficacy. In the unfavorable case, he dare not hope, he does not try
—and he is caught in a vicious circle that is likely to mire him in
incompetence, fatalism, and failure. It seemed to me that many of
our practical dilemmas of race, poverty, and education, among
others, amount essentially to questions of how to foster the benign
sort of circular process and how to break into and disrupt or re-
direct the vicious sort. We have clues, very promising ones, but
not answers.

With many gaps and omissions, I have brought the story to
my present concerns. I am still preoccupied with formulating more
clearly the psychological problems underlying the general human
problem of how man may become more fully the master of his fate,
an origin of social causation in De Charms' (1968) sense rather
than a pawn. If psychology can be made to address this issue coherently and dependably, the field should become unmistakably
relevant—to the problems of our time as well as to student interests.

From the standpoint of this problem, traditional behavioristic psychology misses the mark by leaving no place for human freedom. It reduces man to a reactor, not an actor, and treats as illusion

or paradox the free will that makes choice and planning and responsibility intelligible. Classical psychoanalysis does little better in its unbalanced emphasis on unconscious determination. Both aspire, however, to a scientific causal analysis. In deploring the human irrelevance of behaviorism and psychoanalysis, the so-called humanistic psychologies of the "third force" (Rogers and Maslow and May) have tended at times to throw out the scientific baby with the bathwater. They accept human agency and choice as a philosophical postulate, but their respect for the integrity of human experience often leads them into disrespect for the canons of science as a self-critical cumulative enterprise.

I find grounds for hope for a more humanly cogent personality and social psychology in indications from several quarters that we are at the threshold of becoming able to treat self-determination—free will if you like—not as an illusion or paradox, not as a metaphysical assumption outside the grasp of science, but as an empirical variable on which some people rank higher than others, a variable that is linked to causes and consequences that can be understood and turned to the enhancement of human freedom. In my teaching, I refer to Claude Brown's *Manchild in the Promised Land* (1965) to illustrate the variable that I am talking about. The "case of Claude" can be read as a dramatic story of the process by which the Harlem street boy gradually gains the conviction, utterly foreign to him at the beginning, that he can be the architect of his own life, not the pawn of a cruel fate. In the special case of this variable, the conviction is father of the fact. A psychology that can deal with it empirically and systematically is both humanistic *and* scientific. It is to nudging psychology along in this direction that I should now particularly like to contribute.

This sort of ambition one realizes only partially and imperfectly in actuality, though it can infuse a good many of one's activities and make them personally meaningful. On a more realistic scale, there are a number of ways in which a problem-focused social psychologist, a generalist with interdisciplinary inclinations, can contribute toward headway on the serious problems that present an unprecedented challenge to mankind, an ominous package of threats that is also the basis for high hopes if we can only gird ourselves to face them.

Psychologists can draw upon their knowledge of research and theory to help reformulate the practical problems involved in war, population, pollution, and the rest—putting them in new terms that may make them amenable to solution. (We know from psychological research on thinking and problem-solving that putting the question correctly is more than half the battle.) Psychologists can undertake applied research that is directly focused on pieces of the urgent problems. Psychologists can use their technical research skills in carefully evaluating social programs, so that we can learn from our mistakes as well as from our successes. For my own part, I have been trying to bring my sociopsychological training to bear on pieces of the social problems that involve student protest and campus conflict, racist prejudice, and the population explosion.

As a social psychologist, I see a good deal of potential gain and little loss from taking much of our sense of direction from such human problems, so long as we approach them with a persistent effort to understand and to generalize. There are fields of inquiry— especially the physical sciences—where a heavy focus on applied work is stultifying. In psychology, such areas in which a strong intrinsic line of development dictates the required next steps are not so common. I think of aspects of physiological psychology, developmental psycholinguistics, and the study of cognitive growth and then begin to falter. In much of psychology, especially social psychology, the lines of development are far less clear. There have been obvious gains in the sophistication of our questions, in our awareness of relevant variables, and in the level of our information, but fad and fashion in concepts and methods have too often substituted for (and mimicked) the missing lines of development inherent in the emerging structure of the science at its frontier. Wherever this state of affairs prevails, it seems to me, advance in generalizable understanding is just as likely to come as a by-product of work at urgent human and social problems as it is from a head-on assault in "basic" research. (I do not at all criticize psychologists whose strong sense of scientific direction turns them away from social problems: we need more of them. For every psychologist who feels such an imperative sense of direction, however, there must unfortunately be dozens of others looking for a suitable topic for a publishable study: hence our cluttered and so often unrewarding journals.)

Since all important social problems entail conflicts of important human interests, in principle none of them could be *solved* by psychological—or social scientific—knowledge even if we were vastly more knowledgeable than we are. Any and all solutions will necessarily be forged in the political arena, with scientific knowledge only one ingredient in the process. But it can become a much more important ingredient than it characteristically has been. I therefore think it a fitting close to this account of one social psychologist's activities, as well as to this volume, to invoke a favorite maxim of Kurt Lewin—a major influence on me as on all social psychologists of my generation, although I had little direct contact with him: "There is nothing as practical as a good theory."

I close with Lewin's maxim and example because it seems to me that the most difficult challenge of teaching today is to awaken students to the *relevance* of hard intellectual and scientific work and of persistent commitment to the difficult process of democratic politics. The unprecedented problems of the present world, the unsettling rapidity of change, have made many of us lose our bearings. The credentials of science, like those of the Establishment, are suspect. A new romanticism has arisen in reaction to the previous suppression of feeling and human value, to the aridity of technological society, and to the intractability of human problems. Yet the problems before us require head as well as heart if they are to be solved. Since so many of them hinge on human cussedness, the challenge to a humane yet scientific social psychology is immense.

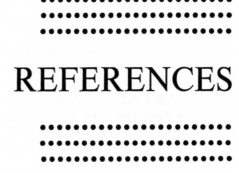

REFERENCES

ABELSON, R. P., ARONSON, E., MC GUIRE, W. J., NEWCOMB, T. M., ROSEN-
BERG, M. J., AND TANNENBAUM, P. H. (Eds.) *Theories of Cognitive Consistency: A Sourcebook.* Chicago: Rand McNally, 1968.

Ad Hoc Committee on Ethical Standards in Psychological Research. *Ethical Principles in the Conduct of Research with Human Participants.* Washington, D.C.: American Psychological Association, 1973.

ADORNO, T. W., FRENKEL-BRUNSWIK, E., LEVINSON, D. J., AND SANFORD, R. N. *The Authoritarian Personality.* New York: Harper and Row, 1950.

ALKER, H. "Is Personality Situationally Specific or Intrapsychically Consistent?" *Journal of Personality,* 1972, *40,* 1–16.

ALLPORT, F. H. *Institutional Behavior: Essays Toward a Reinterpretation of Contemporary Social Organization.* Chapel Hill: University of North Carolina Press, 1933.

ALLPORT, G. W. "The Ego in Contemporary Psychology." *Psychological Review,* 1943, *50,* 451–478.

ALLPORT, G. W. "Attitudes." In C. Murchison (Ed.), *A Handbook of Social Psychology.* Worcester, Mass.: Clark University Press, 1935. Reprinted in G. W. Allport, *The Nature of Personality.* Reading, Mass.: Addison-Wesley, 1950.

ALLPORT, G. W. *Becoming: Basic Considerations for a Psychology of Personality.* New Haven, Conn.: Yale University Press, 1955.

ALLPORT, G. W. *Pattern and Growth in Personality.* New York: Holt, Rinehart, and Winston, 1961.

ALMOND, G. A., AND VERBA, S. *The Civic Culture: Political Attitudes and Democracy in Five Nations.* Princeton, N.J.: Princeton University Press, 1963.

American Psychological Association Task Force on Psychology, Family Planning and Population Policy. "Population and Family Planning: Growing Involvement of Psychologists." *American Psychologist,* 1972, *27,* 27–30.

ANGYAL, A. *Foundations for a Science of Personality.* New York: Commonwealth Fund, 1941.

ASCH, S. E. *Social Psychology.* Englewood Cliffs, N. J.: Prentice-Hall, 1952.

ASTIN, A. W. "New Evidence on Campus Unrest: 1969–70." *Educational Record,* winter 1971, 41–46.

BACK, K. *Beyond Words: The Story of Sensitivity Training and the Encounter Movement.* New York: Russell Sage, 1972.

BALDWIN, J. M. *Social and Ethical Interpretations in Mental Development.* New York: Macmillan, 1913.

BAYER, A. E., AND ASTIN, A. W. "Violence and Disruption on the U.S. Campus: 1968–69." *Educational Record,* fall 1969, 337–350.

BAYER, A. E., AND ASTIN, A. W. "Campus Unrest, 1970–71: Was It Really All That Quiet?" *Educational Record,* fall 1971, 301–313.

BAYER, A. E., ASTIN, A. W., AND BARUCH, R. F. "Social Issues and Protest Activity: Recent Student Trends." *ACE Research Reports,* 1970, *5*(2).

BECKER, G. M., AND MC CLINTOCK, C. G. "Value: Behavioral Decision Theory." *Annual Review of Psychology,* 1967, *18,* 239–286.

BEM, D. J. "Self-Perception: An Alternative Interpretation of Cognitive Dissonance Phenomena." *Psychological Review,* 1967, *74,* 183–200.

BERELSON, B. "Democratic Theory and Public Opinion." *Public Opinion Quarterly,* 1952, *16,* 313–330.

BETTELHEIM, B. "Obsolete Youth." *Encounter,* 1969, *23*(3), 29–42.

BLOCK, J. H. *The Child-Rearing Practices Report.* Berkeley, Calif.: University of California Institute of Human Development, 1965. (Mimeographed.)

BLOCK, J. H. "Generational Continuity and Discontinuity in the Understanding of Societal Rejection." *Journal of Personality and Social Psychology,* 1972, *22,* 333–345.

BLOCK, J. H., HAAN, N., AND SMITH, M. B. "Socialization Correlates of Student Activism." *Journal of Social Issues,* 1969, *25*(4), 143–177.

BLOS, P. *On Adolescence: A Psychoanalytic Interpretation.* New York: Free Press, 1962.

BOWER, E. M. "Primary Prevention of Mental and Emotional Disorders. A Conceptual Framework and Action Possibilities." *American Journal of Orthopsychiatry,* 1963, *33,* 832–848.

BRAUNGART, R. G. "SDS and YAF: Backgrounds of Student Political Activists." Paper presented to the American Sociological Association, August 1966.

BREHM, J. W. *A Theory of Psychological Reactance.* New York: Academic, 1966.

BROWN, C. *Manchild in the Promised Land.* New York: Macmillan, 1965.

CALLAHAN, D. *Ethics and Population Limitation: An occasional paper of the Population Council.* New York: The Population Council, 1971. (Distributed by Key Book Service, Inc., 425 Asylum St., Bridgeport, Connecticut 06610)

CAMPBELL, A., AND CONVERSE, P. E. (Eds.) *The Human Meaning of Social Change.* New York: Russell Sage, 1971.

CAMPBELL, A., CONVERSE, P. E., MILLER, W. E., AND STOKES, D. E. *The American Voter.* New York: Wiley, 1960.

CAMPBELL, D. T. "Social Attitudes and Other Acquired Behavioral Dispositions." In S. Koch (Ed.), *Psychology: A Study of a Science.* Vol. 6. New York: McGraw-Hill, 1963.

CAMPBELL, D. T. "Reforms as Experiments." *American Psychologist,* 1969, *24,* 409–429.

CAMPBELL, D. T. "Methods for the Experimenting Society." Distinguished Scientific Contribution Award Address presented at the meeting of the American Psychological Association, Washington, D.C., September, 1971.

"Campus '65." *Newsweek,* Mar. 22, 1965, p. 54.

CHEIN, I. *The Science of Behavior and the Image of Man.* New York: Basic Books, 1972.

CHILMAN, C. S. *Growing Up Poor: An Over-View and Analysis of Child-Rearing and Family Life Patterns Associated with Poverty.* Washington, D.C.: Division of Research, Welfare Administration, U.S. Department of Health, Education, and Welfare, 1966.

CHILMAN, C. S. "Probable Social and Psychological Consequences of an

American Population Policy Aimed at the Two-Child Family." *Annals of the New York Academy of Science,* 1970, *175,* 868–879.

CHRISTIE, R. "Eysenck's Treatment of the Personality of Communists." *Psychological Bulletin,* 1956, *53,* 411–430.

CHRISTIE, R., AND GEIS, F. L. (Eds.) *Studies in Machiavellianism.* New York: Academic, 1970.

CLAUSEN, J. A. "Values, Norms, and the Health Called 'Mental': Purposes and Feasibility of Assessment." In S. B. Sells (Ed.), *The Definition and Measurement of Mental Health.* U.S. Public Health Service Publication No. 1873. Washington, D.C.: National Center for Health Statistics, 1968.

COLEMAN, J. S. *The Adolescent Society: The Social Life of the Teenager and Impact on Education.* New York: Free Press, 1961.

COLEMAN, J. S. *Adolescents and the Schools.* New York: Basic Books, 1965.

COLLINS, B. E. "Four Separate Components of the Rotter I-E Scale: Belief in a Difficult World, A Just World, a Predictable World, and a Politically Responsive World." *Journal of Personality and Social Psychology,* in press.

CONVERSE, P. E. "The Nature of Belief Systems in Mass Publics." In D. Apter (Ed.), *Ideology and Discontent.* New York: Free Press, 1964.

CONVERSE, P. E., AND SCHUMANN, H. " 'Silent Majorities' and the Vietnam War." *Scientific American,* 1970, *222,* 17–25.

COOLEY, C. H. *Human Nature and The Social Order.* New York: Scribner, 1902.

CROWE, B. L. "The Tragedy of the Commons Revisited." *Science,* 1969, *166,* 1103–1107.

DARITY, W. A. "Family Planning and the Black Community." Paper presented at the meeting of the American Psychological Association, Washington, D.C., Sept. 4, 1971.

DAVIS, K. "Population Policy: Will Current Programs Succeed?" *Science,* 1967, *158,* 730–739.

DAVIS, K., AND BLAKE, J. "Social Structure and Fertility: An Analytical Framework." *Economic Development and Cultural Change,* 1956, *4,* 211–235.

DE CHARMS, R. *Personal Causation: The Internal Affective Determinants of Behavior.* New York: Academic, 1968.

DEUTSCH, M. "Socially Relevant Science: Reflections on Some Studies of Interpersonal Conflict." *American Psychologist,* 1969, *24,* 1076–1092.

DILLEHAY, R. C. "On the Irrelevance of the Classical Negative Evidence Concerning the Effect of Attitudes on Behavior." *American Psychologist,* 1973, *28,* 887–891.

DOOB, L. W. "The Behavior of Attitudes." *Psychological Review,* 1947, *54,* 135–156.

DOUVAN, E., AND WALKER, A. M. "The Sense of Effectiveness in Public Affairs." *Psychological Monographs,* 1956, *70* (22, Whole No. 429), 1–19.

DUVAL, S., AND WICKLUND, R. A. *A Theory of Objective Self-Awareness.* New York: Academic, 1972.

EISENBERG, L. "The *Human* Nature of Human Nature." *Science,* 1972, *176,* 123–128.

EISENSTADT, S. *From Generation to Generation.* New York: Free Press, 1956.

ERIKSON, E. H. *Young Man Luther: A Study in Psychoanalysis and History.* New York: Norton, 1958.

ERIKSON, E. H. "Identity and the Life Cycle." *Psychological Issues,* 1959 (Whole No. 1).

ERIKSON, E. H. "Reality and Actuality." *Journal of the American Psychoanalytic Association,* 1962, *10,* 451–474.

ERIKSON, E. H. "Youth: Fidelity and Diversity." In E. Erikson (Ed.), *Youth: Change and Challenge.* New York: Basic Books, 1963.

ERIKSON, E. H. *Insight and Responsibility.* New York: Norton, 1964.

ERIKSON, E. H. "The Problem of Ego Identity." *Journal of the American Psychoanalytic Association,* 1965, *4,* 55–121.

EYSENCK, H. J. *The Psychology of Politics.* London: Routledge, 1954.

EZEKIEL, R. S. "The Personal Future and Peace Corps Competence." *Journal of Personality and Social Psychology,* 1968, *8*(2), Monograph Supplement Pt. 2.

FAWCETT, J. T. *Psychology and Population.* New York: The Population Council, 1970.

FAWCETT, J. T. (Ed.) *Psychological Perspectives on Population.* New York: Basic Books, 1973.

FESTINGER, L. *A Theory of Cognitive Dissonance.* Evanston, Ill.: Row, Peterson, 1957.

FESTINGER, L. "Behavioral Support for Opinion Change." *Public Opinion Quarterly,* 1964, *28,* 404–417.

FEUER, L. W. *The Conflict of Generations.* New York: Basic Books, 1969.

FISHBEIN, M. "Attitude and the Prediction of Behavior." In M. Fishbein (Ed.), *Readings in Attitude Theory and Measurement.* New York: Wiley, 1967.

FISHER, S., AND CLEVELAND, S. E. *Body Image and Personality.* Princeton, N.J.: Van Nostrand, 1958.

FISHKIN, J., AND KENISTON, K. *Moral Development and Political Ideology.* 1972 (unpublished manuscript).

FLACKS, R. "The Liberated Generation: An Exploration of the Roots of Student Protest." *Journal of Social Issues,* 1967, *23* (3), 52–75.

FOOTE, N. N., AND COTTRELL, L. S., JR. *Identity and Interpersonal Competence: A New Direction in Family Research.* Chicago: University of Chicago Press, 1955.

FRANK, J. D. *Persuasion and Healing: A Comparative Study of Psychotherapy.* Baltimore, Md.: Johns Hopkins, 1961. (Rev. ed., 1972.)

FRANKEL, C. "The Nature and Sources of Irrationalism." *Science,* 1973, *180,* 927–931.

FREUD, S. *Group Psychology and the Analysis of the Ego.* [1921]. *Standard Edition.* London: Hogarth, 1955, *18,* 65–143.

FROMM, E. *Escape from Freedom.* New York: Farrar and Rinehart, 1941.

GALES, K. E. A. "A Campus Revolution." *British Journal of Sociology,* 1966, *17,* 1–19.

GELINEAU, V. A., AND KANTOR, D. "Pro-Social Commitment Among College Students." *Journal of Social Issues,* 1964, *20* (4), 112–130.

GLOCK, C. Y. "Images of Man and Public Opinion." *Public Opinion Quarterly,* 1964, *28,* 539–546.

GOFFMAN, E. *The Presentation of Self in Everyday Life.* Garden City, N.Y.: Doubleday Anchor Books, 1959.

GOFFMAN, E. *Relations in Public: Microstudies of the Public Order.* New York: Basic Books, 1971.

GOLDSTEIN, K. *The Organism.* New York: American Book, 1939.

GREENSTEIN, F. *Personality and Politics.* Chicago: Markham, 1969.

GRINKER, R. R., SR. "A Dynamic Story of the 'Homoclite.'" In J. H. Masserman (Ed.), *Science and Psychoanalysis,* 1963, *6,* 115–134.

GRINKER, R. R., SR. "Normality Viewed as a System." *Archives of General Psychiatry,* 1967a, *17,* 320–324.

GRINKER, R. R., SR. *Toward a Unified Theory of Human Behavior* (1956). (2nd ed.) New York: Basic Books, 1967b.

GRINKER, R. R., SR. "The Continuing Search for Meaning." *American Journal of Psychiatry*, 1970, *127*, 25–31.

GRINKER, R. R., SR., with the collaboration of Grinker, R. R., Jr., and Timberlake, J. "'Mentally Healthy' Young Males (Homoclites)." *Archives of General Psychiatry*, 1962, *6*, 405–453.

GRODDECK, G. *The Book of the It: Psychoanalytic Letters to a Friend.* London: Daniel Co., 1935.

GURIN, G., VEROFF, J., AND FELD, S. *Americans View Their Mental Health: A Nationwide Opinion Survey.* New York: Basic Books, 1960.

GURIN, R., GURIN, G., LAO, R. C., AND BEATTIE, M. "Internal-External Control in the Motivational Dynamics of Negro Youth." *Journal of Social Issues*, 1969, *25* (3), 29–53.

HAAN, N. "A Proposed Model of Ego Functioning: Coping and Defense Mechanisms in Relation to IQ Change." *Psychological Monographs*, 1963, *77* (8, Whole No. 571).

HAAN, N. "Activism as Moral Protest: Moral Judgments of Hypothetical Moral Dilemmas and an Actual Situation of Civil Disobedience." In L. Kohlberg and E. Turiel (Eds.), *The Development of Moral Judgment and Action.* New York: Holt, Rinehart, and Winston, 1972.

HAAN, N., SMITH, M. B., AND BLOCK, J. H. "Moral Reasoning of Young Adults: Political-Social Behavior, Family Background, and Personality Correlates." *Journal of Personality and Social Psychology*, 1968, *10*, 183–201.

HAMBURG, D. A., AND ADAMS, J. E. "A Perspective on Coping Behavior: Seeking and Utilizing Information in Major Transitions." *Archives of General Psychiatry*, 1967, *17*, 277–284.

HARDIN, G. "The Tragedy of the Commons." *Science*, 1968, *162*, 1243–1248.

HARDIN, G. "Editorial: The Survival of Nations and Civilization." *Science*, 1971, *172*, 1297.

HARTMANN, H. *Ego Psychology and the Problem of Adaptation.* New York: International Universities Press, 1958.

HAWTHORNE, G. *The Sociology of Fertility.* London: Collier-Macmillan, 1970.

HEATH, D. H. *Explorations of Maturity.* New York: Appleton-Century-Crofts, 1965.

HEIDER, F. *The Psychology of Interpersonal Relations.* New York: Wiley, 1958.

HEIST, P. "Intellect and Commitment: The Faces of Discontent." In O. W. Knorr and W. J. Minter (Eds.), *Order and Freedom on Campus.* Boulder, Colo.: Western Interstate Commission for Higher Education, 1965.

HEIST, P. "The Dynamics of Student Discontent and Protest." Paper presented to American Psychological Association, September 1966.

HILGARD, E. R., AND SMITH, M. B. "Distributed Practice in Motor Learning: Score Changes Within and Between Daily Sessions." *Journal of Experimental Psychology,* 1942, *30,* 136–146.

HILL, R., STYCOS, J. M., AND BACK, K. *The Family and Population Control: A Puerto Rican Experiment in Social Change.* Chapel Hill: University of North Carolina Press, 1959.

HOFFMAN, M. L. "Techniques and Processes in Moral Development." Mimeographed report, 1964.

HOLLINGSHEAD, A. B., AND REDLICH, F. C. *Social Class and Mental Illness: A Community Study.* New York: Wiley, 1958.

HOLT, R. R. "Freud's Mechanistic and Humanistic Images of Man." *Psychoanalysis and Contemporary Science, 1,* 1972.

HORN, J. F., AND KNOTT, P. D. "Activist Youth in the 1960's: Summary and Prognosis." *Science,* 1971, *171,* 977–985.

HOVLAND, C. I. "Reconciling Conflicting Results Derived from Experimental and Survey Studies of Attitude Change." *American Psychologist,* 1959, *14,* 8–17.

HOVLAND, C. I., AND JANIS, I. L. *Personality and Persuasibility.* New Haven, Conn.: Yale University Press, 1959.

HOVLAND, C. I., JANIS, I. L., AND KELLEY, H. H. *Communication and Persuasion.* New Haven, Conn.: Yale University Press, 1953.

HOVLAND, C. I., LUMSDAINE, A. A., AND SHEFFIELD, F. D. *Experiments in Mass Communication: Studies in Social Psychology in World War II.* Vol. 3. Princeton, N.J.: Princeton University Press, 1949.

HYMAN, H. H. *Survey Design and Analysis.* New York: Free Press, 1955.

HYMAN, H. H. "Surveys in the Study of Political Psychology." In J. N. Knutson (Ed.), *Handbook of Political Psychology.* San Francisco: Jossey-Bass, 1973.

INHELDER, B., AND PIAGET, J. *The Growth of Logical Thinking from Childhood to Adolescence.* New York: Basic Books, 1958.

INSKO, C. A. *Theories of Attitude Change.* New York: Appleton-Century-Crofts, 1967.

JAHODA, M. "Toward a Social Psychology of Mental Health." In M. J. E. Senn (Ed.), *Symposium on the Healthy Personality*. New York: Josiah Macy Jr. Foundation, 1950.

JAHODA, M. *Current Concepts of Positive Mental Health*. New York: Basic Books, 1958.

JAMES, W. "The Consciousness of Self." In *The Principles of Psychology*. Vol. 1. New York: Holt, 1890.

JAMES, W. *The Principles of Psychology*. 2 Vols. New York: Holt, 1890.

JANIS, I. L. "Effects of Fear Arousal on Attitude Change: Recent Developments in Theory and Experimental Research." In L. Berkowitz (Ed.), *Advances in Experimental Social Psychology*. Vol. 3. New York: Academic, 1967.

JANIS, I. L., AND MANN, L. "A Conflict-Theory Approach to Attitude Change and Decision Making." In A. G. Greenwald, T. Brock, and T. M. Ostrom (Eds.), *Psychological Foundations of Attitudes*. New York: Academic, 1968.

JANIS, I. L., AND SMITH, M. B. "Effects of Education and Persuasion on National and International Images." In H. C. Kelman (Ed.), *International Behavior: A Social Psychological Analysis*. New York: Holt, 1965.

JENCKS, C., AND RIESMAN, D. *The Academic Revolution*. New York: Viking, 1968.

Joint Commission on Mental Illness and Health. *Action for Mental Health: Final Report of the Joint Commission*. New York: Basic Books, 1961.

JUNG, C. G. "The Relations Between the Ego and the Unconscious." In C. G. Jung, *Collected Works*. Vol. 7. Princeton, N.J.: Princeton University Press, 1953. (Originally published in 1945).

KARLINS, M., AND ABELSON, H. I. *Persuasion: How Opinions and Attitudes are Changed*. (2nd ed.) New York: Springer, 1970.

KATZ, D., AND SCHANCK, R. L. *Social Psychology*. New York: Wiley, 1938.

KATZ, D., AND STOTLAND, E. "A Preliminary Statement to a Theory of Attitude Structure and Change." In S. Koch (ed.), *Psychology: A Study of a Science*. Vol. 3. New York: McGraw-Hill, 1959.

KATZ, J., AND OTHERS. *No Time for Youth: Growth and Constraint in College Students*. San Francisco: Jossey-Bass, 1968.

KELLER, A. B., SIMS, J. H., HENRY, W. E., AND CRAWFORD, T. J. "Psychological Sources of 'Resistance' to Family Planning." *Merrill-Palmer Quarterly*, 1970, *16*, 286–302.

KELLEY, H. H. "Two Functions of Reference Groups." In G. E. Swanson, T. M. Newcomb, and E. L. Hartley (Eds.), *Readings in Social Psychology* (2nd. ed.) New York: Holt, Rinehart, and Winston, 1952.

KELLY, G. A. *The Psychology of Personal Constructs.* 2 Vols. New York: Norton, 1955.

KELMAN, H. C. "Compliance, Identification, and Internalization: Three Processes of Opinion Change." *Journal of Conflict Resolution,* 1958, 2, 51–60.

KELMAN, H. C. *A Time to Speak: On Human Values and Social Research.* San Francisco: Jossey-Bass, 1968.

KENISTON, K. *The Uncommitted: Alienated Youth in American Society.* New York: Harcourt Brace Jovanovich, 1965.

KENISTON, K. *Young Radicals: Notes on Committed Youth.* New York: Harcourt Brace Javonovich, 1968.

KENISTON, K. *Youth and Dissent: The Rise of a New Opposition.* New York: Harcourt Brace Jovanovich, 1971.

KERPELMAN, L. C. *Activists and Nonactivists: A Psychological Study of American College Students.* New York: Behavioral Publications, 1972.

KEY, V. O., JR. (with the assistance of M. C. Cummings, Jr.) *The Responsible Electorate: Rationality in Presidential Voting.* Cambridge, Mass.: Harvard University Press, 1966.

KIESLER, C. A., COLLINS, B. E., AND MILLER, N. *Attitude Change: A Critical Analysis of Theoretical Approaches.* New York: Wiley, 1969.

KIRSCHT, J. P., AND DILLEHAY, R. C. *Dimensions of Authoritarianism: A Review of Research and Theory.* Lexington: University of Kentucky Press, 1967.

KNUTSON, A. L. "The Definition and Value of a New Human Life." *Social Science and Medicine,* 1967, 1, 7–29.

KNUTSON, A. L. "A Human Life and Abortion." In J. T. Fawcett (Ed.), *Psychological Perspectives on Population.* New York: Basic Books, 1973.

KOCH, S. "Epologue." In S. Koch (Ed.), *Psychology: A Study of Science.* Vol. 3. New York: McGraw-Hill, 1959.

KOCH, S. "The Image of Man in Encounter Groups." *American Scholar,* 1973, 42, 636–652.

KOHLBERG, L. "The Development of Children's Orientations Towards a Moral Order. I. Sequence in the Development of Moral Thought." *Vita Humana,* 1963, 6, 11–33.

KOHLBERG, L. "Development of Moral Character and Moral Ideology." In M. L. Hoffman and L. W. Hoffman (Eds.), *Review of Child Development Research*. Vol. 1. New York: Russell Sage, 1964.

LA PIERE, R. T. "Attitudes Versus Actions." *Social Forces,* 1934, *13,* 230–237.

LASSWELL, H. D. *Psychopathology and Politics.* Chicago: University of Chicago Press, 1930.

LASSWELL, H. D., AND KAPLAN, A. *Power and Society: A Framework for Political Inquiry.* New Haven, Conn.: Yale University Press, 1950.

LATANÉ, B., AND DARLEY, J. M. *The Unresponsive Bystander: Why Doesn't He Help?* New York: Appleton-Century-Crofts, 1970.

LAZARFELD, P. F., BERELSON, B., AND GAUDET, H. *The People's Choice.* New York: Duell, Sloan and Pearce, 1944.

LEFCOURT, H. M. "Internal Versus External Control of Reinforcement." *Psychological Bulletin,* 1966, *65,* 206–220.

LEFCOURT, H. M. "Internal Versus External Control of Reinforcement Revisited: Recent Developments." In B. A. Maher (Ed.), *Progress in Experimental Personality Research,* Vol. 6. New York: Academic, 1972.

LERNER, M. "Hippies and Radicals." *Daily Californian,* Oct. 27, 1966. 6.

LEWIN, K. *Field Theory in Social Science.* New York: Harper and Row, 1951.

LEWIS, O. *Five Families: Mexican Case Studies in the Culture of Poverty.* New York: Basic Books, 1959.

LEWIS, O. *La Vida: A Puerto Rican Family in the Culture of Poverty— San Juan and New York.* New York: Random House, 1966.

LIFTON, R. J. *Thought Reform and the Psychology of Totalism: A Study of "Brainwashing" in China.* New York: Norton, 1961.

LINDZEY, G., AND ARONSON, E. (Eds.) *The Handbook of Social Psychology* (2nd ed.) 5 Vols. Reading, Mass.: Addison-Wesley, 1968–1969.

LINTON, R. *The Study of Man: An Introduction.* New York: Appleton-Century-Crofts, 1936.

LIPE, D. "Incentive, Fertility Control, and Research." *American Psychologist,* 1971, *26,* 617–625.

LIPSET, S. M. "Student Opposition in the United States." *Government and Opposition,* 1966, *1,* 351–374.

LIPSET, S. M., AND SCHAFLANDER, G. *Passion and Politics: Student Activism in America.* Boston: Little, Brown, 1971.

LITTLE, B. R. "Psychological Man as Scientist, Humanist and Specialist." *Journal of Experimental Research in Personality*, 1972, *6*, 95–118.

LOEVINGER, J. "Three Principles for a Psychoanalytic Psychology." *Journal of Abnormal Psychology*, 1966, *71*, 432–443.

LYND, H. M. *On Shame and the Search for Identity*. New York: Harcourt Brace Javonovich, 1958.

MACAULAY, J., AND BERKOWITZ, L. (Eds.) *Altruism and Helping Behavior*. New York: Academic, 1970.

MC CLOSKY, H. "Personality and Attitude Correlates of Foreign Policy Orientation." In J. N. Rosenau (Ed.), *Domestic Sources of Foreign Policy*. New York: Free Press, 1967.

MACCOBY, N. "The New Scientific Rhetoric." In W. Schramm (Ed.), *The Science of Communication: New Directions and New Findings in Communication Research*. New York: Basic Books, 1963.

MAC DONALD, A. P., JR. "Internal-External Locus of Control and the Practice of Birth Control." *Psychological Reports*, 1970, *21*, 206.

MC DOUGALL, W. *Introduction to Social Psychology* (14th ed.) Boston: Luce, 1921.

MC GUIRE, W. J. "Inducing Resistance to Persuasion." In L. Berkowitz (Ed.), *Advances in Experimental Psychology*. Vol. 1. New York: Academic, 1964.

MC GUIRE, W. J. "The Nature of Attitudes and Attitude Change." In G. Lindzey and E. Aronson (Eds.), *The Handbook of Social Psychology* (2nd ed.) Vol. 3. Reading, Mass.: Addison-Wesley, 1968.

MC GUIRE, W. J. "The Yin and Yang of Progress in Social Psychology: Seven Koan." *Journal of Personality and Social Psychology*, 1973, *26*, 446–456.

MAHER, B. (Ed.) *Clinical Psychology and Personality: The Selected Papers of George Kelly*. New York: Wiley, 1969.

MASLOW, A. H. "Self-Actualizing People: A Study of Psychological Health." In *Personality Symposia: Symposium No. 1 on Values*. New York: Grune and Stratton, 1950.

MASLOW, A. H. *Motivation and Personality*. New York: Harper and Row, 1954.

MASLOW, A. H. *Religions, Values, and Peak-Experiences*. Columbus: Ohio State University Press, 1964.

MASLOW, A. H. *Eupsychian Management: A Journal*. Homewood, Ill.: Dorsey-Irwin, 1965.

MASLOW, A. H. *The Psychology of Science: A Reconnaissance.* New York: Harper and Row, 1966.

MASLOW, A. H. *Toward a Psychology of Being.* (2nd ed.) Princeton, N. J.: Van Nostrand, 1968.

MASLOW, A. H. *The Farther Reaches of Human Nature.* New York: Viking, 1971.

MAY, R. *Love and Will.* New York: Norton, 1969.

MAY, R. *Power and Innocence: A Search for the Sources of Violence.* New York: Norton, 1972.

MEAD, G. H. *Mind, Self, and Society.* Chicago: University of Chicago Press, 1934.

MEADOWS, D. H., MEADOWS, D. L., RANDERS, J., AND BEHRENS, W. W. *The Limits to Growth.* New York: Universe Books, 1972.

MERTON, R. K. "The Self-Fulfilling Prophecy." In R. K. Merton, *Social Theory and Social Structure* (Rev. ed.) New York: Free Press, 1957.

MERTON, R. K. *Social Theory and Social Structure.* (Rev. ed.) New York: Free Press, 1957.

MERTON, R. K., AND KITT, A. S. "Contributions to the Theories of Reference Group Behavior." In R. K. Merton and P. F. Lazarsfeld (Eds.), *Continuities in Social Research: Studies in the Scope and Method of "The American Soldier."* New York: Free Press, 1950.

MILLER, D. R., AND SWANSON, G. E. *The Changing American Parent.* New York: Wiley, 1958.

MILLER, D. R., AND SWANSON, G. E. *Inner Conflict and Defense.* New York: Holt, Rinehart, and Winston, 1960.

MILLER, G. A. "Psychology as a Means of Promoting Human Welfare." *American Psychologist,* 1969, *24,* 1063–1075.

MISCHEL, W. *Personality and Assessment.* New York: Wiley, 1968.

MORRIS, C. W. *Paths of Life: Preface to a World Religion.* New York: Harper and Row, 1942.

MORRIS, C. W. *Varieties of Human Value.* Chicago: University of Chicago Press, 1956.

MUNK, M. "New Left: Background of Young Radicals." *National Guardian,* Sept. 18, 1965, *3.*

MURPHY, G., AND LIKERT, R. *Public Opinion and the Individual.* New York: Harper and Row, 1938.

MURPHY, G., MURPHY, L. B., AND NEWCOMB, T. M. *Experimental Social Psychology.* (Rev. ed.) New York: Harper and Row, 1937.

MURPHY, L. *The Widening World of Childhood: Paths Toward Mastery.* New York: Basic Books, 1962.

MURRAY, H. A. *Explorations in Personality.* New York: Oxford University Press, 1938.

MUSGROVE, F. *Youth and the Social Order.* Bloomington: Indiana University Press, 1965.

MYRDAL, G. (with assistance of R. Sterner and A. Rose). *An American Dilemma: The Negro Problem and Modern Democracy.* Vols. 1 and 2. New York: Harper and Row, 1944.

NAMBOODIRI, N. K., AND POPE, H. "Social Norms Concerning Family Size." Paper presented at annual meeting of the Population Association of America. Boston, April 1968.

OFFER, D. *The Psychological World of the Teenager: A Study of Normal Adolescent Boys.* New York: Basic Books, 1969.

OFFER, D., AND SABSHIN, M. *Normality: Theoretical and Clinical Concepts of Mental Health.* New York: Basic Books, 1966.

OSGOOD, C. E. *Alternative to War or Surrender.* Urbana: University of Illinois Press, 1962.

OSGOOD, C. E., SUCI, G. J., AND TANNENBAUM, P. H. *The Measurement of Meaning.* Urbana: University of Illinois Press, 1957.

PARSONS, T. "Youth in the Context of American Society." In E. Erikson (Ed.), *Youth: Change and Challenge.* New York: Basic Books, 1963.

PETERSON, R. E. "Organized Student Protest in 1964–1965." Paper presented to American Psychological Association, September 1966.

PETERSON, R. E. *The Scope of Organized Student Protest in 1964–1965.* Princeton, N.J.: Educational Testing Service, 1966.

PETERSON, R. E. *The Scope of Organized Student Protest in 1967–1968.* Princeton, N.J.: Educational Testing Service, 1968.

PIAGET, J., AND WEIL, A. M. "Le Développement Chez l'Enfant de l'Idée de Patrie et des Relations avec l'Etranger." *Bulletin International des Sciences Sociales* (UNESCO), 1951, *3*, 605–621.

PLATT, J. R. *The Step to Man.* New York: Wiley, 1966.

PLATT, J. R. "How Men Can Shape Their Future." *Futures,* 1971, *3* (1) 32–47.

POHLMAN, E. T. *Incentives and Compensations in Birth Planning.* Chapel Hill, N.C.: Carolina Population Center, 1971.

POHLMAN, E. T. "Birth Planning Incentives." In J. T. Fawcett (Ed.), *Psychological Perspectives on Population.* New York: Basic Books, 1973.

RAE-GRANT, Q. A. F., GLADWIN, T., AND BOWER, E. M. "Mental Health,

Social Competence, and the War on Poverty." *American Journal of Orthopsychiatry*, 1966, *36*, 652–664.

RAINWATER, L. *And the Poor Get Children*. New York: Quadrangle Books, 1960.

RAINWATER, L. *Family Design: Marital Sexuality, Family Size, and Contraception*. Chicago: Aldine, 1965.

RAND, A. *Atlas Shrugged*. New York: Random House, 1957.

RAND, A. *The Virtues of Selfishness*. New York: New American Library, 1964.

REES, M. "Editorial: A Humane Approach to Population Problems." *Science*, 1971, *173*, 381.

REICH, C. *The Greening of America*. New York: Random House, 1970.

RIESMAN, D., in collaboration with Denney, R., and Glazer, N. *The Lonely Crowd: A Study of the Changing American Character*. New Haven, Conn.: Yale University Press, 1950.

RING, K. "Experimental Social Psychology: Some Sober Questions About Frivolous Values." *Journal of Experimental Social Psychology*, 1967, *3*, 113–123.

ROGERS, C. *On Becoming a Person*. Boston: Houghton Mifflin, 1961.

ROKEACH, M. *The Open and Closed Mind: Investigations into the Nature of Belief Systems and Personality Systems*. New York: Basic Books, 1960.

ROKEACH, M. *Beliefs, Attitudes, and Values: A Theory of Organization and Change*. San Francisco: Jossey-Bass, 1968.

ROMMETWEIT, R. "Language Games, Syntactic Structures and Hermeneutics." In J. Israel and H. Tajfel (Eds.), *The Context of Social Psychology: A Critical Assessment*. New York: Academic, 1972.

ROSENBERG, M. J. "An Analysis of Affective-Cognitive Consistency. In M. J. Rosenberg, C. I. Hovland, W. J. McGuire, R. P. Abelson, and J. W. Brehm, *Attitude Organization and Change: An Analysis of Consistency Among Attitude Components*. New Haven, Conn.: Yale University Press, 1960.

ROSENBERG, M. J. "Attitude Change and Foreign Policy in the Cold War Era." In J. N. Rosenau (Ed.), *Domestic Sources of Foreign Policy*. New York: Free Press, 1967.

ROSENBERG, M. J., AND ABELSON, R. P. "An Analysis of Cognitive Balancing." In M. J. Rosenberg, C. I. Hovland, W. J. McGuire, R. P. Abelson, and J. W. Brehm, *Attitude Organization and Change: An Analysis of Consistency Among Attitude Components*. New Haven, Conn.: Yale University Press, 1960.

ROSENBERG, M. J., VERBA, S., AND CONVERSE, P. E. *Vietnam and the Silent Majority: The Dove's Guide.* HAR/ROW Books. New York: Harper and Row, 1970.

ROSENTHAL, R., AND ROSNOW, R. L. (Eds.) *Artifact in Behavioral Research.* New York: Academic, 1969.

ROSENZWEIG, S. "E. G. Boring and the *Zeitgeist: Eruditione Gesta Beavit.*" *Journal of Psychology,* 1970, *75,* 59–71.

ROSZAK, T. *The Making of a Counter-Culture.* Garden City, N.Y.: Doubleday, 1969.

ROTTER, J. B. "Generalized Expectancies for Internal Versus External Control of Reinforcement." *Psychological Monographs,* 1966, *80* (1, Whole No. 609), 1–28.

RYDER, N. B. "The Cohort as a Concept in the Study of Social Change." *American Sociological Review,* 1965, *30,* 843–861.

SABSHIN, M. "Psychiatric Perspectives on Normality." *Archives of General Psychiatry,* 1967, *17,* 258–264.

SAMPSON, E. E., AND KORN, H. A. *Student Activism and Protest: Alternatives for Social Change.* San Francisco: Jossey-Bass, 1970.

SANFORD, N. "Authoritarian Personality in Contemporary Perspective." In J. N. Knutson (Ed.), *Handbook of Political Psychology.* San Francisco: Jossey-Bass, 1973.

SARBIN, T. R., AND ADLER, N. "Self-Reconstitution Processes: A Preliminary Report." *The Psychoanalytic Review,* 1970–1971, *57,* 599–616.

SARNOFF, I. "Psychoanalytic Theory and Social Attitudes." *Public Opinion Quarterly,* 1960, *24,* 251–279.

SARTRE, J-P. *Existentialism and Human Emotion.* New York: Philosophical Library, 1957.

SCHEIN, E. H., SCHNEIER, I., AND BARKER, C. H. *Coercive Persuasion: A Socio-Psychological Analysis of "Brainwashing" of American Civilian Prisoners by the Chinese Communists.* New York: Norton, 1961.

SCHIFF, L. F. "The Obedient Rebels: A Study of College Conversions to Conservatism." *Journal of Social Issues,* 1964, *20* (4), 74–95.

SCHIFF, L. F. "Dynamic Young Fogies, Rebels on the Right." *Trans-Action,* November 1966, pp. 30–36.

SCHILDER, P. *The Image and Appearance of the Human Body.* London: Kegan, Paul, Trench, Trubner, 1935.

SCHOFIELD, W. "The Role of Psychology in the Delivery of Health Services." *American Psychologist,* 1969, *24,* 565–584.

SCOTT, W. A. "Attitude Measurement." In G. Lindzey and E. Aronson

(Eds.), *The Handbook of Social Psychology* (2nd. ed.) Vol. 2. Reading, Mass.: Addison-Wesley, 1968.

SEARS, D. O. "Political Behavior." In G. Lindzey and E. Aronson (Eds.), *The Handbook of Social Psychology* (2nd ed.) Vol. 5. Reading, Mass.: Addison-Wesley, 1969.

SEEMAN, M. "Alienation, Membership, and Political Knowledge." *Public Opinion Quarterly*, 1966, *30*, 354–367.

SELLS, S. B. (Ed.) *The Definition and Measurement of Mental Health*. U.S. Public Health Service Publication No. 1873. Washington, D.C.: National Center for Health Statistics, 1969.

SHAND, A. F. *The Foundations of Character*. London: Macmillan, 1914.

SHERIF, C. W., SHERIF, M., AND NEBERGALL, R. E. *Attitude and Attitude Change: The Social Judgment Approach*. Philadelphia: Saunders, 1965.

SHERIF, M. *Social Interaction: Process and Products*. Chicago: Aldine, 1967.

SHERIF, M., AND CANTRIL, H. *The Psychology of Ego-Involvements: Social Attitudes and Identifications*. New York: Wiley, 1947.

SHERIF, M., AND HOVLAND, C. I. *Social Judgment: Assimilation and Contrast Effects in Communication and Attitude Change*. New Haven, Conn.: Yale University Press, 1961.

SKINNER, B. F. *Walden Two*. New York: Macmillan, 1948.

SKINNER, B. F. *Verbal Behavior*. New York: Appleton-Century-Crofts, 1957.

SKINNER, B. F. *The Technology of Teaching*. New York: Appleton-Century-Crofts, 1968.

SKINNER, B. F. *Beyond Freedom and Dignity*. New York: Knopf, 1971.

SLATER, P. E. *The Pursuit of Loneliness*. Boston: Beacon Press, 1970.

SMITH, M. B. *Functional and Descriptive Analysis of Public Opinion*. Unpublished Ph.D. thesis. Harvard University, 1947a.

SMITH, M. B. "The Personal Setting of Public Opinions: A Study of Attitudes Toward Russia." *Public Opinion Quarterly*, 1947b, *11*, 507–523.

SMITH, M. B. "Optima of Mental Health: A General Frame of Reference." *Psychiatry*, 1950, *13*, 503–510. (Also in Smith, 1969c, pp. 156–164.)

SMITH, M. B. "Research Strategies Toward a Conception of Positive Mental Health." *American Psychologist*, 1959, *14*, 673–681. (Also in Smith, 1969c, pp. 165–178.)

SMITH, M. B. " 'Mental Health' Reconsidered: A Special Case of the

Problem of Values in Psychology." *American Psychologist*, 1961, *16*, 299–306. (Also in Smith, 1969c, pp. 179–190.)

SMITH, M. B. "An Analysis of Two Measures of Authoritarianism Among Peace Corps Teachers." *Journal of Personality*, 1965a, *33*, 513–535. (Also in Smith, 1969c, pp. 117–135.)

SMITH, M. B. "Motivation, Communications Research, and Family Planning." In M. C. Sheps and J. C. Ridley (Eds.), *Public Health and Population Change*. Pittsburgh: University of Pittsburgh Press, 1965b. (Also in Smith, 1969c, pp. 292–305.)

SMITH, M. B. "Explorations in Competence: A Study of Peace Corps Teachers In Ghana." *American Psychologist*, 1966a, *21*, 555–566. (Also in Smith, 1969c, pp. 191–209.)

SMITH, M. B. Review of *The Psychology of Science: A Reconnaissance*, by A. H. Maslow. *Science*, 1966b, *153*, 284–285.

SMITH, M. B. "Attitude Change." In *International Encyclopedia of the Social Sciences*. Vol. 1. New York: Free Press, 1968a. (Also in Smith, 1969c, pp. 458–467.)

SMITH, M. B. "A Map for the Analysis of Personality and Politics." *Journal of Social Issues*, 1968b, *24* (3), 15–28.

SMITH, M. B. "Competence and Socialization." In J. A. Clausen (Ed.), *Socialization and Society*. Boston: Little, Brown, 1968c. (Also in Smith, 1969c, pp. 210–250.)

SMITH, M. B. "Conference Report: International Conference on Social-Psychological Research in Developing Countries." *Journal of Personality and Social Psychology*, 1968d, *8*, 95–98.

SMITH, M. B. "Personality in Politics: A Conceptual Map, with Application to the Problem of Political Rationality." In O. Garceau (Ed.), *Political Research and Political Theory: Essays in Honor of V. O. Key, Jr.* Cambridge, Mass.: Harvard University Press, 1968e. (Also in Smith, 1969c, pp. 14–32.)

SMITH, M. B. "Samuel A. Stouffer." In *International Encyclopedia of the Social Sciences*. Vol. 15. New York: Free Press, 1968f. (Also in Smith, 1969c, pp. 61–65.)

SMITH, M. B. "Morality and Student Protest." In M. B. Smith, *Social Psychology and Human Values: Selected Essays*. Chicago: Aldine, 1969a.

SMITH, M. B. "Racism, Education, and Student Protest." *Illinois School Journal*, 1969b, *49*, 207–214.

SMITH, M. B. *Social Psychology and Human Values: Selected Essays*. Chicago: Aldine, 1969c.

SMITH, M. B. "Competence and 'Mental Health': Problems in Conceptualizing Human Effectiveness." In S. B. Sells (Ed.), *The Definition and Measurement of Mental Health.* U.S. Public Health Service Publication No. 1873. Washington, D.C.: National Center for Health Statistics, 1969d.

SMITH, M. B. "Is Experimental Social Psychology Advancing?" Review of *Advances in Experimental Social Psychology,* L. Berkowitz (Ed.) Vols. 1–5. *Journal of Experimental Social Psychology,* 1972, *8,* 86–96.

SMITH, M. B. "Criticism of a Social Science." Review of *The Context of Social Psychology.* J. Israel and H. Tajfel (Eds.) *Science,* 1973a, *180,* 610–612.

SMITH, M. B. "Environmental Degradation and Human Behavior: Can Psychology Help?" *Representative Research in Social Psychology,* 1973b, *4,* 227–234.

SMITH, M. B., BRUNER, J. S., AND WHITE, R. W. *Opinions and Personality.* New York: Wiley, 1956.

SMITH, M. B., HAAN, N., AND BLOCK, J. H. "Social-Psychological Aspects of Student Activism." *Youth and Society,* 1970, *1,* 261–288.

SMITH, M. B., AND HOBBS, N. "The Community and the Community Mental Health Center." *American Psychologist,* 1966, *21,* 499–509.

SOLOMON, F., AND FISHMAN, J. "Youth and Peace: A Psychosocial Study of Student Peace Demonstrators in Washington, D.C." *Journal of Social Issues,* 1964, *20* (4), 54–73.

SPENGLER, J. "Population Problem: In Search of a Solution." *Science,* 1969, *166,* 1234–1238.

SPOCK, B. *The Commonsense Book of Baby and Child Care.* New York: Duell, Sloan and Pearce, 1946.

STAGNER, R. "Traits Are Relevant: Logical and Empirical Issues." Paper presented in symposium on "Traits, Persons, and Situations: Some Theoretical Issues," American Psychological Association, Montreal, 1973.

STEINER, I. D. "Perceived Freedom." In L. Berkowitz (Ed.), *Advances in Experimental Social Psychology.* Vol. 5. New York: Academic, 1971.

STONE, C. P., AND SMITH, M. B. "Serial Discrimination by Rats at the Choice-Points of Elevated Mazes." *Journal of Comparative Psychology,* 1941, *31,* 79–95.

STOUFFER, S. A., COTTRELL, L. S., JR., DEVINNEY, L. C., JANIS, I. L., LUMSDAINE, M. H., SMITH, M. B., STAR, S. A., SUCHMAN, E. A., AND WILLIAMS, R. M., JR. *The American Soldier: Studies in Social*

Psychology in World War II. Adjustment in Army Life, Vol. 1. Combat and Its Aftermath, Vol. 2. Princeton, N.J.: Princeton University Press, 1949.

SZASZ, T. S. *The Myth of Mental Illness: Foundations of a Theory of Personal Conduct*. New York: Harper-Hoeber, 1961.

TAYLOR, D. W. "Decision Making and Problem Solving." In J. W. March (Ed.), *Handbook of Organizations*. Chicago: Rand McNally, 1965.

THIBAUT, J. W., AND KELLEY, H. H. *The Social Psychology of Groups*. New York: Wiley, 1959.

THOMAS, E. J., AND BIDDLE, B. J. *Role Theory: Concepts and Research*. New York: Wiley, 1966.

THOMAS, W. I., AND ZNANIECKI, F. *The Polish Peasant in Europe and America*. Vol. 1. Boston: Badger, 1918.

THURSTONE, L. L. "Attitudes Can Be Measured." *American Journal of Sociology*, 1928, *33*, 529–554.

TOFFLER, A. *Future Shock*. New York: Random House, 1970.

WATTS, W. A., AND WHITTAKER, D. "Free Speech Advocates at Berkeley." *Journal of Applied Behavioral Science*, 1966, *2*, 41–62.

WATTS, W. A., AND WHITTAKER, D. "Profile of a Nonconformist Youth Culture: A Study of Berkeley Non-Students." *Sociology of Education*, 1968, *41*, 178–200.

WESTBY, D., AND BRAUNGART, R. "Class and Politics in the Family Backgrounds of Student Political Activists." *American Sociological Review*, 1966, *31*, 690–692.

Westinghouse Learning Corporation and Ohio University. *The Impact of Head Start: An Evaluation of the Effects of Head Start on Children's Cognitive and Affective Development*. Athens, Ohio, 1969. 2 Vols.

WESTOFF, C. F., POTTER, R. G., AND SAGI, P. C. *The Third Child*. Princeton, N.J.: Princeton University Press, 1963.

WESTOFF, C. F., POTTER, R. G., SAGI, P. C., AND MISHLER, E. G. *Family Growth in Metropolitan America*. Princeton, N.J.: Princeton University Press, 1961.

WEXLER, J. G. "Campus Revolution: Social and Political Responsibilities." *Illinois School Journal*, 1969, *49*, 171–179.

WHEELIS, A. *The Quest for Identity*. New York: Norton, 1958.

WHITE, R. K. *Nobody Wanted War: Misperception in Vietnam and Other Wars*. Garden City, N.Y.: Doubleday, 1968.

WHITE, R. W. *Lives in Progress: A Study of the Natural Growth of Personality*. New York: Dryden, 1952.

WHITE, R. W. "Motivation Reconsidered: The Concept of Competence." *Psychological Review*, 1959, *66*, 297–333.

WHITE, R. W. "Ego and Reality in Psychoanalytic Theory: A Proposal for Independent Ego Energies." *Psychological Issues*, 1963, *3* (3).

WHITTAKER, D., AND WATTS, W. A. "Personality Characteristics of a Nonconformist Youth Subculture: A Study of the Berkeley Non-Student." *Journal of Social Issues*, 1969, *25* (2), 65–89.

WICKER, A. W. "Attitudes Versus Actions: The Relationship of Verbal and Overt Behavioral Responses to Attitude Objects." *Journal of Social Issues*, 1969, *25* (4), 41–78.

WILDAVSKY, A. *The Politics of the Budgetary Process*. Boston: Little, Brown, 1964.

WILLIAMSON, J. B. "Subjective Efficacy as an Aspect of Modernization in Six Developing Nations." Unpublished Ph.D. dissertation. Harvard University, 1969. Cited in J. T. Fawcett, *Psychology and Population*. New York: The Population Council, 1970.

WITKIN, H. A., DYK, R. B., FATERSON, H. F., GOODENOUGH, D. R., AND KARP, S. A. *Psychological Differentiation: Studies of Development*. New York: Wiley, 1962.

WYLIE, R. C. *The Self Concept*. Lincoln: University of Nebraska Press, 1961.

WYLIE, R. C. "The Present Status of Self Theory." In E. F. Borgatta and W. W. Lambert (Eds.), *Handbook of Personality Theory and Research*. Chicago: Rand McNally, 1968.

YANKELOVICH, D., INC. *The Changing Values on Campus: Political and Personal Attitudes of Today's College Students*. New York: Pocket Books, Washington Square Press, 1972.

YANKELOVICH, D., AND BARRETT, D. *Ego and Instinct: The Psychoanalytic View of Human Nature—Revised*. New York: Random House, 1970.

ZIMBARDO, P. G. "The Human Choice: Individuation, Reason, and Order Versus Deindividuation, Impulse, and Chaos." In W. J. Arnold and D. Levine (Eds.), *Nebraska Symposium on Motivation: 1969*. Lincoln: University of Nebraska Press, 1969.

ZIMBARDO, P., AND EBBESEN, E. B. *Influencing Attitudes and Changing Behavior*. Reading, Mass.: Addison-Wesley, 1969.

ZUBIN, J. "Clinical, Phenomenological, and Biometric Assessment of Psychopathology with Special Reference to Diagnosis." In S. B. Sells (Ed.), *The Definition and Measurement of Mental Health*. U.S. Public Health Service Publication No. 1873. Washington, D.C.: National Center for Health Statistics, 1968.

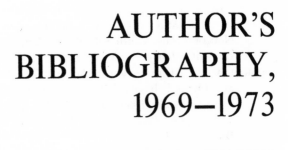

AUTHOR'S BIBLIOGRAPHY, 1969–1973

A complete bibliography for 1938–1968 may be found in the first item below, pages 421–428.

1969

Social Psychology and Human Values: Selected Essays. Chicago: Aldine, 1969.

"The Schools and Prejudice: Findings." In C. Y. Glock and E. Siegelman (Eds.), *Prejudice U.S.A.* New York: Praeger, 1969. Reprinted in Smith (1969).

"Competence and 'Mental Health': Problems in Conceptualizing Human Effectiveness." In S. B. Sells (Ed.), *The Definition and Measurement of Mental Health.* U.S. Public Health Service Publication No. 1873. Washington, D.C.: National Center for Health Statistics, 1969.

"Racism, Education and Student Protest." *Illinois Schools Journal,* 1969, *49* (3), 207–214.

With N. Haan, and J. H. Block. "Social-Psychological Aspects of Student Activism." *Youth and Society,* 1969, *1,* 261–288,

With J. H. Block, and N. Haan. "Socialization Correlates of Student Activism." *Journal of Social Issues,* 1969, *25* (4), 143–177.

Foreword to *The Psychological Impact of School Experience: A Comparative Study of Nine-Year-Old Children in Contrasting Schools,* by P. Minuchin, B. Biber, E. Shapiro, and H. Zimiles. New York: Basic Books, 1969.

Review of *Negro and White Children: A Psychological Study in the Rural South,* by E. E. Baughman and W. G. Dahlstrom. *Science,* 1969, *163,* 461–462.

1970

"Morality and Student Protest." In M. Wertheimer (Ed.), *Confrontation: Psychology and the Problems of Today.* Glenview, Ill.: Scott, Foresman, 1970.

With R. I. Evans, T. Pettigrew, and J. S. Harding. Edited transcription of symposium entitled "Gordon Allport: His Unique Contributions to Contemporary Personality and Social Psychology." In R. I. Evans, *Gordon Allport: The Man and His Ideals.* New York: Dutton, 1970.

Comment on R. Reiff, "Psychology and Public Policy." *Professional Psychology,* 1970, *1,* 324–326.

Comments on the symposium "Factors Underlying Student Unrest," in F. F. Korten, S. W. Cook, and J. I. Lacey (Eds.), *Psychology and the Problems of Society.* Washington, D.C.: American Psychological Association, 1970.

Review of *Mass Behavior in Battle and Captivity: The Communist Soldier in the Korean War.* Research Studies Directed by William C. Bradbury, S. M. Meyers and A. D. Biderman (Eds.) *American Journal of Sociology,* 1970, *75,* 870–871.

Review of *A Time to Speak: On Human Values and Social Research,* by H. C. Kelman. *American Sociological Review,* 1970, *35,* 342–343.

Review of *Race and the Social Sciences,* I. Katz and P. Gurin (Eds.) *Contemporary Psychology,* 1970, *15,* 716–718.

1971

"A Psychologist's Perspective on Public Opinion Theory." *Public Opinion Quarterly,* 1971, *35* (1), 36–43.

"Allport, Murray, and Lewin on Personality Theory: Notes on a Con-

frontation." *Journal of the History of the Behavioral Sciences,*
1971, *7,* 353–362.

Foreword to E. E. Baughman, *Black Americans: A Psychological Analysis.* New York: Academic, 1971.

Letter, "Blaming the Victim." *Washington Monthly,* April 1971, 3.

Review of *The Behavioral and Social Sciences: Outlook and Needs,* E.
R. Hilgard and H. W. Riecken (Eds.) and *Psychology,* K. E.
Clark and G. A. Miller (Eds.) *Contemporary Psychology,* 1971,
16, 196–197.

Review of *Social Character in a Mexican Village: A Sociopsycho-
analytic Study,* E. Fromm and M. Maccoby. *Contemporary Psychology,* 1971, *16,* 635–637.

1972

"Normality: For an Abnormal Age." In D. Offer and D. X. Freedman (Eds.), *Modern Psychiatry and Clinical Research: Essays
in Honor of Roy R. Grinker, Sr.* New York and London: Basic
Books, 1972.

"Toward Humanizing Social Psychology." In T. S. Krawiec (Ed.),
The Psychologists. Vol. 1. New York: Oxford, 1972. Condensed
version in *Psychology Today,* 1972, *6* (4), 67–70, 88.

"Ethical Implications of Population Policies: A Psychologist's View."
American Psychologist, 1972, *27,* 11–15.

Foreword to R. Froman, *Racism.* New York: Delacorte Press, 1972.

Review essay: "Is Experimental Social Psychology Advancing?" Review of *Advances in Experimental Social Psychology,* L. Berkowitz (Ed.) Vols. 1–5. *Journal of Experimental Social Psychology,* 1972, *8,* 86–96.

Review of *Beyond Freedom and Dignity,* by B. F. Skinner. *American
Scientist,* 1972, *60,* 80–81.

1973

"Political Attitudes." In J. N. Knutson (Ed.), *Handbook of Political
Psychology.* San Francisco: Jossey-Bass, 1973.

"A Social Psychological View of Fertility." In J. T. Fawcett (Ed.),
Psychological Perspectives on Population. New York: Basic
Books, 1973.

With S. W. Cook, L. H. Hicks, G. A. Kimble, W. J. McGuire, and P.
H. Schoggen (Ad hoc Committee on Ethical Standards in Psychological Research). *Ethical Principles in the Conduct of Re-*

search with Human Participants. Washington, D.C.: American
Psychological Association, 1973.

With J. Block and N. Haan. "Activism and Apathy in Contemporary
Adolescents." In J. F. Adams (Ed.), *Understanding Adolescence: Current Developments in Adolescent Psychology* (2nd
ed.) Boston: Allyn and Bacon, 1973.

"Environmental Degradation and Human Behavior: Can Psychology
Help?" *Representative Research in Social Psychology,* 1973, *4,*
227–234.

"On Self-Actualization: A Transambivalent Examination of a Focal
Theme in Maslow's Psychology." *Journal of Humanistic Psychology,* 1973, *13* (2), 17–33.

"Is Psychology Relevant to New Priorities?" *American Psychologist,*
1973, *28,* 463–471.

"Comment on D. G. Mandelbaum, The Study of Life History:
Ghandi." *Current Anthropology,* 1973, *14,* 203–204.

"Comment on White's Paper." (R. W. White, "The Concept of
Healthy Personality: What Do We Really Mean?") *The Coun-
seling Psychologist,* 1973, *4* (2), 48–51.

"Editorial: Protection of Human Subjects—Ethics and Politics." *APA
Monitor,* December 1973, *4* (12), 2.

Review of *The Science of Behavior and the Image of Man,* by I.
Chein. *Psychology Today,* 1973, *6* (12), 14–15.

Review of *The Context of Social Psychology: A Critical Assessment,*
J. Israel and H. Tajfel (Eds.) *Science,* 1973, *180* (4086), 610–
612.

Review of *The Broken Rebel: A Study in Culture, Politics, and Authoritarian Character,* by R. Wilkinson. *Political Science Quarterly,* 1973, *88,* 347–348.

ACKNOWLEDGMENTS

The chapters originally appeared in the following books or journals. In each case, permission to reprint my copyrighted material is gratefully acknowledged.

Chapter Two: "A Psychologist's Perspective on Public Opinion Theory." *Public Opinion Quarterly,* 1971, *35* (1), 36–43. Copyright © 1971 by Columbia University Press. Revised from a paper presented in the symposium "Toward a Theory of Public Opinion," American Association for Public Opinion Research, May 22, 1970.

Chapter Three: "Political Attitudes." In J. N. Knutson, ed., *Handbook of Political Psychology.* San Francisco: Jossey-Bass, 1973. Copyright © 1973 by Jossey-Bass Inc., Publishers, San Francisco, and Jossey-Bass Limited, London.

Chapter Four: "Activism and Apathy in Contemporary Adolescents." In J. F. Adams, ed., *Understanding Adolescence* (2d ed.). Boston: Allyn and Bacon, 1973. Copyright © by Allyn and Bacon, Inc. Also in J. F. Adams, ed., *Human Behavior in a Changing Society.* Boston: Holbrook Press, 1973. Copyright © by Holbrook Press, Inc. I am grateful to my colleagues for permission to reprint this chapter, which was prepared in connection with our study at the Institute of Human Development, University of California, Berkeley, on the moral orientations of student activists, supported by grants from the Rosenberg Foundation and the foundation's Fund for Research in Psychiatry.

Chapter Five: "A Social-Psychological View of Fertility." In J. T. Fawcett, ed., *Psychological Perspectives on Population*. New York: Basic Books, 1973. Copyright © 1973 by Basic Books, Inc., Publishers, New York.

Chapter Six: "Ethical Implications of Population Policies: A Psychologist's View." *American Psychologist*, 1972, *27*, 11–15. Copyright © 1972 by the American Psychological Association. Reprinted by permission.

Chapter Seven: "Competence and 'Mental Health': Problems in Conceptualizing Human Effectiveness." In S. B. Sells, ed., *The Definition and Measurement of Mental Health: A Symposium.* Washington, D.C.: National Center for Health Statistics, 1969.

Chapter Eight: "Normality: For an Abnormal Age." In D. Offer and D. X. Freedman, eds., *Modern Psychiatry and Clinical Research: Essays in Honor of Roy R. Grinker, Sr.* New York: Basic Books, 1972. Copyright © 1972 by Basic Books, Inc., Publishers, New York.

Chapter Nine: "On Self-Actualization: A Transambivalent Examination of a Focal Theme in Maslow's Psychology." *Journal of Humanistic Psychology*, 1973 (2), 17–23. Copyright © 1973 by American Association of Humanistic Psychology. Written at the invitation of Bertha Maslow and originally intended for a volume of critical essays on Maslow's work.

Chapter Ten: "The Iceberg and the Mirror: Perspectives on Selfhood." Revised from a paper for the symposium "Henry A. Murray at Eighty." American Psychological Association, Montreal, Aug. 27, 1973.

Chapter Eleven: "Is Psychology Relevant to New Priorities?" *American Psychologist*, 1973, *28*, 463–471. Copyright © 1973 by the American Psychological Association. Reprinted by permission. Revised from the invited keynote address presented at the annual meeting of the Western Psychological Association, Portland, Ore., Apr. 27, 1972.

Chapter Twelve: "Psychology and Ethics: Future Prospects

and Challenges." Prepared for the Symposium on Psychology and Ethics, Loyola University, Chicago, May 2, 1973. To be published in E. C. Kennedy, ed., *The Loyola Symposium on Ethics and Psychology.* New York: Chandler Publishing Company, 1975. I am especially grateful to Father Kennedy and to Chandler Publishing Company for permission to include the chapter here.

Chapter Thirteen: "Toward Humanizing Social Psychology." In T. S. Krawiec, ed., *The Psychologists.* Vol. 1. New York: Oxford University Press, 1972. Copyright © 1972 by Oxford University Press.

For material internal to Chapter Three, I gratefully acknowledge permission to use passages from my article "Attitude Change," in *International Encyclopedia of the Social Sciences,* Vol. 1 (New York: Macmillan and Free Press, 1968), copyright © 1968 by Crowell Collier and Macmillan, Inc.; Figure 1 from my article "A Map for the Analysis of Personality and Politics," *Journal of Social Issues,* 1968, *24* (3), 25, copyright © 1968 by the Society for the Psychological Study of Social Issues; and an extended quotation from P. Zimbardo and E. B. Ebbesen, *Influencing Attitudes and Changing Behavior* (Reading, Mass.: Addison-Wesley, 1970), copyright © 1970, Addison-Wesley Publishing Company, Inc.; and passages from my chapter, "Personality in Politics: A Conceptual Map, with Applications to the Problem of Political Rationality," from O. Garceau (Ed.), *Political Research and Political Theory* (Cambridge, Mass.: Harvard University Press), copyright © 1968 by the president and fellows of Harvard College.

"Ethical Principles in the Conduct of Research with Human Participants," included in Chapter Twelve, is extracted from pp. 1–2 of the publication of the same title by the Ad Hoc Committee on Ethical Standards in Psychological Research (Washington, D.C.: American Psychological Association, 1973), copyright © 1973 by the American Psychological Association; reprinted by permission.

INDEXES

Name

ABELSON, H. I., 29
ABELSON, R. P., 23, 27, 28, 36-37, 40
ADAMS, J. E., 148
ADLER, N., 44
ADORNO, T. W., 26, 42, 50
ALKER, H., 187
ALLPORT, F. H., 13
ALLPORT, G. W., 2, 19, 23, 24, 145, 173, 182, 234, 235-236, 240, 244
ALMOND, G. A., 17, 55
ANGYAL, A., 153
ARONSON, E., 1, 23, 28, 36
ASCH, S. E., 35-36, 39, 145
ASTIN, A. W., 14, 60, 63

BACK, K., 3, 104, 165, 170, 203, 225
BALDWIN, J. M., 183
BARKER, C. H., 43
BARRETT, D., 185
BARTON, W., 131
BARUCH, R. F., 14
BAUMRIND, D., 209-211, 215
BAYER, A. E., 14, 63
BEATTIE, M., 159
BECKER, G. M., 102
BEHRENS, W. W., 193, 216, 224
BEM, D. J., 20, 188
BENEDICT, R., 177

BERELSON, B., 15-16, 25
BERKOWITZ, L., 227
BETTELHEIM, B., 90
BIDDLE, B. J., 186
BLAKE, J., 97
BLOCK, J. H., 57-94
BLOS, P., 68
BORING, E. G., 224, 234, 235
BOWER, E. M., 132, 134, 136
BRAUNGART, R. G., 59, 63-64, 75, 76, 82, 83
BREHM, J. W., 17
BROWN, C., 155-158, 162, 251
BRUNER, J., 17, 45, 49-50, 239-240

CALLAHAN, D., 116, 117, 119
CAMPBELL, A., 25, 49, 197
CAMPBELL, D. T., 13, 20, 28, 35, 197
CANTRIL, H., 43
CHEIN, I., 20, 54-55, 170, 172, 185-186, 201, 202, 223
CHILMAN, C. S., 112, 155
CHRISTIE, R., 24, 43
CLAUSEN, J. A., 146, 249
CLEVELAND, S. E., 182
COLEMAN, J. S., 62
COLLINS, B. E., 23, 28-29, 41, 159

283

Subject